Growing Language Through Science, K–5

To science for the wonder and delight it offers.

To Dennis, my husband, best friend, and super teacher, the light of my life.

To Dr. M. Houman Fekrazad, for his scientific knowledge and compassion, who gave me a second chance at life.

Growing Language Through Science, K–5

Strategies That Work

Judy Reinhartz

Foreword by Katherine I. Norman

CORWIN
A SAGE Company

CORWIN
A SAGE Company

FOR INFORMATION:

Corwin
A SAGE Company
2455 Teller Road
Thousand Oaks, California 91320
(800) 233-9936
www.corwin.com

SAGE Publications Ltd.
1 Oliver's Yard
55 City Road
London EC1Y 1SP
United Kingdom

SAGE Publications India Pvt. Ltd.
B 1/I 1 Mohan Cooperative Industrial Area
Mathura Road, New Delhi 110 044
India

SAGE Publications Asia-Pacific Pte. Ltd.
3 Church Street
#10-04 Samsung Hub
Singapore 049483

Acquisitions Editor: Erin Null
Associate Editor: Desirée A. Bartlett
Editorial Assistant: Andrew Olson
Production Editor: Melanie Birdsall
Copy Editor: Talia Greenberg
Typesetter: C&M Digitals (P) Ltd.
Proofreader: Eleni-Maria Georgiou
Indexer: Molly Hall
Marketing Manager: Amanda Boudria

Printed in the United States of America

A catalog record of this book is available from the Library of Congress.

ISBN: 978-1-4833-5831-4

This book is printed on acid-free paper.

SFI Certified Sourcing
www.sfiprogram.org
SFI-00453

15 16 17 18 19 10 9 8 7 6 5 4 3 2 1

Contents

PART IV. ASSESSING LEARNING

Visit the companion website at
http://resources.corwin.com/ReinhartzGrowingLanguage
for downloadable resources.

Foreword

Growing Language Through Science, K–5: Strategies That Work is an excellent and much-needed resource for all teachers of language learners in the science classroom. Too often, students whose first language is not English are taken out of the science classroom for additional tutoring with the idea that science is "too difficult" for them, thus depriving them of a science content background that might lead to future careers in science and technology. On a more global scale, such actions rob our nation and society of the contributions that these individuals may make in the future in science and related fields. It is past time to take action to ensure that all of our young people receive a solid foundation in science, not only for future careers, but to contribute intelligently to our society. To fail to do so is to fail our youth, our nation, and our future.

Growing Language Through Science, K–5: Strategies That Work focuses on the codevelopment of science and language learning in grades K–5. With the implementation of the Common Core State Standards and the Next Generation Science Standards, this book provides a rich resource for school systems, districts, and teachers to help students in learning both science and language. The NGSS were developed for the purpose of providing *all* students an internationally benchmarked science education. This includes the thousands of students in our classrooms who are English learners. The book affords a teacher a way to accomplish this goal and to develop and supplement an outstanding science program in their own classroom through exercises, investigations, games, ideas, and other activities. All of these are based on the way students learn science effectively. The NGSS includes critical thinking and communication skills that students need for postsecondary success and citizenship in a world "fueled by innovations in science and technology." The NGSS integrates these practices with the science content. This book provides a practical approach for K–5 teachers to accomplish the goals of the NGSS and to facilitate language learners' understanding and practice of these skills.

Up until recently, with the arrival of the NGSS and the Common Core's emphasis on students reading texts in science, many elementary teachers left science out of the school day due to high stakes testing associated with teaching and learning language arts and mathematics. Because of this, many experienced K–5 teachers have not taught science and are very uncomfortable with the thought of doing so. *Growing Language Through Science, K–5: Strategies That Work* offers an easy-to-follow road map for both experienced teachers and new teachers to develop and implement a very successful science program in their classrooms. The English Language Arts Standards of the Common Core stress critical-thinking, problem-solving, and analytical skills, and the book suggests easy-to-follow methods for teachers to teach these skills to their students. The book provides the link between the English Language Development Standards, which identify the relationship between what students need to know and be able to do as they move toward full fluency in English, and the Next Generation Science Standards.

On a personal level, the book is dear to me because of the emphasis it places on the natural curiosity children have for science and the importance of the teacher in building on this curiosity and motivation to learn science. My own pursuit of a PhD and a career in science education was fueled by the knowledge that children have an innate desire to understand our natural world, but that too often the desire and curiosity about science is doused by the way science is taught. *Growing Language Through Science, K–5: Strategies That Work* presents practical strategies that capitalize on students' desires to learn. The book connects research and best practice for the elementary school grades in teaching and learning both science and language, and it provides the way for learners to experience success in a language-rich science program.

—Katherine I. Norman
Professor, California State University, Stanislaus
Former President of the Association for
Science Teacher Education

Preface

Perhaps the greatest idea that America has given the world is education for all.

—R. Hutchins

Teacher learning is an evolutionary process in which this learning must be linked to classroom practice. Building on this connection, teachers are more likely to implement what they have learned to contribute to the academic success of their students. This book endeavors to change the dynamics of teacher learning and subsequent student learning. My hope is to empower and engage teachers in purposeful and relevant instructional experiences that link current research with effective science classroom practice.

Features of the Book

The contents of this book are derived from (1) a sequence of professional development sessions with teachers and principals, (2) conference presentations, (3) consultations with school administrators and teachers at individual campuses, (4) some 47 years of teaching experience, and (5) coaching school leaders to find ways to better support English learners in science. The ideas and strategies in this book have been "field tested" over many years in elementary, middle, and high school monolingual, dual-language, and bilingual science classrooms, as well as in university courses across the country.

Learning science is a tall order for students who come to school with different cultural and language backgrounds and varying levels of proficiency in English. This presents a challenge for both students and their teachers. To complicate matters, science has a demanding academic vocabulary, including multisyllabic words that are often hard to pronounce, complex definitions to understand and remember, and visuals that are often difficult to comprehend. Accordingly, "doing science" sets the stage for students to use communicative language in the classroom. This approach moves science away from strictly using textbooks and other print materials to integrating science literature and more kinesthetic experiences into the learning process.

As teachers expand their instructional repertoire, their students learn in a comfortable environment that encourages them to test their science knowledge and language skills. Whether it is singing a song about clouds, exploring shadows using outlines of their bodies on the school grounds at different times of day, reading short science fun facts on the inside of Snapple caps, and/or recording observations of different objects in their science notebooks, students have multiple opportunities to enjoy learning science and to use their listening, speaking, reading, and writing skills.

This book is based on three fundamental principles to grow language in grades K–5 science classrooms:

1. Building teacher capacity to meet students' instructional needs
2. Valuing students' educational, cultural, and linguistic diversity
3. Appreciating and understanding the interdependence of teaching and learning

It also lays the foundation for contextualizing language by framing instruction within the 5E model (Engage, Explore, Explain, Elaborate, and Evaluate). Students put their language to work as they participate in each of the 5Es, and in doing so, they develop and expand their scientific understanding.

A key feature of this book, the codevelopment of science and language learning, stems from working with science teachers, dual and bilingual teachers, and their students, as well as from my ongoing research. This book distinguishes itself from other supplementary K–5 instructional resources in three distinct ways. First, it serves as a bridge connecting research and practice within the existing and evolving social, cultural, and linguistic landscapes of elementary schools. Second, the book provides a window into language-rich science classrooms, rendering a smoother transition for English learners to experience success in science. Third, it presents a language-centered approach using a variety of exercises, investigations, and games that teachers can easily adopt to supplement their existing science programs, thereby further benefitting all their students.

Highlights for Setting the Stage for Growing Language in Science

Learning science is a cumulative process that commences in the early grades and builds a developmental path for learning science and growing language. Understanding this learning progression is essential for planning and teaching science topics in ways that are described in the *Framework for K–12 Science Education: Practices, Crosscutting Concepts, and Core Disciplinary Ideas.*

The *Framework* sets the tone for what it means to be proficient in science. Teaching and learning science build on the notion that science knowledge is based on evidence that is continually being extended, refined, and revised. It is this vision that I embrace, and that is reflected throughout the book. In the *Framework,* there are three grade bands—K–5, 6–8, and 9–12—and this book focuses on the first, grades K–5.

The book includes a vast array of strategies in the form of exercises, investigations, and activities that teachers can use to enrich their science programs. Many of these have been uploaded to the companion website for easy access. The book also complements the current national, state, and district curricula and science and language standards in providing a structure for lifelong teacher learning.

Young students have a joy of learning and get excited about almost everything; they are curious about what they hear or see, and about how things work. As a first grader has said about science, it is "figyoring theings oat." Students' natural curiosity propels them to explore, using their senses, language skills, and cognitive abilities. And the quality of these exciting "science journeys" that students want to talk about and share is determined by their teachers.

Tapping into students' natural curiosity gives science teachers an advantage that many other teachers do not enjoy. Science becomes the ideal environment in which to grow language because, as Rachel Carson notes in *Silent Spring,* students want to share what interests them. And it is through this sharing, using the communication skills of listening, speaking, reading, and writing, that they increase their language proficiency.

The book begins with a brief discussion of the role that curiosity plays in science. Students come to school having an innate desire to learn, and they bring this desire to the science classroom, which makes a world of difference in growing their language. Science is a motivator and an academic engine for utilizing language. But it is the teacher who is crucial in fostering students' natural curiosity by implementing best inquiry practices that capitalize on the students' desire to learn.

This book seeks to heighten teachers' awareness of the critical role that language plays in science. When planning lessons, knowing the science is important, but so is awareness of language use for communication and learning, such as in print materials, argumentation, and discourse, that come into play when learning science. Science serves as a catalyst for students to use their language skills in relevant and purposeful ways both in the classroom and at home with family members.

Design and Organization of the Book

Throughout the book, figures and illustrations serve to enrich the textual discussions. Each chapter has a quotation, an introduction, a conclusion, and a section that includes opportunities for readers to think further about the content in and across chapters. Taking the time to reflect offers opportunities to think about the information presented in the light of the reader's instructional practices. Implementing reflection practices often becomes a challenge because it requires "wait time" for teachers to think and make informed decisions. There are many ways to engage in reflective practices:

Chatting with others, including your students	*Jotting down* ideas to be explored later	*Pausing* and routinely stepping back
Observing your classroom and students	*Documenting* what you and your students are doing	*Seeing* through the eyes of your students
Partnering with colleagues, parents, and administrators	*Reading* to keep current	*Joining* network blogs and sharing your issues and ideas

The references cited in each chapter can be found in one list at the end of the book. Last, there is a companion website, http://resources.corwin.com/ReinhartzGrowingLanguage, that includes not only additional resources, but also several documents from the chapters in both Word and PDF formats.

The book has four major parts and ten chapters. Part I, Science Teaching and Learning Using a Language Lens, includes three chapters. Chapter 1 serves as an introduction to the current science education landscape and diversity of learners and levels of language proficiency. Chapter 2 addresses the importance of effective teaching and learning principles from research and connecting them with practice. And Chapter 3 presents the 5E instructional model against the backdrop of teaching and learning through inquiry.

Part II, Science and Language in the Science Classroom: A Good Pairing, includes five chapters that present the content and inquiry strategies that teachers can use to promote science and language learning. Chapter 4, The Power of Questions, lays the groundwork for all of Part II. Chapter 5, Doing Science, includes sample lessons and ideas for hands-on exercises, as well as a discussion of three types of investigations: descriptive, comparative, and experimental. Chapter 6, Navigating Through the Practices, Crosscutting Concepts, and Core Science Ideas: Physical Sciences and Earth and Space Sciences, and Chapter 7, Life Sciences Across the Grades, address topics from different science disciplines, as well as engineering design, and incorporate activities for teaching them. Children's literature, used extensively throughout the book, is included in Chapters 6 and 7 to enhance and demonstrate how such texts can be utilized to augment science learning and contribute to language growth. Chapter 8, Games: A Context for Meaningful Learning and Communication Language Usage, brings Part II to a close. Integrating educational games to promote science learning is a clever way to get students to play and use their communication skills, while in reality they are learning.

Part III, Enhancing the School–Home Connection, is comprised of one chapter. Chapter 9, School–Home Science Connection, explores ways to bring children and their parents together through the study of science. Doing science at home reinforces the idea that science is everywhere, not just in school. At the same time, this chapter offers teachers ways to increase parental involvement in school activities and their children's education, which is critical to their academic success.

Part IV, Assessing Learning, also contains one chapter. Chapter 10, How Do We Know That Students Know?, describes the assessment process as well as strategies that drive teaching and student learning. The focus on assessment is on learning and how to support students in meeting the learning expectations that begin with planning rather than after teaching.

The Epilogue brings the book to a close. It offers some final thoughts about the importance of engagement that can lead to growing language through science as teachers and their students travel the learning journey together.

There are several figures that are too long for inclusion in the chapters that can be found on the website. Last, the index is arranged by science topics and the strategies for teaching them, providing an easy way to access desired information. May your science journey be as fruitful as that of your students, because together the final results can be amazing!

To keep your journey an ongoing experience, a companion website, http://resources.corwin.com/ReinhartzGrowingLanguage, has been designed to house resources and figures, including some in Word form so that you can modify them to meet the needs of your particular students. Content will be added to the website periodically to keep the bright ideas flowing.

Acknowledgments

I want to thank all the people who devoted time and effort to make this book possible, with special thanks to Juanita Esparza, who encouraged the integration of language and science and made possible the implementation of these ideas.

Publisher's Acknowledgments

Corwin gratefully acknowledges the contributions of the following reviewers:

Thelma A. Davis
Principal
Clark County School District
Las Vegas, NV

Jon Maxwell, PhD
Elementary Math and Science Curriculum Coordinator
Katy Independent School District
Katy, TX

Lyneille Meza
Coordinator of Data and Assessment
Denton Independent School District
Denton, TX

Louise Wilkinson
Distinguished Professor of Education
Syracuse University
Syracuse, NY

About the Author

Judy Reinhartz's career spans nearly five decades in K–16 education, as an elementary and middle school science teacher; a secondary school science teacher and department science chair; and a professor of undergraduate and graduate science education, curriculum development, research, educational leadership and supervision, and instructional strategy courses. She is also a researcher; a writer of numerous articles, chapters, and books; a presenter and consultant; and director of centers for science, research, effective teaching and learning, grant-funded science academies and institutes, and clinical experiences and student teaching.

Judy has developed a culture of inquiry and worked with diverse populations of students, teachers, college faculty, staff, members of the business community, and parents in varied educational settings at the local, state, national, and international levels. Throughout her career, she has been a champion for teaching science. She has presented a myriad of research into practice studies at professional meetings and conducted professional development for teachers and administrators, many targeting science teaching to diverse learners.

Judy was an associate dean and is professor emeritus at the University of Texas at El Paso, and her degrees include a PhD from the University of New Mexico, master's from Seton Hall University, and bachelor's from Rutgers University. She is the recipient of the AMOCO Outstanding Teacher Award (now called the Chancellor's Council Award for Excellence in Teaching) from the University of Texas at Arlington, where she also was a professor for many years. She also received the Crystal Apple Award for Contributions to

Education from Tarleton State University, the Kyle Killough Award for Contributions to Teacher Centers, the Ted Booker Award for Outstanding Contributions to Teacher Education, the Service Award for Contributions to the Mid-Cities Chapter of Phi Delta Kappa, and from Texas Society for College Teacher Educators, the Special Recognition for Contributions to Teacher Education.

As a consultant, she has worked with many elementary and middle school faculty at specific school campuses on the Texas/Mexico border to promote language through science.

Upon leaving one of Judy's presentations, a teacher commented, "I am leaving with an arsenal of science ideas that I never would have thought of on my own [smiley face]." And on an evaluation a student said of Judy, "Her excitement is contagious. Science did not interest me until this class. Now, it's my favorite subject to teach."

PART I

Science Teaching and Learning Using a Language Lens

1

Setting the Stage for Growing Language Through Science

Awaken people's curiosity. It is enough to open minds; do not overload them. Put there just a spark.

—Anatole France

Introduction

When adults are asked the question *What is science?* many often answer with "scientific method," "facts," or "theories." When elementary school students are presented with the same question, their answers usually are quite different—"fun," "doing and making things," "playing with balls and ramps"—and they enthusiastically share that they want to become scientists when they grow up. So students have a different view of science than adults typically do. For the purposes of this book, defining science is simple. It is a blend of the two: learning a body of knowledge, and learning by doing. When you teach science content using hands-on strategies, your students have multiple opportunities to use their skills of listening, speaking, reading, and writing.

Science as a core academic subject can be a challenge for teachers to teach and students to learn. There are many reasons why this is the case. Science has an extensive vocabulary and a vast amount of information to teach and learn. Its textbooks tend to have complex sentences and confusing visuals. And if that is not intimidating enough, students are expected to read, comprehend, and follow multistep directions and procedures for conducting science investigations (Carrejo, Cortez, & Reinhartz, 2010). So comprehending science can be a daunting task for any K–5 student; but for English learners (ELs) the challenge can be so much greater. How can science grow language?

Natural Curiosity

Unlocking students' natural curiosity is a major part of the solution. It is an important advantage that teachers have in science. Students have a desire to learn more about the world around them; they are naturally curious about it. According to Suzuki (2011), "their world is full of wonder and newness" (p. 6). And Rachel Carson put it best in her book *The Sense of Wonder* (1965): When children have an inborn sense of wonder, to keep it alive they need the companionship of others with whom they can share their joys, excitement, and the mysteries they uncover.

As Carson notes, young students have a joy of learning and get excited about almost everything; they are curious about what they have heard or seen, how things work, and the things in the night sky. Students' natural curiosity propels them to explore, using their senses of touch, hearing, sight, smell, and taste (where safe and appropriate).

And it is this excitement that they want to talk about: to share with others what they have discovered, and to describe in words or pictures what they touch, hear, see, smell, and taste.

Science is a natural motivator and an academic engine for utilizing language, but it is the teacher who is key in fostering students' innate curiosity by creating a risk-free environment, implementing the best inquiry practices that capitalize on their desire to learn, valuing students for who they are and what they bring to the science classroom, and following the 5E (Engage, Explore, Explain, Elaborate, Evaluate) instructional model. These themes will be discussed in greater detail throughout the book.

Facilitating Language Through Science: An Ideal Environment for Growth

Today, there is an increasing number of students coming to the United States from many different countries, and in the school year 2011–2012 they represented 9.1%—or an estimated 4.4 million (National Center for Education Statistics, 2014). It is therefore essential that teachers be aware of their cultural assets as well as their educational needs. This statistic helps to make a case for knowing and understanding language arts as well as for mastering science content and skills. This book seeks to heighten teachers' awareness of the critical role that language plays in their classroom. When planning lessons, knowing the science is of importance, but so is familiarity with language use for communication and learning in printed materials, argumentation, and discourse.

This chapter offers a bridge between language and science content learning. Science serves as a catalyst for students to use their language skills in relevant and purposeful ways. For many teachers, it is a dichotomous situation—language instruction first followed by content instruction, but not both. This approach involves language instruction, leaving the content out of the equation. Thus, language is taught in isolation, lacking the context for using it. Another option calls for the utilization of sheltered instructional strategies in science to support language learners. It is the latter approach—immersing students in language-rich science environments, which encourages academic success—that this book promotes. To make it work, teachers must be aware of both the science and the language standards.

Until recently, the research landscape generally has ignored the challenges that language learners face in content areas, particularly science.

The question that teachers struggle with continually is, "How do you teach science to students whose English skills are at a beginning or intermediate level?" Himmel (2012) argues that teachers who have English learners in their classrooms should implement strategies that teach content and be aware of the language skills that are needed to carry out tasks. She reminds us that content teachers often "do not see themselves as language teachers, and so they are not sure where to begin" (np). This book offers teachers a variety of strategies that embed scaffolds and sheltered-based instruction, demonstrating how science serves as an ideal environment for growing language while learning it.

What Standards Mean for Teachers and Their Students

Overview of the Standard-Based Movement

The rationale for the standard-based movement is to raise the educational bar for all students and to hold them accountable to the same academic expectations. The movement began with the publication of *A Nation at Risk* in 1983, and waves of reforms followed (Commission on Excellence in Education, 1983). Project 2061 was initiated in 1985. A key question driving this reform was *How can the current educational system address changes in our world so that students can think critically and lead responsible and productive lives shaped by science and technology?* (Rutherford & Ahlgren, 1989).

A panel of scientists, mathematicians, and technologists made recommendations, resulting in the 1989 publication of *Science for All Americans,* which integrated findings from Project 2061 (Rutherford & Ahlgren, 1989). This book defined science literacy; it laid out some principles for effective STEM teaching and learning, and identified the common themes or general concepts such as systems, models, patterns of change, and scale that cut across science, mathematics, and technology for grades K–12. Last, it described the "Habits of Mind [that include] attitudes, skills, and ways of thinking that are essential to science literacy" (np). *Science for All Americans* (1989) was a hallmark for science reform and laid the groundwork for the Next Generation Science Standards (NGSS, 2013).

The standard-based movement continued to gain momentum in 1994 and then again in 2001, with the passage of the Improving America's Schools Act and the No Child Left Behind Act, respectively. The reform movement continued into the 21st century with the Council of Chief State School Officers (CCSSO) and the National

Governors Association (NGA) in 2009 collaborating on a set of K–12 standards that defined the knowledge and skills students need to graduate from high school and to be college and/or job ready.

The Common Core State Standards (2012) were developed by key state educational policy leaders, and were reviewed by several educational groups and associations. English language arts and literacy (ELA/literacy) standards begin in grade 6 for history/social studies, science, and technical subjects. The goal of the standards is to promote communication skills across the content areas. It leaves it to the states to decide how to implement the CCSS with the K–5 student population.

Recently, in 2011 the National Research Council (NRC) published *A Framework for K–12 Science Education: Practices, Crosscutting Concepts, and Core Ideas* (hereafter referred to as *Framework*). This document is a cooperative effort involving the National Science Teachers Association, the American Association for the Advancement of Science, and Achieve, Inc. It lays the foundation for a common set of science standards called the Next Generation Science Standards (NGSS). Building on the information in *Science for All Americans,* NGSS identifies science ideas and exercises that high school graduates need to know and be able to do. The final draft of NGSS was published in 2013.

Science Standards

The national science standards (NGSS) have transformed STEM education (science, technology, engineering, and mathematics) by defining the essence of science teaching and learning. The standards include three components, called "dimensions." These are composed of the following:

Dimension 1: Science and engineering practices

Dimension 2: Crosscutting concepts

Dimension 3: Disciplinary core ideas

Figure 1.1 illustrates how they fit together, and in doing so, how they support our understanding of science, engineering, and inquiry teaching and learning.

Dimension 1 describes the major practices that scientists use to investigate and build models to learn more about their world. It also includes a set of practices that engineers employ to design and build systems. The standards use the word *practices* deliberately to imply the need for both scientific investigations as well as knowledge that is specific to the practices. In Dimension 1, there are eight

Figure 1.1 Three Dimensions From the Science Framework

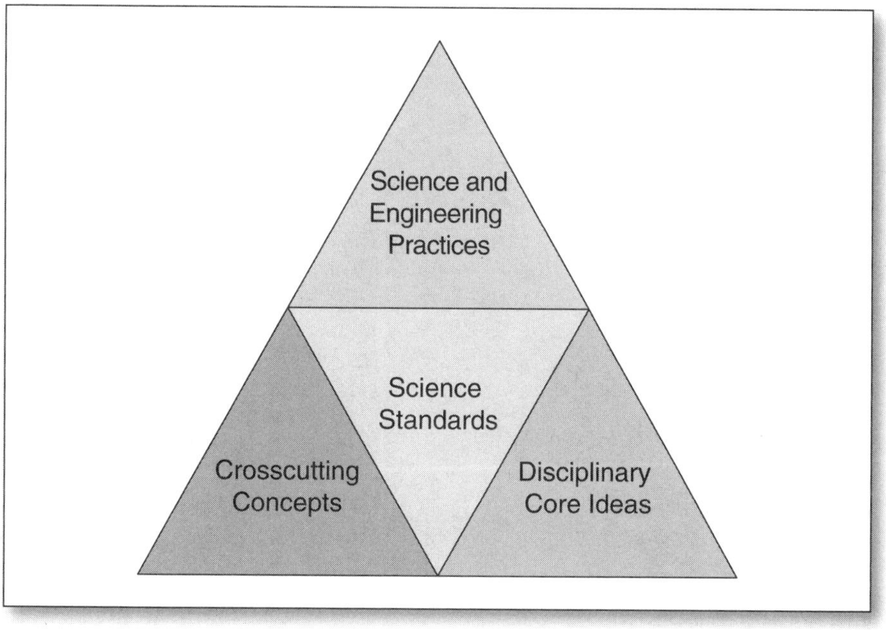

domains that include a range of different cognitive, social, and physical practices. In addition, it describes the essential practices of inquiry that exemplify what students are expected to *do,* not just learn. Figure 1.2 presents Dimension 1 and its eight domains.

Dimension 2 includes the concepts applicable across the eight domains. These concepts focus on the big ideas across all science disciplines—physical science, life science, earth and space science, and engineering—and serve as magnets for connecting facts and bits of information. The forerunners of these concepts are cited in *Science for All Americans,* where they are called "common themes" (systems, models, patterns of change, constancy, and scale) that cut across science, mathematics, and technology. These crosscutting concepts are patterns, cause and effect, scale, systems, energy and matter, structure and function, and stability and change in science. The concepts provide coherence for gaining a greater understanding of the world, be it the patterns that exist or the role of cause and effect. It is essential that students recognize, understand, and appreciate the roles that the crosscutting concepts play in the science disciplines. See Figure 1.2 for more details.

Dimension 3 includes the four major science disciplines, along with their respective "core" ideas. When planning a series of lessons on matter, for example, it is important that the core ideas in physical science relate to the crosscutting concepts of cause and effect and scale, proportion, and quantity. Figure 1.2 can serve as a handy reference when planning science lessons.

Figure 1.2 Three Dimensions of the Science Framework

Dimension 1: Scientific and Engineering Practices	Dimension 2: Crosscutting Concepts	Dimension 3: Disciplinary Core Ideas
1. Asking questions (for science) and defining problems (for engineering) 2. Developing and using models 3. Planning and carrying out investigations 4. Analyzing and interpreting data 5. Using mathematics and computational thinking 6. Constructing explanations (for science) and designing solutions (for engineering) 7. Engaging in argument from evidence 8. Obtaining, evaluating, and communicating information	1. Patterns, similarity, and diversity 2. Cause and effect: Mechanism and explanation 3. Scale, proportion, and quantity 4. Systems and system models 5. Energy and matter: Flows, cycles, and conservation 6. Structure and function 7. Stability and change	Physical Sciences PS 1: Matter and its interactions PS 2: Motion and stability: Forces and interactions PS 3: Energy PS 4: Waves and their applications in technologies for information transfer Life Sciences LS 1: From molecules to organisms: Structures and processes LS 2: Ecosystems: Interactions, energy, and dynamics LS 3: Heredity: Inheritance and variation of traits LS 4: Biological evolution: Unity and diversity Earth and Space Sciences ESS 1: Earth's place in the universe ESS 2: Earth's systems ESS 3: Earth and human activity Engineering, Technology, and the Applications of Science ETS 1: Engineering design ETS 2: Links among engineering, technology, science, and society

Source: "Science and Language for English Language Learners in Relation to Next Generation Science Standards and With Implications for Common Core State Standards for English Language Arts and Mathematics," by O. Lee, H. Quinn, and G. Valdés, 2013, *Educational Research.* doi: 10.3102/0013189X13480524

English Language Development Standards

The goal of the 2012 amplification of the English Language Development (ELD) standards for grades K–12 is to promote a mutual understanding and use of language development standards among content area teachers who have ELs (English learners) in their classes (World-Class Instructional Design and Assessment [WIDA], 2012). The standards formalize the language expectations for these learners across different learning environments to ensure that they succeed linguistically as well as in content areas.

Since ELs are expected to meet the same standards as other students, content teachers should have an understanding of the ELD standards. Teachers need to integrate the four language domains—listening, speaking, reading, and writing—into their lesson plans. These standards are divided into grade-band clusters—preK–K, 1–2, 3–5, and 6–8—and into English language proficiency levels. Many school districts use the WIDA standards for revising and/or developing their English language curriculum.

Being aware of district, state, and national standards in science and English language proficiency is a necessary first step in addressing the learning issues of ELs. The science standards identify the science topics and tasks to be learned (creating models, classifying objects, comparing cycles in nature, etc.), and the English language development standards identify the language skills and functions needed to communicate this understanding (comprehension, applying science content to a specific topic, etc.). By doing so, students achieve academic language fluency in science.

These standards are especially helpful to teachers of English learners because of their attention to the language domains applicable across the content areas. By addressing language functions embedded in content learning, teachers present students with many opportunities to use language in meaningful contexts and ways. These language functions include addressing the following:

- Use of language comparisons when describing two different animals (e.g., more than, less than).
- Sequence of steps to complete an investigation (e.g., first, second, last).
- Information that is recorded on a graphic organizer (e.g., double bubble map) so that the students can identify main ideas and organize them accordingly.
- Summarization of ideas both orally and in writing to demonstrate what the students have learned.

Aligning Science and Language Standards in Lesson Objectives

Writing measureable and student-friendly science *and* language objectives represents an important step in support of language learners in the science classroom. Therefore, it is essential that science- and language-learning tasks be aligned. The next key step is to review the standards for the language skills needed for the lesson. For example, if sequential language is required to complete a science task, then teachers should preview it with the students, using sentence frames (_______ *is done first. What is done second?*). Students working in pairs can retell to their partner the story of the science model just constructed. So when planning a 5E lesson, including effective language objectives is an essential companion to the science objectives.

Writing content objectives that provide different avenues to acquire the skills and concepts named in the content standards is essential. Questions to consider include: *Are there provisions for using the home language to show the mastery of content knowledge? Do the students have a conceptual understanding of the lesson content? At what levels of language proficiency are the students?*

In Figure 1.3 California's Content Standards (2012) for third-grade science, along with the language objective, are presented (Himmel, 2012).

As shown in Figure 1.3, the science standard on the three forms of matter spawned the science objective, which corresponds directly to the language objective (Himmel, 2012). By aligning and embedding science content objectives with language arts objectives, language becomes an integral part of the science lesson.

Figure 1.3 Third-Grade Science, States of Matter

Content Area Standard	Content Objective	Language Objective
California: Students know that matter has three forms: solid, liquid, and gas.	Students will be able to distinguish between liquids, solids, and gases, and provide an example of each.	Students will be able to *orally describe* characteristics of liquids, solids, and gases to a partner.

Source: "Language Objectives: The Key to Effective Content Area Instruction for English Learners," by J. Himmel, 2012, *Colorín Colorado*, http://www.colorincolorado.org/article/49646. Used with permission.

Writing Language Lesson Objectives

When considering language objectives for science, teachers should differentiate instruction so that ELs can access and be successful at learning grade-level content. Writing language objectives means determining expectations for the students' levels of language proficiency; most important, it offers numerous opportunities for students to use English.

Himmel (2012) and Short, Himmel, Gutierrez, and Hudec (2012) offer guidelines for writing language objectives. These guidelines can be helpful in identifying ways to think about what language skills are needed for specific science lesson topics. Including language objectives when planning lessons will strengthen the science connection with language:

1. **Identify key science academic and concept words.** Think about the language functions of describing, explaining, comparing, and/or charting information that relate to the science topic. What will the students be expected to learn in science and be asked to do to demonstrate that learning using language?
2. **Pinpoint the language skills needed to accomplish the science tasks.** Will the students be reading from a textbook to identify the parts of a plant? Will the students be reading to find specific terms such as *roots, stems,* and/or *leaves*? Will the students be reporting orally to their peers on what they observed during a tomato plant investigation? Do they have the skills to report their observations orally and/or in writing? If the answer to any of these questions is "no," then language arts objectives are needed to carry out the science tasks.
3. **Check the grammar or language structures that are common to science.** The language arts objectives should involve students in experiences that use comparative phrases to analyze related concepts (e.g., identify the car that traveled the fastest, slowest).
4. **Be aware of the tasks that students will complete.** What language skills will students need to know to explain the steps to an investigation? Embedded in the language objectives should be skills needed to explain the steps involved, either orally or in writing.

5. **Review strategies that foster language learning in science.** If a new science topic is introduced, teachers should model how to preview the textbook chapter, looking for words that are in bold, indented, etc. Modeling strategies for an upcoming topic is an appropriate language objective to help students complete the science task.

Another important consideration when writing language objectives relates to the academic language that is unique to specific content areas. For science, academic language refers to the terms, such as *variables, cycles, interdependence,* and *interactions,* along with diagrams and visuals (e.g., phases of the moon) that provide representations of complex concepts.

Gottlieb and Ernst-Slavit (2014) go further in explaining academic language by identifying three additional dimensions that include discourse, sentence, and word/phrase levels. These dimensions of academic language are not clear-cut, but overlap and influence one another. Figure 1.4 presents these dimensions and general areas of coverage using language arts as well as science examples for grade 2. Teachers who are cognizant of the dimensions in Figure 1.4 when planning lessons are better prepared to (1) identify content and language targets, (2) capitalize on students' linguistic and cultural assets, (3) write purposeful science and language objectives, (4) utilize instructional supports that differentiate content (CCSS and NGSS) and various levels of language proficiency, and (5) select instructional activities that highlight language development in the science classroom (Gottlieb & Ernst-Slavit, 2013).

Using the science example featured in column four of the figure, the academic language for science is focused on ecosystems, with the rain forest as a case study. For the science objectives, students will do the following: (1) identify the layers of the *rain forest,* (2) name at least three *animals* that have *adapted* to living in the rain forest, and (3) explain what a *habitat* and an *ecosystem* are. For the language objectives, students will: (1) explain *orally* and *in writing* the layers that make up the rain forest, (2) use academic language to *name* the animals that live in the rain forest, and (3) use *compare and contrast structures* to describe the different layers of the rain forest and the animals that live there. Instructional supports include completing graphic organizers or anchor charts, listening to relevant songs and watching the "Rainforest Rap" (http://www.youtube.com/watch?v=m4bNrIIe0bk), matching words or phrases mounted on a word/phrase wall, completing sentence frames, and working in groups or with science buddies.

Figure 1.4 Dimensions of Academic Language: Language Arts and Science

Dimensions of Academic Language	General Areas of Coverage	Examples of Academic Language for Language Arts, Grades K–2	Examples of Academic Language in Science, Grade 2	Academic Language for Language Arts, Grades 3–5 and 6–8
Discourse level Different forms in language arts: print-based, digital, visual/ multimedia, spoken	**Voice** Cohesion across sentences (e.g., through connectors) Coherence of ideas Organization of text or speech Transitions of thoughts	Folktales Blogs Rhetorical markers Story boards	Definitions Activities: • Read aloud • Shared reading • Discussion • Venn diagram, compare/contrast • Science notebook writing • Animal poster • Science textbook	Editorials Soliloquies Scripts Research reports
Sentence level	Types of sentences: simple, compound, complex, compound-complex Types of clauses: relative, coordinate, embedded Prepositional phrases Syntax (forms and grammatical structures) Passive voice (subject is acted upon)	Prepositional phrases Connectives Sequence words	I learned that the rain forest is a _____. The rain forest has four _____. The layers of the rain forest are _____, _____, and _____. In the _____ live animals like _____, _____, and _____. The rain forest is an important _____.	Metaphors Similes Analogies Allusions
Word/phrase/ expression level	Vocabulary: general, specialized, technical, academic words and expressions Multiple meanings Idiomatic expressions Double entendres	"Characters" "Text" "Titles" "Rhyming words"	Academic words: *ecosystem, habitat, layers, rain forest, canopy, forest floor, understory, emergent layer, mammals, birds, fish, amphibians, reptiles*	"Hyperlinks" "Stanzas" "Perspectives" "Root words"

Source: Adapted from *Academic Language in Diverse Classrooms: Promoting Content and Language Learning,* by M. Gottlieb and G. Ernst-Slavit, 2014, pp. 3, 4, and 128. Thousand Oaks, CA: Corwin.

Acquiring and Learning a Language

Researchers make an important distinction between "acquiring a language" and "learning" one. Students *acquire a language* as they grow up among family members and in their neighborhoods, being unaware of the rules underlying it. *Learning a language,* on the other hand, is a conscious process of understanding the structure and grammar rules, and using them when communicating.

Gottlieb and Ernst-Slavit (2014) define an acquired language as "the language that they [students] use to make significant relationships and to construct meaning about the world"; it is the home language that ties "students to their cultures, traditions, and ways of learning and being" (p. 11). The authors go on to say that when "viewing language(s) and cultures as assets, [teachers] can build on the knowledge students have about the world and about how language works" (p. 12).

One place to begin to address the language and content issues impacting language learners is the levels of language proficiency and development. The purpose for understanding these levels is to apply this knowledge to support ELs in the science classroom. Different states and organizations use different labels for each level of proficiency, but regardless of the labels, the student language performance remains similar (Arizona, 2013; California, 2012; Teachers of English to Speakers of Other Languages [TESOL], 2005; Texas, 2011; Wisconsin, 2008).

The next step is to determine what students are expected to do as they move within these levels. It is important to recognize that these levels of language proficiency serve as a guide to address language-learning strategies within the content classrooms. These levels guide teachers in assessing student progress as they listen to student-to-student interactions, review student paperwork and entries in science notebooks, and determine the quality of contributions made during class discussions and activities.

Growing Language Across Different Proficiency Levels

For our purposes, five levels of language proficiency have been selected. Within these levels, teacher and student behaviors contributing to science academic success are included. Remember that this is not a definitive list, but a starting point to support ELs in the science classroom based on their language proficiency levels.

The levels include beginning, beginning/intermediate, intermediate, advanced, and advanced high (Texas English Language Proficiency

Assessment System [TELPAS], 2011), along with general descriptors of what students should be able to do and/or will be able to do at any entry point. A brief description of each level follows:

> **Beginning.** Students listen, watch their teacher model skills and instructions, learn vocabulary, use interactive word/phrase walls, draw and label pictures, respond to questions, employ nonverbal communication skills, and engage in tactile experiences with different materials.
>
> **Beginning/intermediate.** Students have an emerging set of communication skills, and they use short phrases when they speak. They begin to learn vocabulary as they describe pictures and graphics, respond to yes/no questions, provide brief labels for objects and materials, write simple responses, and begin to participate in class discussions.
>
> **Intermediate.** Students continue to develop communication skills by using phrases, content information, and definitions to explain vocabulary of content, and they respond to clear directions and engage in social conversations with peers.
>
> **Advanced.** Students continue to expand their language fluency by highlighting information in printed materials; begin to use analytic thinking skills involving predicting, hypothesizing, and synthesizing information that is crucial in learning science; and record in their science notebooks, using their own words and ideas derived from participating in hands-on investigations.
>
> **Advanced high.** Students have the ability of English speakers, writers, and readers. They continue to build bridges between what they are experiencing—touching, seeing, smelling, tasting (if safe), and hearing—and find ways to express this knowledge in English following the language rules.

Language development standards combined with the science content objectives determine the best path for identifying the students' language proficiency level(s).

Figure 1.5 presents differentiated science content objectives using the TELPAS levels for science, grade 2, on the topic of "animal and plant adaptations."

It is evident from reading these objectives that the expectations for each level are different, and that they become progressively more difficult.

After identifying the language skill levels needed, the next part of planning involves finding strategies to differentiate instruction.

Figure 1.5 Differentiated Science Content Objectives According to TELPAS Proficiency Levels

Standard Area: Science	Grade Level: 2	Topic: Animal and Plant Adaptations
	Content	
Intermediate	**Advanced**	**Advanced high**
Describe, compare, and *contrast* characteristics of animals or plants that help them survive in a certain ecosystem from real-life observations, experiences, or pictures.	*Organize* information on characteristics of animals or plants that help them survive in a certain ecosystem from real-life observations, experiences, or pictures.	*Evaluate* and *compose* information on characteristics of animals or plants that help them survive in a certain ecosystem from real-life observations, experiences, or pictures.
Content Objectives for Students With Conceptual Understanding Identify and describe the different internal and external characteristics of plants and animals needed to survive in various environments from real-life observations, experiences, or pictures. Classify and analyze plant and animal adaptations as they create their own design for an informative poster.		
Content Objectives for Students Challenged by the Concepts Working in bilingual pairs, identify and describe the different internal and external characteristics of plants and animals needed to survive in various environments from real-life observations, experiences, or pictures. Classify and analyze plant and animal adaptations referencing an outline and pictures provided by the teacher to create an informative poster.		

Source: Based on ELPS descriptors (http://ritter.tea.state.tx.us/rules/tac/chapter074/ch074a.html#74.4) and TEKS (http://www.tea.state.tx.us/index2.aspx?id=6148).

For example, by using an open-ended exercise of designing plant or animal posters showing adaptations to their environment, language learners have many opportunities to successfully complete the assignment. Knowing the science and language standards and what they have in common is central to the growing language in the science classroom.

Bringing It All Together

Figure 1.6 includes the five language proficiency levels, along with a general statement of teacher behaviors and what students should be able to do in science.

Figure 1.6 Language and Science Framework

Levels of Language Acquisition	Teaching Behaviors and Strategies Making Science Sense and Using Language	Student Behaviors Making Science Sense and Using Language
Beginning/ New to English Students are involved in hands-on exercises to promote interest and to foster listening and speaking skills when given opportunities to: *respond to questions* and *use models.*	Teachers implement best practices. They do the following: • Establish an engaging, supportive, and nonthreatening classroom climate by not overly calling attention to language-related issues. • Model skills and instructions using gestures to differentiate size, mass, color, and texture. • Plan meaningful science lessons that actively involve students in observing, exploring, and investigating to test their ideas, just like scientists. • Plan lessons using models to promote receptive and productive language. • Ask questions that encourage students to use social and academic language. • Use visuals/pictures, objects, and other materials to spark interest and focus students' attention. • Use a variety of print and nonprint resources. • Have students assume group roles (PI, MM, MD, RR) as they participate in descriptive investigations and review the ways to demonstrate that group members are working together, making good decisions as a group, and showing respect for one another. • Ask yes/no, "skinny" questions that require one-word responses. • Collect science picture books for students to peruse in the classroom. • Use science notebooks for students to draw pictures, glue pictures to matching names, and tell stories using pictures, prior experiences, and props.	Students "doing" science. They do the following: • Sing songs and repeat rhymes and chants. • Are active listeners and demonstrate by using a pointer (flyswatter) to pick out pictures that match terms. • Respond to yes/no questions using nonverbal communication skills. • Use the skills of observing, exploring, and predicting when given materials/objects. • Use models to explain science events/phenomena. • Use visuals to describe and/or explain what they are thinking. • Activate prior knowledge by using different visuals, real objects, graphic organizers, and print materials. • Respond using single words or simple phrases to describe and explain models. • Learn science using an interactive word/phrase wall and surprise boxes, drawing pictures, and participating in anchor chart development. • Put their heads together when working in pairs/groups to accomplish a task. • Demonstrate cooperation by working together, listening to one another (showing respect), assuming their assigned roles, and making group decisions.

(Continued)

Figure 1.6 (Continued)

Levels of Language Acquisition	Teaching Behaviors and Strategies Making Science Sense and Using Language	Student Behaviors Making Science Sense and Using Language
Beginning/ Intermediate Students continue to use manipulatives to expand their listening and speaking skills and to develop academic language when given opportunities to: *construct explanations* and *describe using evidence they uncover.*	• Construct anchor charts with students to brainstorm lists and complete graphic organizers for science topics (plants, animals, motion, habitats, energy, light, etc.) to organize information and summarize concepts. • Continue to ask "skinny" questions and begin to add "rich" ones to stimulate ideas. • Respond to students in a non-evaluative way by withholding judgment. • Use "wait time" to give students "think" time to respond and formulate their answers. • Use response protocol to increase classroom talk. • Model what is to be done. • Use science notebooks for students to record information collected during investigations, draw pictures, and plot data on graphs. • Have students assume group roles as they participate in descriptive and comparative investigations. • Conduct whole-class discussions based on what students did in the *engage* and *explore* phases of the 5E lesson. • Offer social language opportunities by having students work in pairs and small groups. • Set up a model to demonstrate, for example, the solar system. • Prepare science loops (*Who has? I have . . .*) to review science information using pictures.	• Use short phrases when answering questions or talking with group members. • Follow directions to science investigations. • Act like scientists and plan and implement investigations based on their own ideas. • Make observations when exploring materials and use their senses when examining objects during investigations. • Write/draw pictures in their science notebooks with different purposes in mind: observing, implementing steps to an investigation, filling in graphic organizers, and describing/explaining their models. • Label visuals, graphic organizers, and diagrams using cards, a pointer, or flyswatter. • Assume group roles and responsibilities. • Participate in class discussions. • Label objects and materials in their models. • Participate in simulations, games, and role-playing. • Read familiar, patterned text, as in songs, rhymes, and poems. • Compare ideas in greater depth. • Participate in science loop to review science information using pictures.

Levels of Language Acquisition	Teaching Behaviors and Strategies Making Science Sense and Using Language	Student Behaviors Making Science Sense and Using Language
Intermediate Students are involved in exercises to develop comprehension and analysis skills when reading science narratives and expository text to increase exposure to different types of written materials when given opportunities to: *plan and carry out investigations* and *analyze and interpret data*.	• Implement the "think alouds" and pair-share strategies as a way to get students to explain and describe how they made their decisions and chose their answers. • Provide students opportunities to unpack their thinking by assuming different roles and playing games. • Model science information during the lesson. • Have students assume group roles (PI, MM, MD, RR) as they participate in descriptive, comparative, and experimental investigations. • Ask students to use during the lesson a card with red on one side and green on the other to communicate if they understood the science being presented. • Use science notebooks regularly so students can label diagrams, identify hypotheses, and respond to relationships when conducting comparative and experimental investigations, including creating and testing hypotheses, identifying variables, creating a data table, plotting data on a graph, and writing the results and conclusions of what they found. • Collect gently used nonfiction science books at different reading levels for students to review and read. • Plan tasks and questions to start students thinking speculatively. • Use and have students develop models to demonstrate their conceptual understanding. • Prepare science loops (*Who has? I have . . .*) to review science information.	• Participate in pair/group activities and orally respond using the language of science when presenting their ideas. • Begin to use the appropriate language rules when speaking and writing. • Record information on "t" tables and plot the data on graphs. • Complete double bubble graphic organizers and Venn diagrams. • Assume group roles and responsibilities. • Are active listeners and demonstrate their understanding by keeping the green side of the card up on their desks; if they do not understand, they put the red side up. • Respond to clear directions and work with partners/group members to accomplish a task. • Complete sentence frames and write captions to visuals/diagrams and simple sentences. • Design models to explain and describe a science concept. • Peruse and read nonfiction science books for pleasure and to carry out assignments. • Ask questions that get them to think, *If I do ____, then ____ will happen.* • Construct models and begin to write their stories to demonstrate the science behind them. • Participate in science loop.

(Continued)

Figure 1.6 (Continued)

Levels of Language Acquisition	Teaching Behaviors and Strategies Making Science Sense and Using Language	Student Behaviors Making Science Sense and Using Language
Advanced Students are involved in science talk, group work, and independent reading activities when given opportunities to: *engage in claims and evidence exercises*; *construct explanations*; and *obtain, evaluate, and communicate information*.	• Ask "rich" questions such as *What is the relationship between ____ and ____?* when conducting experimental investigations. • Ask PMI, big science, and what-if questions. • Involve students in investigations that ask them to consider alternatives and different variables. • Initiate class discussions using the response protocol to encourage students to use descriptive language. • Use science notebooks to get students to record what is presented during the lesson and assess their level of understanding. • Review tables and graphs in science notebooks. • Have students assume group roles (PI, MM, MD, RR) as they participate in experimental, descriptive, and comparative investigations. • Ask students to develop claims supported by evidence in print materials, including books provided. • Plan exercises to encourage the use of analytic thinking that involves hypothesizing, synthesizing, creating, and evaluating information using models. • Prepare science loops (*Who has? I have . . .*).	• Experiment with variables (independent and dependent) when responding to relationship questions. • Respond to a variety of questions, including "skinny" and "rich" questions. • Come up with new questions based on results. • Write in their science notebooks in their own words about what evidence they gathered during investigations. • Contribute orally to discussions using more descriptive language and examples. • Select and read nonfiction science books. • Continue to record data in tables and construct graphs to plot data. • Assume group roles and responsibilities. • Explain information included in graphic organizers and diagrams using analytic thinking skills. • Participate in science loop. • Demonstrate increased levels of language accuracy during and after they complete science tasks. • Write narrative and expository texts. • Build models to demonstrate science ideas.

Levels of Language Acquisition	Teaching Behaviors and Strategies Making Science Sense and Using Language	Student Behaviors Making Science Sense and Using Language
Advanced High Students read with greater comprehension, write in more depth, use advanced science vocabulary, and follow language rules when given opportunities to: *ask and answer their own questions, plan and carry out investigations, analyze and interpret data,* and *construct explanations from evidence collected.*	• Ask students to summarize what they have read and to identify the main points in their science textbook, handout, and/or science nonfiction book. • Continue modeling social and academic language and remind the students of the rules regarding cooperation, etc. • Ask higher-order questions to get students to interpret, analyze, and evaluate the models they created. • Use science notebooks for students to record information, and draw sketches/pictures with labels. • Collect a series of nonfiction science books at different reading levels for students to review and read. • Foster conceptual understanding (patterns, cause and effect, scale, systems, energy and matter, structure and function, stability and change) through using big-idea questions. • Have students assume group roles (PI, MM, MD, RR) when they participate in experimental investigations. • Prepare science loops.	• Read with greater comprehension by adding examples and other ideas that are not presented in print material when paraphrasing the information. • Use appropriate grammatical structures when responding orally in whole-class/small-group tasks and discussions. • Use appropriate grammatical structures, writing more creative descriptions and explanations in their science notebooks. • Interpret and analyze models and make changes in their models, thereby changing their thinking and coming up with new questions and ideas. • Write stories that explain their models. • Demonstrate conceptual understanding in their stories and notebook entries. • Demonstrate understanding of idiomatic and academic language when reading and playing games. • Generate questions to drive new investigations. • Assume group roles and responsibilities. • Participate in science loop.

It offers a guide for teachers to engage all the students in the science classroom. Once the students' levels of language proficiency are determined, teachers can ascertain realistic student expectations and select the corresponding instructional strategies.

Conclusion

Learning science is a tall order for students who come to school with different language backgrounds and proficiencies. Teachers need to tap into the students' innate desire to learn, and to capitalize on this desire when planning and teaching. Science becomes an ideal environment to grow language because students want to share what interests them, and it is through this sharing—using communication skills of listening, speaking, reading, and writing—that they increase their language proficiencies.

To make science a fertile language-growing environment, teachers need to factor in not only content, but language standards and objectives when planning lessons. Growing language does not automatically happen. Figure 1.2 offers an overview of the science standards that can be of assistance when writing content objectives. Figure 1.4 provides insight into the complex nature of academic language that can prove helpful when reflecting on what students will do to demonstrate their degree of understanding, and how they will do it. And Figure 1.6 provides a glimpse into the classroom through the ways that show how language and science come together.

In addition, the science dimensions are embedded in Figure 1.6 so that teachers have a jump-start on ways to think about how to promote language in their science classrooms. Figure 1.6 offers a wealth of ideas for engaging students in science and involving them in listening, speaking, reading, and writing exercises.

Your Turn

1. In what ways can you demonstrate in your classroom that science is a natural motivator for promoting language development?
2. Had you previously considered students' curiosity a motivator? In your planning, how will you build on this natural curiosity?
3. When planning and teaching, how will you use the knowledge of language and science standards in ways to make science learning more language-friendly? How will you consider what the students should do to demonstrate what they know?

4. Review the five guidelines for writing language objectives. Write at least two language objectives and two science objectives for your next science lesson. Implement them with your students and see how they work.
5. Analyze the three levels of science objectives in Figure 1.5 and identify the differences between them based on the language proficiency levels. What can you conclude? Are the differentiations between them great or subtle? Why do you think so? How will you use this information when writing content and language objectives?
6. How can you use the framework presented in Figure 1.6 as a road map to codevelop and contextualize language in your science classroom? Pick at least one language level, and using the other two columns, describe how you would use the information to teach a specific science topic.
7. What are you already doing and what more can you do to grow language in your science class in a more sustainable way? List at least three ways to share with colleagues and/or an administrator.

2

Effective Science Teaching and Learning

Bridging Research and Practice

To teach is to learn twice.

—J. Joubert

Introduction

Much has been written on the topic of "good teaching," and specifically good science teaching. But what is good science teaching? Many find it hard to define or explain. Put simply, teaching is implementing a common map of instructional behaviors that contribute to student learning. In the 1970s and 1980s, lists of teaching behaviors were extensive and often included being clear and enthusiastic, engaging students in productive ways, using a variety of strategies and questions, and interacting with students (Brophy & Good, 1986; Rosenshine & Furst, 1971).

Decades later, Rosenshine (2012) compiled 10 instructional principles "that all teachers should know" (p. 12), principles that will sound familiar because research studies continue to attribute them to effective teaching:

1. Begin the lesson with a short review of previous learning.
2. Present new information in small steps with student practice after each step.
3. Ask a large number of questions and check the responses of all students.
4. Provide models.
5. Guide student practice.
6. Check for student understanding.
7. Obtain a high success rate.
8. Provide scaffolds for difficult tasks.
9. Require and monitor independent practice.
10. Engage students in weekly and monthly reviews. (p. 12)

Good Science Teaching and Learning

Science teaching for 21st-century schools embraces these principles, particularly using models, a variety of questions, reviews, practice, and scaffolds, but it goes one step further. According to the *Hechinger Report* (2011), the essential ingredients for good science teaching stress the human aspect, which includes knowing the content, making connections, exciting students, being flexible, explaining why something is important, and extending the walls of the classroom.

When thinking of a typical classroom, a picture of students in seats, listening to their teachers, and working on assignments comes to mind. In the effective science classroom, students are sitting at tables completing graphic organizers and contributing to anchor charts to get acquainted with the topic, and then working with a partner or in small groups to carry out a series of exercises using their observation and investigative skills. The common denominator for the science classroom is "learning by doing," and the teacher's taking advantage of students' desire to know how things work and why (Sawyers, 2011).

The literature is replete, however, with accusations that the educational system extinguishes students' natural curiosity (Tabarrok, 2011). Teachers who do try to capitalize on student curiosity are often criticized because such strategies are suggestive of "fluff" learning. When teachers are asked if these accusations are accurate, they do admit that there is pressure to teach a vast amount of science content and to get acceptable scores on local and state-mandated tests. Often, teachers call this "teaching to the test."

Frequently, teachers are caught in the middle, walking a fine line between implementing principles of good science teaching gleaned from research and the more short-term goal of increasing test scores. These so-called "fluff" strategies are cited in the research as effective ways to reach students, and using these strategies will achieve the results that school administrators desire while making science informative and fun (Marzano, Warrick, & Simms, 2014).

Chapter 2 charts a course for implementing strategies that have a proven track record, which leads to student science and language successes. Teachers do not have to follow a formulaic path to achieve high test scores, nor do they have to abandon what is known about good teaching. Both can be achieved by building on students' natural curiosity.

Good Science Teaching

There are many terms used to describe "good" teaching, such as *best* or *authentic* practices. The standards lay the foundation for good science teaching that involves implementing the science and engineering practices described in Dimension 1, and using crosscutting concepts and teaching disciplinary core ideas.

Rosenshine's (2012) principles of instruction include many of the same practices outlined in the new science standards. For example, two of these principles—asking a large number of questions and providing models—are also in the standards. According to several research studies, "the most successful teachers spend more . . . time asking questions" because they assist students in practicing new information and connecting it to prior learning (p. 17), as well as "providing students with models [that] . . . can help them learn to solve problems faster" (p. 15).

The hallmarks of good teaching include being learner-centered, inquiry-centered, knowledge-centered, assessment-centered, and home-community-centered. Teachers promote a culture of questioning and taking risks, and students experience varied instructional strategies, engage in challenging tasks that involve high-level thinking, provide opportunities to observe and explore, build models and test hypotheses, and address students' initial understanding and preconceptions about science topics ("Best Practices," np).

Remember the old adage, "Tell me and I forget, show me and I remember, involve me and I understand"? It is the last phrase, "involve me and I understand," that is the essence of good science teaching because of its connection to inquiry. In an inquiry-centered classroom, students have multiple opportunities to question and convert information into useful knowledge. To generate a culture of inquiry teaching and learning requires a context and framework for focusing on various levels of questions. For more details about using questions consult Chapter 4.

Inquiry learning is nothing new to students, for they have been doing it since they were born. But good science teaching means implementing strategies that go beyond students' accumulating information; it means supporting them as they generate useful knowledge that cuts across science concepts and is applied in different science disciplines. Keeping inquiry learning alive in the science classroom gives students permission to continue to nurture their natural curiosity and to develop inquiring attitudes and habits of mind. Good teachers strike a balance between "how students come to know" and "what they need to know."

Science experiences in grade school provide memories that can last a lifetime: of those special times exploring insects, for example; or of examining flowers, leaves, and branches of trees; or that special teacher who made it all possible. As the K–5 curriculum continues to contract, with more and more emphasis placed on fewer and fewer subjects, science is often left out of prime time. Liliana Aguas (2013), a second-grade dual language teacher, comments on a 2011 study involving teachers in California who spend an hour or less a week teaching science. Two-thirds of these teachers confessed that they did not feel prepared to teach science, and that "science was not their thing." Their comments are not uncommon, but this does not have to be the case. To change this paradigm, teachers need a doable plan to follow.

It All Begins With a Plan

Why would teaching be any different than any other part of life? Consider giving a party for a very special occasion; seldom does this event just "happen." For a social event to be a success, the host does many things in advance. A guest list is created, plans for refreshments and decorations are made, and a budget is developed based on the list of materials needed. Also, the number of guests must be determined. The success of the event ultimately depends on the kinds of plans and decisions that are made beforehand.

Teaching works very much the same way. The 5E instructional model is a handy planning and teaching framework for identifying desired student science and language outcomes, strategies to accomplish the lesson's science and language objectives, and resources and materials needed. Just as in planning a party, the excitement and anticipation build as teachers assemble their plans and use them to guide student learning.

Many teachers find teaching science challenging and often wonder, *Where do I begin? How do I teach the science topic, and in what order? What resources do I need? What is the most effective way to teach this topic, concept, or skill?* As teachers begin the planning process, they frequently seek answers to these questions.

The answers lie in the 5Es. Each of the five phases—*engage, explore, explain, elaborate,* and *evaluate*—provides a framework for teachers to transform science content into meaningful learning experiences for all their students. The 5Es offer teachers a blueprint for organizing science inquiry–based teaching and learning that foster communicative language. The five phases are presented in Chapter 3, and a sample science lesson identifying science and language behaviors is included in Figure 3.4.

Planning Includes Safety Too

Since good science teaching includes laboratory investigations, interactive experiences, and field trips, school officials and teachers should take responsibility for establishing and maintaining safety standards. School authorities are responsible for providing safety equipment (i.e., fire extinguishers), personal protective equipment (i.e., goggles and eye wash stations), and Material Safety Data sheets. Laboratory teaching space should meet the building and fire safety codes, all students should be supervised, and accommodations should be made for those with special needs. Teachers should not permit eating or drinking of any kind in the lab. For more information about safety in the science classroom consult the National Science Teachers Association website, http://www.nsta.org/safety/.

One of the best ways to avoid mishaps in the science classroom is to plan lessons focusing on safety. Setting safety expectations for students is essential. Safety is achieved by having students assume roles and responsibilities, spacing out materials to avoid congestion, having a system for collecting materials, labeling what is needed for tasks, and stressing the importance of cooperating with and showing respect for one another. Reviewing the safety protocols before each investigation should become routine.

Students also should learn what tools and safety equipment scientists use and wear. For example, safety goggles are a must, and students who function as maintenance directors should make sure that they are worn. Role-playing helps students to better understand what they are required to do, how to use the equipment in case of an accident, and why the protocols are needed.

Last, students and their parents and guardians should receive a written letter explaining the safety protocols that will be followed during science instruction. It is a good idea to send a brief letter home for parents or guardians to sign to ensure that they have been made aware of this information. Keeping students safe at school should be foremost in teachers' minds, and the science classroom is no exception.

Planning and Managing the Physical Space

The classroom furniture in science should be arranged to maximize language enhancement. Tables and chairs are configured to encourage students to communicate—put their heads together—to make decisions, solve problems, and show respect for one another. This arrangement allows everyone to participate, and no one is left out. If tables are not available, students should group their desks in a circle, again providing everyone a chance to participate. Having a flat surface on which students may work is necessary to prevent materials from rolling over or spilling.

Using colors to organize materials by tables or groups can be a useful management technique. Color-coding materials that belong to specific tables or groups of students makes it easier for them to obtain the appropriate materials for an activity and for teachers to monitor the work that is being done. For example, the purple table or group has everything in purple; a container for supplies, a zippered pouch, and folders to keep their work together are placed in the center of the work area. A full-color version of Figure 2.1 is available on the companion website, http://resources.corwin.com/ReinhartzGrowingLanguage.

As seen in Figure 2.2, students can sign up for a specific color by using that color pencil and signing their name next to the same color on the sheet. At this level of coding, teachers know what specific students contributed to the group's activities. A color version of this figure also appears on the companion website at http://resources.corwin.com/ReinhartzGrowingLanguage.

Color-coding facilitates teacher assessment by groups as well as by individual students (Guided Language Acquisition Design [GLAD], 2014). Coding serves not only as a way to identify group members' completed work, but also to organize and manage the physical space.

Figure 2.1 Coding Table Materials

Figure 2.2 Coding for Individual Student Writing Contributions

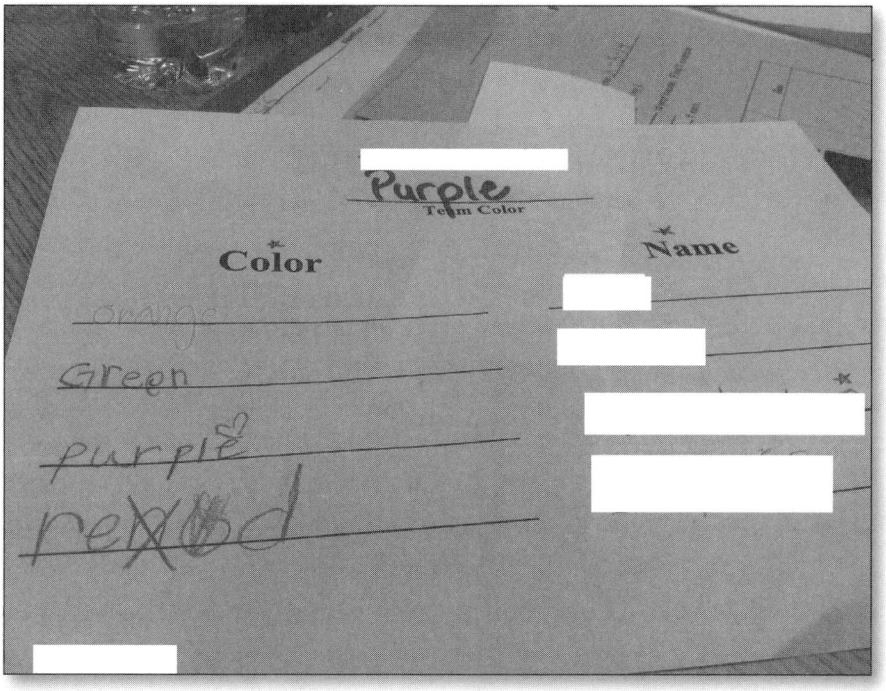

Available for download from **http://resources.corwin.com/ReinhartzGrowingLanguage**

Managing Students in the Science Classroom

In science, students are involved in many small-group experiences, and they should have specific roles and responsibilities during each investigation. For best results in getting students to participate, the size of the group should not be larger than four. Groups with five students will work, but their individual jobs are more limited. The essential roles are *principal investigator* (PI), *material manager* (MM), *maintenance director* (MD), and *reporter recorder* (RR).

Each of these roles is introduced at the beginning of the year, along with a discussion of the safety guidelines. Each group member has a role to play. Before students assume their roles, they are explained and modeled. Then students have an opportunity to role-play their jobs. It is important not to rush students into these roles; they need to be confident about what they are expected do. Make four signs of different colors, one for each job. If possible, laminate them so that they last. Attach plastic clothespins matching the color of the sign for each role.

These signs should be visible during each exercise. A color version of all these roles in Figure 2.3 are found on the companion website at http://resources.corwin.com/ReinhartzGrowingLanguage. While initially roles are assigned, the goal over the course of a school year is to have each student experience the four roles several times. To assist in who is doing what during an investigation, students clip the corresponding color of the clothespin to a convenient place on their clothes. Wearing the clothespin makes it easy to see what each student is supposed to do. When the exercise is over, the MM collects all the clothespins and clips them to the signs with the corresponding colors.

The title of each role gives away what that student is doing—at least for the most part. The PI is essentially the "teacher or expert" in the group who directs what is to be done, checks the work when it is completed, and is the only group member who gets to ask the teacher questions. This last responsibility is particularly important because it encourages the students to work together to decide what questions the PI needs to ask the teacher. In addition, the teacher responds to group questions rather than individual ones, and thus benefits by having to answer fewer questions.

The MM operates the equipment and picks up and returns materials. The MD makes sure the group members follow the safety protocols, directs the clean-up, and invites others to help with it; negotiating skills begin here. The final role is that of the RR, who presents the group's findings, responds to questions if asked, and/or plots the group's results on a class graph or chart. If teachers require only one report or assignment to be turned in, then the RR completes it, and if a short oral presentation is required, then it is this person who makes it. Even if only one report is required, all group members should record this information in their science notebooks.

As shown in the full-color version of Figure 2.3 online at http://resources.corwin.com/ReinhartzGrowingLanguage, the roles are coded as follows: PI is red, MM is yellow, MD is green, and RR is blue.

Using Science Notebooks

Often, the terms *science notebooks* and *journals* are used interchangeably. They do share common elements in that students record information and ideas in both; however, there still are major differences between them. The most significant points of departure relate to format and purpose. The purpose of science notebooks is to get students to use descriptive writing as a way to determine the extent to which they understand investigations and other exercises. Journals, on the

Figure 2.3 Managing the Science Classroom Using Roles and Responsibilities

Principal Investigator (PI)

© Mike Powell/Thinkstock Photos

1. You ask the teacher the questions.
2. You read the directions.
3. You check the work.

Material Manager (MM)

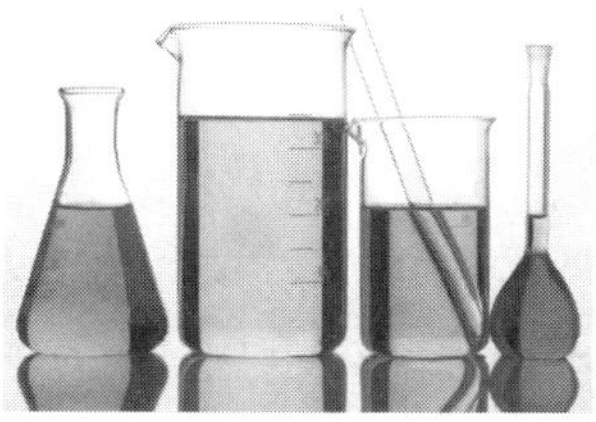

© luchschen/Thinkstock Photos

1. You pick up the materials.
2. You operate the equipment.
3. You return the materials.

Maintenance Director (MD)

© sharonscribbles/Thinkstock Photos

1. You make sure your group is following the safety rules.
2. You direct the clean-up.
3. You ask others to help clean up.

Reporter Recorder (RR)

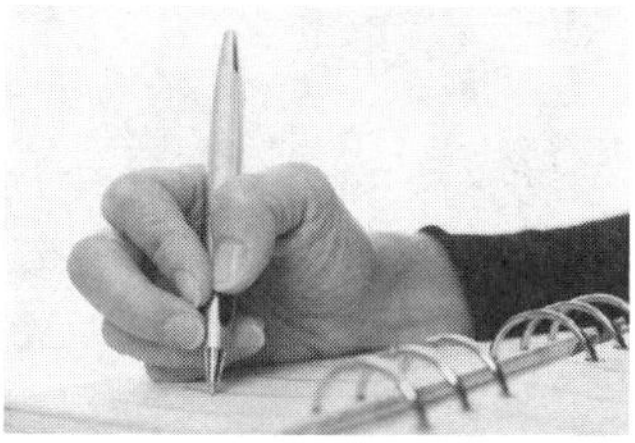

© Fuse/Thinkstock Photos

1. You do the writing.
2. You put the information on the board or chart.
3. You explain the report.

other hand, encourage students to use more free-form writing to get them to express their feelings and thoughts about topics, issues, and experiences. Students should learn how to use both forms of writing. Throughout this book, the term *notebooks* will be used rather than *journals.* Science notebooks, when used consistently, have had a positive impact on students' thinking and writing.

Students need to be taught the purpose of science notebooks and given guidelines for making entries. While scientists use notebooks for a variety of reasons, the most important are to write down information they uncover and questions that come to mind, and to make drawings from investigations including graphs, tables, and charts to organize the information that has been collected. In the picture in Figure 2.4, students have their science notebooks open to record information as they engage in their investigation using Slinky toys. Science notebooks should be considered valuable documents as records of information over time.

There are many different notebook features that can be used to group entries. These include (1) drawings; (2) tables, charts, and graphs; (3) graphic organizers; (4) notes; (5) reflective and analytical entries; and (6) inserts (Science Notebooks in K12 Classrooms). Figure 2.5 includes an example of an insert feature for grades 3 and 4, which includes students' drawings along with digital pictures of stream tables to document their study of land and water.

Students' cognitive and language proficiency levels will determine to a great extent the type of notebook features that will be used. In the primary grades, there will be inserts that have students color

Figure 2.4 Using Science Notebooks

Figure 2.5 Sample Science Notebook Entry

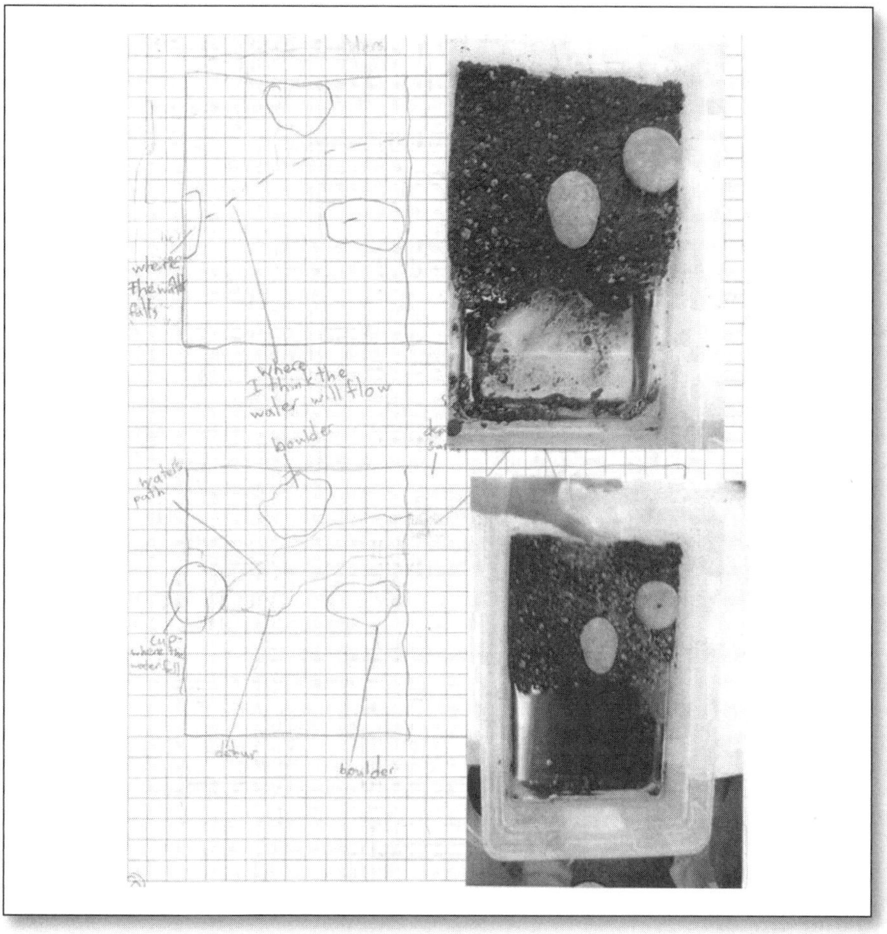

Source: Used with permission from Science Notebooks in K12 Classrooms, http://www.sciencenotebooks.org/student_work/search.php

and match pictures to written labels, drawings or sketches that record what the students observed or noticed, and simple tables constructed from data generated from investigations. In the upper grades, students will record notes in their notebooks, which will be reviewed to ensure that the information is clear and accurate. As shown in the example in Figure 2.5, the science notebook entry is a combination of drawings and digital picture inserts.

To get students to appreciate the importance of science notebooks, they should be organized in such a way that information can be easily accessed. Science notebooks are not old trunks to be continually stuffed and rarely opened and used. Notebooks are data banks that can be referred to over and over again when searching for information.

Ideas for Formatting Science Notebooks. There should be a cover page where the students include their name and any other pertinent information. Personalizing the cover is usually a beginning-of-the-year activity that students relish. The first few pages of the notebook should be left blank for a table of contents, and the pages should be numbered at the bottom. If students make a mistake, they should put one line through it and go on. No pages should be torn out or removed. The students are scientists; therefore, all their information is valuable and should be kept in its original condition. Each entry should be dated and given a title, again for easy access when looking for something and/or studying for a test. When students complete their entries or responses to questions, they should draw a "line of learning" to indicate that they are done. A glossary of science terms can be included in the back of the notebook. Students should write or print neatly and legibly, and in complete sentences if possible—depending on their language level. And finally, all graphics and drawings should be labeled. For more ideas, check out Marcarelli's (2010) book on interactive notebooks.

Using sentence starters or frames will get students thinking about what goes into their science notebooks. Examples include *I expected ____ to happen, but ____ did not; I wonder if I did ____ would I get the same results;* or *I was surprised when ____ occurred.* By completing these starters, students learn to put their thoughts down on paper; this experience gives them time to think about an investigation before it takes place, while it is happening, and even after it is completed. By doing so, students communicate their predictions in writing before interpreting findings and drawing conclusions about what occurred.

Obviously, entries for kindergarteners will look very different from those in the upper grades. Figure 2.6 includes science notebook samples from different grade levels.

Creating Science- and Language-Rich Classroom Environments

According to research, a language-rich science classroom exposes students "deliberately and recurrently to high-quality verbal [and written] input among peers and adults," and in an environment characterized by a high level of adult responsiveness (Justice, 2004). Justice identifies five key elements to create a language-rich classroom: (1) exposure to a variety of oral and print materials; (2) deliberateness in being conscious of student-to-student and student-to-teacher

Figure 2.6 Sample Science Notebook Entries

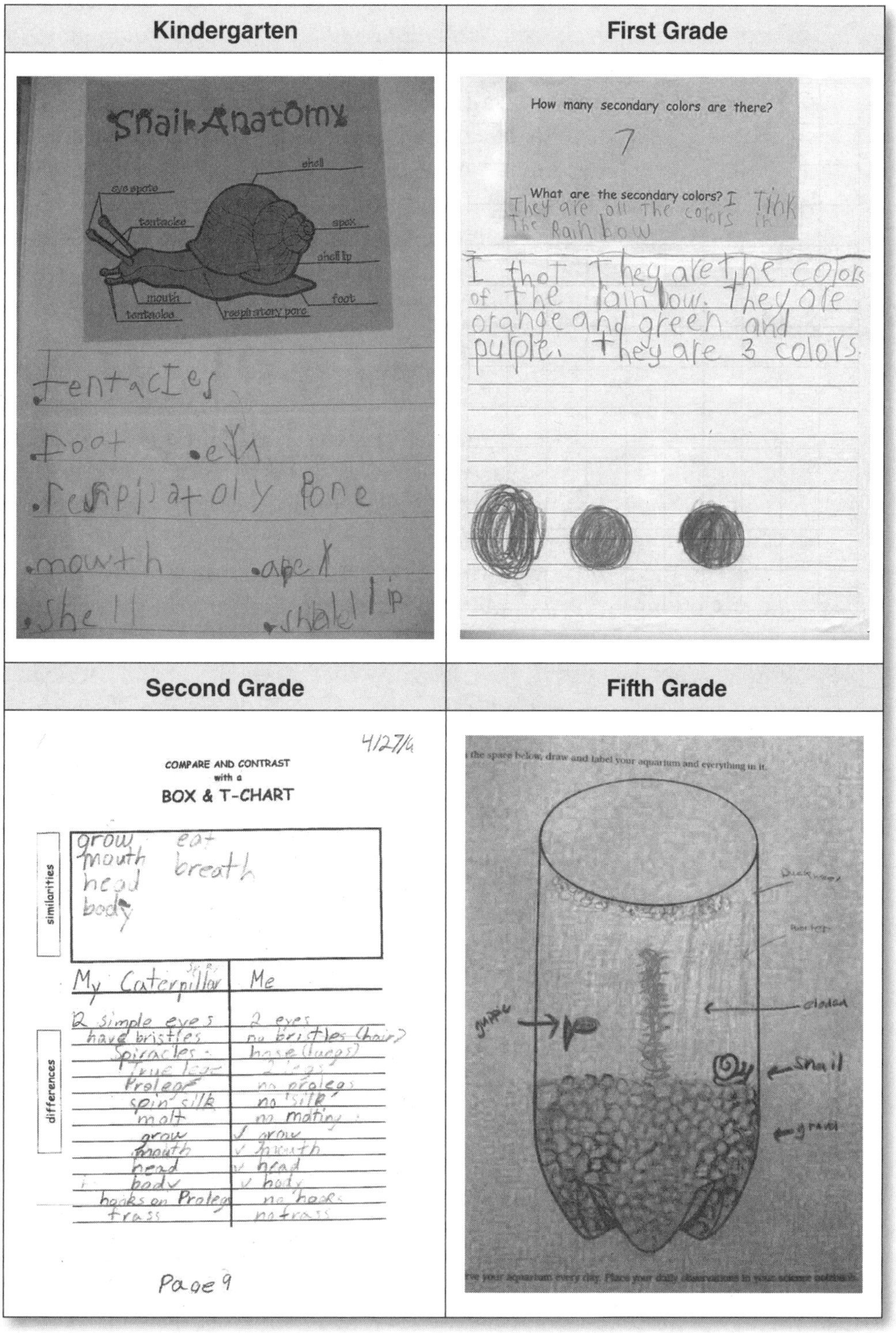

Source: Used with permission from Science Notebooks in K12 Classrooms, http://www.sciencenotebooks.org/student_work/search.php

high levels of interaction; (3) recurrence of these language events over time when learning new vocabulary words; (4) high-quality input from adults such as teachers, older students, school volunteers, or parents; and (5) adult responsiveness to students' communicative acts. These elements are associated with robust language gains from new vocabulary words to using language in functional social and academic settings. Language gains increase in science classrooms when teachers design lessons, structure the physical space, interact with students in deliberate ways, and keep them safe (Carrejo & Reinhartz, 2014b).

Ideas for Growing Language in Science

It is critical to keep track of who contributes to class discussions and who asks and answers questions, and it is equally important to give students many opportunities to share their ideas and to use their oral communication skills. A good place to begin is to present what it means to be respectful during whole-class and small-group activities. Discuss and describe it and create a graphic organizer with the word *respect* in the middle and four boxes or circles around the word with the following information: What does respect "*look like* if someone came into the room?" What does it "*sound like* if someone were listening?" What would it "*feel like*"? "What does it "*cost*"? Modeling examples of disrespect with the students include waving their arms, saying *ooh-ooh,* and jumping up and down. Showing respect is looking at the person speaking, listening to what is being asked or said, and waiting to be called on.

Once students understand what respect is, teachers can use a container holding numbered Popsicle sticks relating to how many students are at each table. Each student at a table or in a group is assigned a number. Teachers control which group answers and how many times, and which students answer questions, by pulling a Popsicle stick out of the container. When a student does not answer, he or she goes back to table or group members to get some ideas. The teacher then cycles back to that student after asking another question or two of other students. If the student still does not have an answer, he or she should be encouraged to use one of the relevant charts posted around the room to put an answer together. Groups of students earn points by responding, and they earn even more points if they follow directions and carry out the tasks. Getting students to work effectively together at their tables or in their groups is extremely important to promoting social and academic language skills, as well as to learning how to collaborate and share with others.

Using this approach ensures that all students get to contribute, not just the ones who have or think they have the answer to a question or something to add to the discussion. It gives teachers a way to assess students' levels of science understanding as well as their language proficiencies.

Fostering Observation Skills. Another way to encourage students to use their science and language abilities is through sharpening their observation skills. Making observation sheets is a good start. This task requires students to use their observation skills by looking at pictures of objects, animals, plants, etc., that are related to a science topic (Guided Language Acquisition Design [GLAD], 2014). There should be several of these sheets at each table or posted around the room. Students look at the three to five pictures mounted on the paper and draw and/or write what they see on a blank section below the pictures. Samples of observation sheets are presented in Figure 2.7.

This table task can be completed while the teacher works with other small groups of students on specific science and language learning skills and/or topics. Before transitioning to another activity, the teacher should move around to individual students and ask them to describe what they observed by focusing on what they drew and/or wrote about specific pictures and why, giving students yet another opportunity to use language. This information gives teachers insight into the students' thoughts and, most important, the proficiency level(s) at which they are functioning.

The ABC Science Book. Another table task to promote language is to have students contribute to their table's "ABC Science Book" (GLAD, 2014). At each table, there is a stack of blank paper with a large capital and small letter of the alphabet in the upper-left corner of each sheet (see Figure 2.8). Students pick individual lettered sheets and draw and/or write things they associate with the specific letters of the alphabet. The goal is to encourage them to think of things related to a science topic that begin with specific letters of the alphabet.

This exercise has many benefits, including becoming acquainted with the alphabet in English and expanding vocabulary by identifying living and nonliving objects with the letters on the sheets selected. When the sheets are put together by tables, books with each letter of the alphabet will result, having pictures and words that students can read to one another during language arts times and/or to adults sometime during the day, thereby providing practice in reading and speaking.

Figure 2.7 Sample Observation Charts

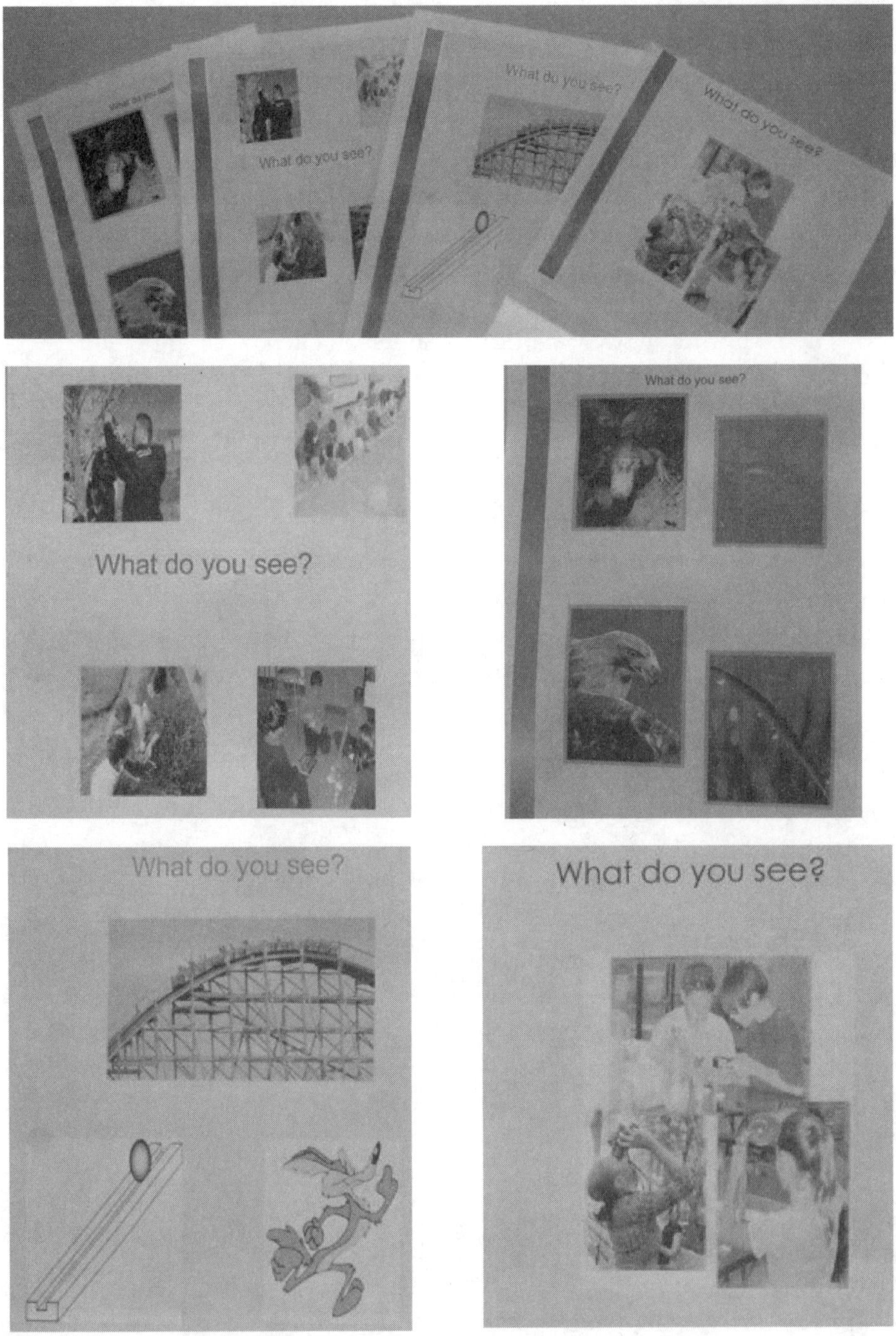

Figure 2.8 Letter A

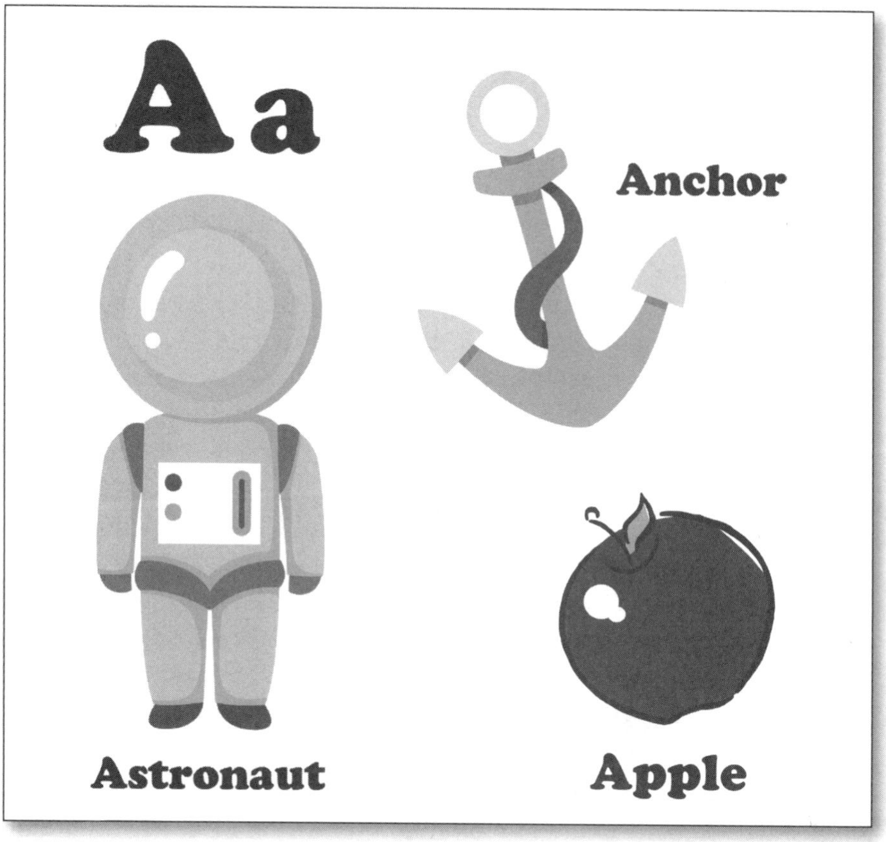

© jehsomwang/Thinkstock Photos; apple image from clipart.com

At first glance, the ABC Science Book sounds like a primary grade exercise, but upon closer examination, it can be adapted for use in the upper grades to promote not only science, but language. Older students select specific lettered sheets and write corresponding science terms such as *electricity, parallel and series circuits,* etc., and relate them to the real world when putting up outdoor lights, for example. Asking students to apply what they have learned to new situations takes them to the next level of thinking and analysis. In this context, the ABC Science Book serves another function for third- through fifth-grade students. These books can be compiled by tables or groups and shared with peers as well as with students in the lower grades, giving them practice in reading and speaking skills.

Science Charades. Working in small groups, students play science charades. They decide who will be the guesser. The student who has been selected as the guesser will turn away from the group. The other members will turn over a 5 × 7 index card revealing a word, phrase, and/or a picture. The information on the cards, such as decomposition, sedimentary rock, flower, cell, etc., comes from the grade-level academic language list. Then, the students act out what is on the card. They take a few minutes to decide how they will communicate nonverbally to the guesser. The guesser then joins the group members and observes them "acting out" the term, phrase, or picture, and guessing what it is.

This activity can be used as a lesson starter to review science information from the previous day or at the end of the day or class. Each student gets a chance to be a guesser and an actor. Take, for example, the word *friction.* Students acting out the word can use nonverbal actions such as rubbing their hands together; and for the word *cold,* they can put on gloves and a coat and scarf as well as appear to be shivering.

Students who play "science charades" need to understand the science information on the card, know what it means, and be able to show what it is by acting it out without saying anything. Such an experience gives students a chance to test not only their nonverbal language skills, but their science knowledge as well.

Songs, Rhymes, and Poems. These can be used at the beginning of, during, or the end of a series of science lessons on a variety of topics. For example, when studying clouds, there are many different songs and rhymes that students can sing and say. Cloud science is a fascinating topic for students. To get ready for lessons about clouds, serve "cloud snacks" (Jell-O cups with whipped topping) and sing a song, such as CLOUDY to the tune of "Bingo" that is featured on the http://www.preschoolexpress.com/music-station08/cloud-songs-rhymes-mar08.shtml website, as well as rhymes. Or teachers can do a choral reading of the "Cloud Poem" with students (Mr. R.'s World of Math and Science website, used with permission):

Cloud Poem

A cloud in the sky,
Had a cool dream,
He learned how to talk,
He learned how to scream!
He learned to warn people,
Walking below,
When raindrops were coming,
And when there'd be snow . . .
I'm made-up of moisture,
Liquid or ice,

And when I fill-up,
Wet is the price!
But then cloud awoke,
All silent it seems,
Clouds couldn't talk,
Unless it's in dreams . . .
Look out below!
Cloud wanted to cry,
But cloud remained silent,
Up in the sky . . .
Cloud couldn't warn,
His voice was well-cloaked,
And people below,
All went home soaked!

Source: Mr. R's World Math and Science Poems at Sciencepoems.net. Used with permission.

Songs, poems, and rhymes provide a great medium for students to have fun with science words, using a repeating pattern and singing it to familiar tunes. Repetition is extremely important to get students to listen and use the language of science, giving them several opportunities to say the words or phrases without fear of making a mistake.

Telling Science Tall Tales. This begins with the teacher partnering with a student to model how the "telling science tall tales" exercise works. Together, they make up a science story. The goal is to have students take turns with a partner, using science terms to tell their science tale. The first sentence, if the topic is on, say, hibernation, might begin with, *There was a bear that lived in. . . .* The students continue to contribute to the story until it comes to what they think is an appropriate end. Eight to ten sentences are optimal. Then, pairs of students share their stories in front of the whole class, and the whole class votes on the best science tall tale. As students cast their vote, they give reasons for their selections. In taking turns to tell science tales, students have to listen and talk in order to contribute fully.

For older students, the stories can focus on outer space, sports, science hobbies, and scientists in history (e.g., Marie Curie). Students can work individually or with a partner to come up with a science tall tale. Students write their tales in their science notebooks, which gets students to organize ideas and coherently write them down; it also encourages creativity in the way their tales are told. By engaging in this exercise, students are putting their science learning to work through storytelling and writing. Writing science stories supports communication and utilizes skills such as organizing ideas, taking notes, recording information, and focusing on specific details.

Anchor Charts. While many teachers are familiar with mind maps, graphic organizers, or commercially prepared charts, they may have limited experiences with anchor charts. Anchor charts are handmade posters or graphic representations that provide visuals for presenting, reviewing, and assessing science processes, vocabulary, equipment, and/or topics. They also serve as a quick reference tool for students to check information on new and ongoing science lessons (Williams, 2009). Using anchor charts in K–5 science classrooms scaffolds learning for *students* in science by doing the following:

1. Providing visual aids to understand science processes, terms, and/or definitions.
2. Serving as a reference tool to remind students of how to approach a task (steps to an experiment).
3. Offering evidence of classroom learning.

Anchor charts are different from commercial posters or visual aids in several ways. Most important, they are constructed by teachers and their students. The students also take ownership of the information because they have contributed to the charts (Tate, 2008; Tate & Phillips, 2011). Brain-based research supports the use of visuals to integrate new learning into memory. When the visuals represent learning events that include the students, they become artifacts of the learning process. If students are codevelopers, they are more likely to use them.

When designing an anchor chart, it is important to remember that it will serve as a tool for "anchoring" key concepts or strategies that students can use in the future. Therefore, the charts need to be simple, using different colors to highlight science words and short phrases that can easily be read. Anchor charts can be any of the following:

- Lists
- Graphic organizers such as Venn diagrams, mind maps, etc.
- Cue cards with a series of visual prompts
- Interactive (over time teachers and students can add or take away information)

Seger (2012) offers essential features of anchor charts. First and foremost, they have a single purpose or focus. Second, they have an organized appearance so that students can read and find information straightforwardly. Anchor charts should serve as learning scaffolds that support students throughout the year. Third, anchor charts should match the students' developmental and language levels. Attention to language, amount of information, length of the phrases, and size of lettering should correspond to the students' learning levels. A chart designed with second graders will be different from one that is constructed with fifth graders in terms of language and complexity. For examples of anchor charts for grade four, see http://fabulous-fourth.blogspot.com/p/anchor-charts.html.

Last, anchor charts are living documents that support ongoing learning. A flip pad made up of individual graphics and/or lists can serve as a class set of anchor charts that reflects science topics and concepts. In this case, students will have easy access to information they need by flipping to the appropriate sheet. Figure 2.9 provides a checklist with a variety of ideas for constructing science anchor charts.

Anchor charts have many uses. Since they are constructed with students, anchor charts are an integral part of science learning, helping to break down complex processes into manageable steps (e.g., chunking). For ELs, anchor charts are especially helpful in providing instructional support.

Using Scaffolds Takes Planning

In the previous section, many different facilitative strategies were presented to excite and engage students in the pursuit of learning science while minimizing stress. Depending on what science content is to be learned and the instructional needs of the students, specific strategies are selected and implemented. These strategies, whether songs, poems, or ABC Science Books, not only promote the use of language; they also serve to scaffold instruction as students move along the path to a deeper understanding of science.

The term *scaffolding* comes from the works of Wood, Bruner, and Ross in 1976, and it is a metaphor for its namesake in the construction industry that is used to describe what teachers do to support student learning. Just as scaffolds are used to support construction workers in raising a building, teachers employ them when students need support in completing a task or in understanding a concept. The goal of using instructional scaffolding is to move students along as they gain traction in working independently. *Fading,* the gradual removal of scaffolds, is likened to training wheels on a bicycle—they are used in the beginning, but they eventually come off.

Figure 2.9 Checklist for Constructing Science Anchor Charts

Identify the purpose for using an anchor chart to scaffold skills such as:	Check off √	Date
1. Identifying cause and effect		
2. Comparing and contrasting		
3. Making connections		
4. Note-taking		
5. Writing notebook entries or any writing assignment checklist for students that includes: *I have used correct grammar.* _____ *My spelling is correct.* _____ *My sentences begin in different ways.* _____ *My sentences are complete, with no run-ons.* _____ *I have capitalized the first word in each sentence, people's names.* _____ *I used a lot of describing words.* _____ *My ideas are written in my own words.* _____		
6. Sequencing steps for problem solving and investigations		
7. Answering investigative questions by defining terms frequently encountered		
8. Writing out steps for answering investigative questions such as, "What do penguins eat?," "Where do the different types of penguin live?"		
9. Collecting and graphing data—How do you collect data?—*first,* write a question, *second,* survey a group of people or collect information from observations, *third* use a "t" table to record data, and *fourth* plot data on a graph (bar graph for younger students, line graph for older students).		
10. Making inferences . . . putting the pieces together (infer, inferring, inference) and making sense out of what data have been collected		
11. Retelling what happened in the activity or investigation *Provided the name of the investigation.* _____ *We worked on* _____. *We described what was done.* _____ *We described the location where the investigation took place (in classroom, outside, etc.).* _____ *We listed the materials used.* _____ *We told what happened using a step-by-step process.* _____ Students answer the following questions: • *What was found?* • *What were the results?* • *What conclusions can be drawn based on the data collected?*		

Source: Modified and adapted from the following sources: http://grrec-k-3literacy.wikispaces.com/file/view/Anchor+Chart+Participants+Handout.pdf; http://www.cornerstoneliteracy.org/newsletter-archive/anchor-charts.

Scaffolds are bridges that are "used to build upon what students already know to arrive at something they do not know. If scaffolding is properly administered, it will act as an enabler, not a disabler" (Benson, 1997, p. 126). They enable students to access difficult information and stay on target with grade-level science content expectations.

For scaffolding to be successful, it takes planning. Teachers need to decide what scaffolds to use; when to use them during the 5Es; and, most important, their purpose(s).

To ameliorate students' frustration and risk, scaffolds offer the needed support for learning. They may include information from anchor charts, pictures, TIP charts (Term, Information, Picture), tables, science word/phrase walls, and graphic organizers that students need to fill the gaps in their prerequisite skills and knowledge. Figure 2.10 lists four basic scaffolding strategies—frameworks, models and gestures, links, and contexts—along with tasks to build student learning that teachers can use in science. Many of the tasks listed in the third column are explained in greater detail in Chapters 5 and 8.

Conclusion

Teachers determine what takes place in classrooms, resulting in student learning. It takes a well-planned, strategic effort to realize the mission outlined in the new science standards that provide a "path for creating opportunities for all students to develop a strong science background" (Badders, 2013, p. 20). Good teaching—and specifically good science teaching—does not just happen; it takes planning. Planning time is the scaffold for good teaching. Planning provides a map to follow to achieve positive student outcomes. Shortchanging planning time tends to shortchange students because teachers have not charted where they want to go, let alone how to get there. Part of the planning process is organizing and managing the physical space as well as the students. Organized science classrooms are safe classrooms where students take on roles and assume their responsibilities that lead to more independent learning, which is the core of effective teaching and learning.

Several language-rich science strategies offered teachers a variety of ways to engage students in using their communication skills as they put their science knowledge to work. Anchor charts scaffold learning for students, and give them ownership of the information that is included.

One of the most important points made addressed the use of scaffolds because they are the bridges that students need to connect with what they do not know. Thus, students can complete science

Figure 2.10 Scaffolding Strategies to Promote Science and Language Learning

Scaffolds	Building Student Learning	Tasks
Frameworks	Create connections between and across science concepts that seem unrelated	Compare/contrast Partner/group work Project-based learning Tutorials Guided practice Hands-on exercises Investigations Games Songs Rhymes Foldables
Models and gestures	Use Concrete experiences Wait time Clear enunciation and articulation Partner/group work Give meaningful feedback Paraphrase Define learning expectations	Think aloud Read aloud Anchor charts/graphic organizers Interactive word/phrase wall TIP (Terms, Information, Pictures) tables Role-playing Discussions Prompts and sentence starters and frames Cues
Links	Awaken prior knowledge Establish personal connections between student and science	Brainstorming Think/read/write-pair-share Guided practice Print/visual-rich science classroom Model building Student-generated materials (books, recordings, storytelling, etc.) Science notebooks T-charts
Contexts	Relevance of new and unfamiliar science information	Manipulatives Science tools and equipment Different media to promote oral and written language Science charades

Source: Adapted and modified from San Diego County Office of Education, Scaffolding Matrix for English Learner Instruction.

assignments without being hindered by gaps in their learning. Teachers need to have a clear picture of learning expectations, write science along with language objectives, develop a rubric based on these expectations to monitor student progress, provide meaningful feedback throughout the learning process, and promote responsibility for achieving independent learning.

Your Turn

1. You have been asked to make a presentation to your faculty on why planning is key to student learning. To get started, here are a few questions to consider:

   Why do you think many teachers find planning a waste of time or say they do not have time to write out their science lesson plan, even when they have limited experience and/or knowledge with the content and/or instructional strategies that promote learning?

   a. What can you do to get your colleagues engaged in the planning process, beginning with writing science and language objectives and selecting appropriate science literature books?

2. In what ways are science notebooks thinking tools? How do notebooks support differentiated learning?

   Review Figure 2.6 (Sample Science Notebook Entries) and identify the key differences that you notice. For example, how does the fifth-grade entry differ from the second-grade entry, and so on?

   a. How can you use science notebooks as a formative assessment tool to demonstrate growth to students and their parents?

3. Take one exercise in the "Ideas for Growing Language" section and make plans to use it in your science classroom. For example, how can telling science tall tales benefit students in growing language in science?

   a. The science topic is: ______________________________.

   b. Description of how you will develop it: ________________.

   c. Science and language objectives for this exercise are: _________.

4. Review Figure 2.10 (Scaffolding Strategies), pick one from each of the three columns that you have not used before, and build your next science lesson around them.

5. In what ways can anchor charts engage students in a science topic?

   a. How are they different from other charts you have used?

   b. What advantages do they offer students?

3

Enhancing Science Teaching and Learning Through Inquiry and the 5Es

© Fuse/Thinkstock Photos

Science at its best is an open-minded method of inquiry.

—Rupert Sheldrake

Introduction

The three dimensions of the Next Generation Science Standards offer insight into how to think about inquiry teaching and learning science in grades K–5. It is within the context of the eight practices in Dimension I of the NGSS that they become meaningful and complement the disciplinary core ideas found in Dimension 3. It is the crosscutting concepts in Dimension 2 that serve as a bridge for connecting them. These three dimensions serve as a template for planning inquiry lessons using the 5Es.

The 5Es inquiry model builds on students' curiosity by valuing their impulse to learn through direct personal experiences that in turn shape their views of their world. For Dyasi, "inquiry can make a difference in the way children acquire and understand scientific concepts" (http://www.nsf.gov/pubs/2000/nsf99148/ch_2.htm). The science standards elaborate on ways that students learn to use scientific inquiry to refine their ideas as they continue to uncover answers to questions they present: *How does a light bulb work? Why do ants leave trails? Where does the moon go during the day?*

Over the past several decades, planning for inquiry has evolved from three and four phases to the current five. Many learning cycle models describe teacher and student behaviors that support and promote student science learning and communicative language (Bentley, Ebert, & Ebert, 2000). In such classrooms, students are active learners who engage in "doing" science as they carry out investigations, solve problems, and receive meaningful feedback from the outcomes of their own inquiry.

Within the phases of the 5E instructional model, teachers provide multiple opportunities to employ scientific and engineering practices, to address discrepant events, and to ask and prioritize questions as a means for delving into crosscutting concepts and see how they relate to the core ideas of the life, physical, earth, and space sciences, and engineering, technology, and the applications of science and engineering disciplines.

Applying the NGSS in the Science Classroom

In today's science classroom, *inquiry* is a buzzword, and many teachers and administrators emphasize the importance of engaging students in hands-on and minds-on learning. Quinn, Lee, and Valdés (2012) note that even in activity-rich, "inquiry-based" classrooms, the sense-making practices included in the *Framework* needed by students to "transition from their naïve conceptions of the world to more scientifically-based conceptions" are often not addressed (p. 2).

Dimension 1: Science and Engineering Practices

The practices describe behaviors of scientists and engineers as they engage in investigations. The term *practices* was selected rather than *skills* because *practices* emphasizes the fact that scientific investigations require not only skills but also knowledge. It is this combination of knowledge and skills that is targeted for each of the practices (Next Generation Science Standards [NGSS], 2013).

The eight domains within Dimension 1 lay out a blueprint for teachers to use as they plan inquiry lessons, identify experiences, and set up science classrooms where students have opportunities to enhance their science and language learning. These domains are not merely to be considered quickly and then dismissed; they are scientific and engineering practices that form the cornerstone of any K–5 science education program. The following list of eight practices offer teachers guidance in implementing them in the science classroom:

1. **Asking questions for science and defining problems for engineering.** It is important to note the difference between science and engineering practices. Inquiry in science generally begins with questions and then addressing them through the investigative process. In engineering, on the other hand, the process often begins with problems, and it is through the use of designs that problems are solved.
2. **Developing and using models.** Models are indispensable tools for scientific thinking in the classroom. They are representations that are used to help explain science concepts, try out designs on a small scale, and make predictions about what will happen in the future. In addition, models can take many forms, such as drawings, diagrams, flow charts, graphs, and three-dimensional objects like the Bohr model of the atom and those of plant and animal cells. Like scientists, students should spend a lot of time building, testing, and revising their models.
3. **Planning and carrying out investigations.** There are many forms of investigations, including descriptive, comparative, and experimental, that are used to research and develop explanations for what occurs in nature.

4. **Analyzing and interpreting data.** This domain focuses on the process of finding answers to questions through analyzing and interpreting data. The analytic process begins with identifying relevant issues and deciding on what methods would be appropriate to answer the question(s) that are driving the investigation(s) and ends with the organization and evaluation of the data collected. This practice is central to the *elaborate* phase of the 5Es and is fundamental to questioning.
5. **Using mathematics and computational thinking.** This fifth practice uses mathematical and computational representations to find solutions and to support and explain claims. This practice is evident in science when students record data by using charts, tables, and graphs to make sense out of findings generated from investigations.
6. **Constructing explanations for science and designing solutions for engineering.** Having students engage in these practices accomplishes a minimum of two goals: developing a deeper understanding of the science topics, and giving students opportunities to use their communication skills.
7. **Engaging in arguments from evidence.** Students are presented with ways to identify the evidence they have collected during an investigation by asking them to state a "claim" and to support that claim with "evidence." The importance of evidence is embedded throughout the book, but the strategies for identifying claims and evidence are presented specifically in Figure 3.5.
8. **Obtaining, evaluating, and communicating information.** The book includes a myriad of examples of how to get and evaluate information based on evidence. Equally important is to share this information with others when talking, writing, and/or reading about it.

These eight practices are important because they guide teachers and students from their less sophisticated preconceptions of the world to more scientifically based conceptions. Teachers who use all eight when planning and teaching are taking a major step in creating inquiry-based science classroom environments. But maintaining a balance among these practices is crucial; they all play an important part in defining problems and learning scientific concepts. The extent to which these practices can be implemented depends in large part on how developmentally appropriate they are for students, as well as the students' levels of language proficiencies.

Dimension 2: Crosscutting Concepts

There are seven crosscutting concepts that are applicable across all domains:

1. Patterns, similarity, and diversity
2. Cause and effect: mechanism and explanation
3. Scale, proportion, and quantity
4. Systems and system models
5. Energy and matter: flows, cycles, and conservation
6. Structure and function
7. Stability and change

Their significance lies in helping students connect disparate pieces of information and gain an understanding of the "big ideas" (e.g., cycles) in science. Presenting science facts is not an end in itself, but a means to an end.

The crosscutting concepts form an organizing schema that brings together various science disciplines into a coherent whole. Within the concept of "energy and matter" there are many different cycles, including the life cycle, the carbon cycle, the water cycle, the day–night cycle, and the seasonal cycle. Comprehending the "big idea" of cycles is important. All cycles share common characteristics and follow sequences that are repeated. For example, the water cycle begins with precipitation that is followed by evaporation, which turns the water to a gas—a process that takes solar energy. A careful look at the word *evaporate* reveals that *vapor* is its root. When water vapor in the atmosphere is cooled, it condenses and forms droplets of water in the form of rain, hail, sleet, and/or snow that fall to Earth. For printable teacher guidelines on various science topics, including the water cycle as it relates to tree farming, see Real Trees 4 Kids (http://www.realtrees4kids.org/teacher.htm).

Dimension 3: Disciplinary Core Ideas

There are core ideas within the four science disciplines of physical sciences; life sciences; earth and space sciences; and engineering, technology, and the applications of science. The number of core ideas varies for each science discipline. For a science idea to be considered "core" it must meet at least two of the following four criteria, which provide insight into why they are central science ideas. A core idea must (1) be of broad importance across several science disciplines; (2) provide a tool for investigating more complex ideas; (3) relate to student interests and life experiences; and (4) be teachable across grade levels (NGSS, 2013). In total, there are 13 disciplinary core ideas.

Figure 3.1 presents a view of all three domains sharing the same science content. For this lesson, the science and language objectives are the following: Students will demonstrate an understanding of how materials combine to form new materials by constructing and using models, and students will make drawings of each model and be able to explain how each changed using different materials. Figure 3.1 is derived from the work of Willard, Pratt, and Workosky (2012) and includes only science objectives.

Including the three dimensions in science lessons is essential to successfully implementing the NGSS along with the accompanying language objective.

Figure 3.1 Three Dimensions Focusing on Matter

Dimension 1: Science and Engineering Practices	Dimension 2: Crosscutting Concepts	Dimension 3: Disciplinary Core Ideas
Domain 2: Developing and using models Students construct and revise their models through investigating different designs to explain how materials combine to form new materials.	Domain 1: Patterns Students test different model designs using cause-and-effect relationships to explain how materials combine to form new materials.	Physical Science 1: Matter and its interactions—properties of matter Students investigate different materials to see how they combine with one another in the models that they have constructed.

Inquiry in the Science Classroom

Wilson, Taylor, Kowalski, and Carlson (2009) note that in classrooms across America, there is "less frequency and emphasis [on inquiry] than [on] traditional teaching methods and teaching goals" (p. 1). They point out that inquiry has had "little impact on teacher practice" (p. 1). Even in many classrooms where "inquiry" teaching is said to exist, students often are involved in prescriptive investigations. Smith-Hagadone (2013) describes this approach to inquiry as "cookbook-type" science because "the teacher prepares the lesson, gets all the materials ready, teaches the students [what to do] . . . and then the students perform what the teacher planned with known outcomes" (p. 52). These teacher-created, hands-on activities are an excellent first step for modeling the investigative process, use of equipment, safety techniques, and basic skills, but students need much more to learn science through inquiry. Implementing inquiry in science classrooms may sound easy, but it has proven to be an elusive undertaking for some teachers.

Foundation of Inquiry-Based Teaching and Learning

The foundation of inquiry-based teaching and learning has its roots in the following works: (1) Dewey's "educative experience" (1938), in which students undergo a seamless connection to their environment as they create and become involved in a science topic; (2) Duckworth's "wonderful ideas" (1987), which focus on concepts to foster new connections with an organizing schema; and (3) Vygotsky's "social discourse" (1978), which gets students to approach difficult problems in a strategic way and to gain control over their own thinking and behavior through talking and sharing. Darling-Hammond, Austin, Orcutt, and Martin (2003) elaborate on Vygotsky's point by saying, "The foundation of instruction is dialogic; in other words, we learn through exchange and discussion with a specific academic goal" (p. 127). The higher levels that are needed to support students in building science proficiency as presented in the works of Dewey, Duckworth, and Vygotsky seem to be absent, and only basic elements of inquiry are found in many of today's science classrooms.

Inquiry Comes in Three Forms

Generally, there are three variations of inquiry-based instruction—structured inquiry, guided inquiry, and open inquiry—that may account for the range or degree to which inquiry is implemented (Colburn, 2004). Teachers who use "structured inquiry" present science content in a prescriptive, step-by-step format. In structured inquiry classrooms, students make some decisions about which observations and data are important and decide what the data mean, but the decisions are limited. Baxter, Ruzicka, and Blackwell (2012) relate how their students used observational and recording skills at the beginning of the year to describe and categorize rocks and minerals. Later in the year, students used their knowledge to classify different unidentified rocks and minerals.

Moving to "guided inquiry" in the science classroom means students make predictions and pose questions. These questions drive the investigations and lead students to collect and record specific data. They also identify procedures that are needed to interpret the data collected based on the question(s) posed. An example of guided inquiry involves exploring the topic of electricity using wire, a battery, and a bulb. First, students predict what will happen when they manipulate these materials. Then, they record their actions in their science notebooks using words and/or drawings. Students are cautioned about wearing their safety goggles and handling the wire, battery, and bulb when connecting them. By engaging in hands-on/minds-on science (making predictions, getting ideas, and operating on these ideas), students experience guided inquiry rather than just passively watching their teachers light the bulb.

The third form is "open inquiry," which takes students to the next level of investigation. Encouraging students to pose questions and test their ideas to find answers requires entering data into their science notebooks, completing a "t" table, plotting the data on a graph, and coming up with a conclusion from looking at these mathematical graphics for patterns and/or trends. Student-driven investigations are the gold standard for open inquiry. They get them to follow their own leads and results in determining a solution and/or answer to their question(s), such as what will happen if only one of the three plants is watered, or what will happen if different soils are used in each of the three pots with corn seeds.

All forms of inquiry share common traits, and one of the most important of these is fostering thinking skills. For Baxter, Ruzicka, and Blackwell (2012), the three types of inquiry "offer students multiple opportunities to develop their own understanding of science concepts" (p. 46). A continuum with structured inquiry at one end and open inquiry at the other is one way to visually represent inquiry teaching and learning (see Figure 3.2). The main difference between inquiry forms is the degree to which students take responsibility for their own learning and develop independent thinking in understanding science concepts.

Figure 3.2 Continuum of Inquiry-Based Instruction

Structured Inquiry ➔ Guided Inquiry ➔ Open Inquiry

Key Elements of Inquiry

For a classroom to live up to the label of *inquiry,* all eight practices from the *Framework* come into play, along with crosscutting concepts and disciplinary core ideas. When planning and implementing 5E lessons, taking into consideration all three dimensions will result in inquiry teaching and learning. So what is inquiry teaching and learning? One way to define it is to ask a set of questions that address the teacher's role, the student's role, and the setup of the science classroom.

What would observers see? During a routine classroom observation, the basic elements of inquiry will come to life. And the observers will note how the classroom is arranged and how it supports inquiry. There are common traits shared by all three forms of inquiry that reveal what students and teachers are doing.

What are teachers doing? Much has been written about the role of teachers in inquiry science classrooms that includes—but is not limited to—modeling, guiding, facilitating, and continuously assessing. As teachers assume these roles, instruction becomes more student-centered and less teacher-directed. Observers entering an inquiry science classroom will see teachers doing the following:

- Modeling behaviors of ways to use tools and materials, design investigations, find answers to questions, record evidence, report results, and draw conclusions based on findings.
- Guiding students to take more responsibilities to initiate and carry out investigations.
- Using descriptive, academic science language during instruction to provide labels for materials, science events, and phenomena.
- Scaffolding explanations by using a variety of instructional strategies with graphics, including hands-on materials and interactive word/phrase walls on white boards with cards containing magnetic strips that can be manipulated to enhance science understanding.
- Assessing science learning using different measures that include listening to student discourse of science terms and for accurate scientific explanations and descriptions, talking to students using social language, asking them questions, and checking their thinking to assist them in ascending the academic learning ladder.

At first glance, observers might think that teachers are not actively involved in the teaching–learning process. But that impression is often far from the truth.

Teachers are playing a major role in (1) planning lessons that over time shift the responsibility for learning to the students, (2) laying down the foundation for student engagement, and (3) asking students questions about how they would solve problems they encounter and how they would plan to solve them. If the seeds of inquiry are to flourish, all these teachers' roles are essential. By shifting the responsibility for learning to the students, teachers demonstrate that they value their ideas.

What are the students doing in an inquiry science classroom? They are:

- Planning and carrying out investigations as they design fair tests to try out their ideas and satisfy their curiosity.
- Collaborating and working with others in an interdependent, positive way.
- Demonstrating a willingness to change their ideas when new evidence becomes available.
- Showing respect for differing points of view.
- Observing, measuring, and recording data using different tools, materials, and science skills.
- Communicating orally and in writing using a variety of methods, including notebooks to record, draw, graph, and chart information that offers explanations for their findings.
- Questioning and seeking information, and assessing the quality of the results and conclusions.

© Fuse/Thinkstock Photos

Based on this list of student behaviors, observers will be kept busy watching students work individually and in pairs and small groups. It will be evident that students assume the roles of scientists and engineers as they take risks and seek solutions to problems.

How does the classroom environment support inquiry? Observers will see the following:

- Furniture in a configuration that encourages student-to-student and teacher-to-student communication.
- Students working in pairs/small groups with their chairs moved closer together, their bodies leaning over the tables to listen to one another, and showing respect by taking turns to talk.
- Students addressing a task and taking turns offering ideas, prioritizing these ideas, and making good decisions in solving the problem at hand.
- A variety of student-generated materials around the room, such as completed class anchor charts, graphic organizers, ABC Science Books, stories on felt boards, science notebooks with sketches from observations and investigations, notes taken from teacher presentations, and science literature books and other resources.
- Students expressing their own ideas and opinions confidently, so that all students can hear in small-group and whole-class venues.
- Teachers asking open-ended, "rich" questions to enhance students' thinking and to encourage them to ask their own questions.
- Students critiquing and questioning their ideas and those of others.

The responses to the three questions are a starting point for knowing what inquiry is and for nurturing it to promote science learning. Not all inquiry classrooms look alike. One important reason why has to do with the forms that inquiry takes in science. Yet another is the degree to which the elements of engaging students in thinking about ways to explore and investigate the world around them, allowing and assisting students to find their own path to learning, and providing students with direct experiences are implemented.

Inquiry and Language Learning

Inquiry classrooms are rich in language-learning opportunities. Such an environment supports language use while making sense of science. Valuing all students' contributions is a prime component of inquiry teaching and learning (Carlsen, 2007; Kelly, 2007). "This view is consistent with contemporary literature in science learning and teaching that highlights what students and teachers *do* with language as they engage in science inquiry and discourse practices" (Lee, Quinn, and Valdés, 2013, p. 9).

Teachers who use "descriptive and academic science language during instruction" provide labels for materials and science concepts and events. In turn, students "collaborate and work with others in an interdependent positive way," using listening and speaking skills as they work through investigations. Last, the furniture is arranged to encourage student communication, giving them opportunities to put their heads together and decide what to do next. In an inquiry classroom, students are active learners who feel comfortable participating in the development of an anchor chart, making a topic foldable, and/or assuming the roles of scientists and engineers investigating problems.

Inquiry Science and the 5E Connection

In 1997 Bybee took the many conceptions of inquiry and published the 5E instructional model. The 5E model embraces inquiry teaching and learning, shifting the role of teachers from managers of hands-on science to facilitators of students' science thinking. The phase names are self-explanatory, giving clues to what the teachers and students are to do. In addition, the model has formed the basis for many science programs, including Full Option Science System (FOSS), Science Curriculum Improvement Study (SCIS), and Insights, as well as teacher education courses and professional development. It is an ideal context for using inquiry practices in the science classroom.

The five phases of the instructional model afford students opportunities to learn through *engagement, exploration, explanation, elaboration,* and *evaluation,* respectively, as they manipulate different materials and objects and think about their ideas, and then follow up on them through investigations. McHenry and Borger (2013) report on studies that have found that the 5E model has had a positive impact on learning scientific thinking and on cultivating an interest in science.

Other studies have confirmed that the 5Es, when compared with traditional teaching strategies such as lectures followed by labs, enhance student understanding. In fact, Cardak, Dikmenli, and Saritas (2008) go one step further by reporting that the 5E model was more successful in (1) getting students to construct concepts in their minds by addressing misconceptions in their prior knowledge; (2) promoting greater understanding of information that requires interpretation; and (3) providing a classroom environment that is rich in real objects, print materials, and interesting visuals.

Taking the 5Es Apart

The 5E model is not only a way to teach; it also offers a framework for planning. When sitting down to plan, it is important to consider the following:

- What is the focus of the unit (or series of lessons)?
- How will the individual lessons start to get the students motivated?
- What will the students be doing in each lesson?
- How will students demonstrate their understanding?
- How will students learn the academic terms and definitions of the lesson against the backdrop of the science practices, concepts, and disciplinary ideas?
- How will teachers know that the students have learned what they experienced?
- What language skills and knowledge are needed for students to demonstrate what they have learned?

By following the 5E model, the answers to these questions become evident. The labels are rather obvious: *Engage* is a time to get the students stimulated and ready to learn. In *explore,* the students are "doing" things to enhance their learning. *Explain* is the time for connecting the dots of the information they have experienced. In *elaborate,* students learn and participate in the steps to an investigation, along with learning to use computational skills to record data and plot them on a graph. Last, in *evaluate,* teachers and students find out what has been learned and understood, and to what degree.

Figure 3.3 is a 5E science lesson-planning template. It includes a place for the lesson topic, the science and language objectives, concepts to be presented, and a place for materials for each phase. In addition, it provides a synopsis of each phase, along with some ideas for scaffolding. The planning template is provided on the companion website, http://resources.corwin.com/ReinhartzGrowingLanguage, in Word format so that it can be modified as the science topics change.

At first glance, the phases of the 5Es give the reader the impression that to use the model successfully, it must be followed as is and in a lockstep fashion. Yes, each phase does lead to the next, but the teachers may want to return to *engage* after students have had a chance to *explore* using hands-on materials. Or teachers may want to move to *elaborate* after the *explore* phase. What is frowned upon is starting with *explain,* because then students do not have a context for learning and understanding the science and concepts. Even though many teachers find beginning with the terminology helpful, this

Figure 3.3 5E Science Lesson-Planning Template

Title of the lesson:

Objectives:

A. Science: ______________________________

____

B. Language: ______________________________

____

Concepts/topics:

Materials for each phase:

Phases	Materials
Engage	
Explore	
Explain	
Elaborate	
Evaluate	

General overview of each phase:

Engage

Actively involves students using a variety of strategies. Answering the following questions will assist in getting to the heart of the lesson:

What is the focus of the lesson?

What is the big idea of the lesson to evoke prior knowledge?

What language skills will be needed to carry out the *engage* phase?

Explore

Builds on prior knowledge by getting students to predict: *If I do ____ then ____ will happen. I think ____ because ____.*

Students use materials—or, if outdoors, the environment—to carry out an investigation/activity.

Which inquiry skills will be promoted?

What language skills will be needed to carry out the *explore* phase?

Explain

Teachers connect the *engage* phase to the *explore* phase by using science terms as they relive/tell/demonstrate the previous experiences.

Teachers construct an anchor chart with students that will be referred to later when talking about what they did, writing about it in their science notebooks, and participating in the science loop in the *evaluate* phase.

(Continued)

Figure 3.3 (Continued)

Students make their ideas/thinking public during small-group and whole-class discussions (taking turns, listening to each other, and talking).

Teachers listen to the interactions and contributions from students to determine level of understanding.

What language skills will be needed to carry out the *explain* phase?

Elaborate

For our purposes, it is the part of the science lesson when students come to know and understand the steps to an experiment. It starts with a question; the type of question posed depends on the cognitive and language levels of the students. The question frame *What is the relationship between ____ and ____?* is a place to begin; refer to Figure 3.5 for a detailed account of the *elaborate* phase.

What language skills will be needed for the *elaborate* phase?

Evaluate

How will the students show what they have learned? How do you know they know?

Use reflection questions: *What new questions do you have now?*

Use sentence frames to get students started: *This reminds me of ____ because ____. It was like ____ because ____.*

Have students participate in the science loop. See Figure 3.6.

What language skills will be needed for the *evaluate* phase?

approach does not align well with inquiry-based teaching. The experiences in the *engage* and *explore* phases provide an important foundation that contextualizes science information.

Engage

This phase begins the inquiry process by getting students involved in the lesson, using and building on prior knowledge and experiences. The experiences form the backdrop for generating curiosity, constructing meaning, and making connections between the past and the present. The goal of *engage* is to capture the students' attention and introduce them to the lesson's concept, topic, and/or inquiry skills. The teacher's role is to set the stage to encourage students to respond to questions, participate in think-pair-share strategies, listen to stories, make observations, and/or contribute to K-W-L/anchor chart exercises. The Know-Want-Learn charts have evolved into Know-Learning-Evidence-Wonder (K-L-E-W) charts, thanks to the work of Hershberger, Zembal-Saul, and Starr (2006). These authors wanted to highlight the essential features of inquiry by involving students in scientifically oriented questions, to give priority to evidence, and to justify their explanations based on it. For them, the letters are described as follows:

1. "K" gets students to answer the questions, *What do we "think" we know? Through inquiry, what do we think we can change?*
2. "L" is the response to the question, *What are we learning?* This is answered by active investigations to find out about a science topic.
3. "E" answers the question, *What evidence supports what we are learning?* The emphasis on evidence is essential to the learning and is a significant departure from the K-W-L chart. The evidence is the data collected and reported.
4. "W" gets students to respond to the question, *What new wonderings can be investigated?* Here, asking testable questions is emphasized.

Another example to begin the *engage* phase is to use the picture like the one below (graphic used with permission from Minerals Education Coalition, 2014):

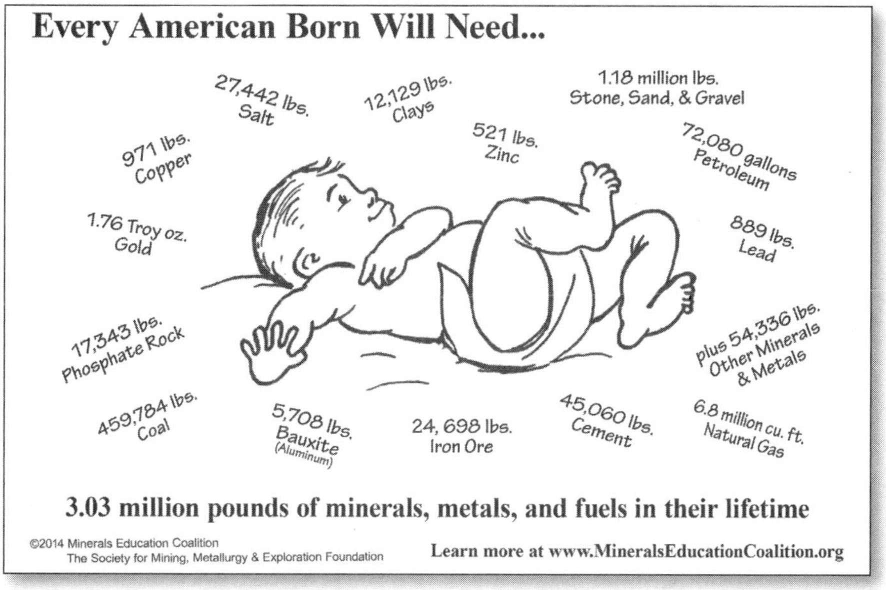

Source: Used with permission from Minerals Education Coalition, 2014. www.MineralsEducationCoalition.org

An earth science lesson focusing on minerals might open by asking students to look at a slide with a graphic of a baby on it. They take the time to observe the baby and the information on the slide. Then, the teacher or a student reads the statement below the baby: "Every child born will need 3.03 million pounds of minerals, metals, and fuels in their lifetime." The teacher asks a series of questions to get them thinking and to spark their curiosity: *What are minerals, metals, and fuels? Where do these materials come from? How are they alike? Different? Why do we need these materials? Why did the artist use a picture of a baby? What do you think the artist was trying to communicate in the picture? What is the artist's point of view?* Once the students are hooked, they are ready to learn more. Figure 3.4 provides an example of how the other four phases build on the *engage* phase presented using the picture of a baby.

Explore

In this phase, students working in groups participate in hands-on experiences that put them to work when making their predictions, offering their hypotheses, thinking through problems, and finding solutions. Manipulating materials is the key to a successful *explore* phase. This is the time when students get their hands on materials, construct models, make observations, and/or take part in an exercise to test their ideas and clarify their understanding.

In the mineral lesson, groups of students are given a box of minerals and the tools (magnifying glass, streak plate, chalk) to examine them. They use these tools to learn about minerals—how hard or soft they are—and to see the differences among them. Together, they make predictions and confirm them by testing each mineral. They draw pictures and write descriptions in their respective science notebooks. And students decide if there are any similarities or differences. Working together in small groups provides an ideal environment for discussing each mineral, voicing their observations, explaining similarities and differences among the specimens, and recording the properties of the minerals they examined (Carrejo & Reinhartz, 2014b).

Explain

In the *explain* phase, teachers use various strategies to give order and names (academic science terms and definitions) to events and topics that the students encountered during the *engage* and the *explore* phases. In addition, students have opportunities to compare ideas, construct

Figure 3.4 5Es, Identifying Student Science and Language Behaviors for the Topic of Minerals

5E Phase	Student Science and Language Behaviors	Science and Language Lesson Presented
Engage	Students will (1) collect information through observations; (2) draw inferences based on information presented and support them with evidence; (3) respond to questions and phenomenon to spark interest; (4) recall information to make connections to prior learning to bring meaning to words and pictures in context; (5) ask, both orally and in writing, higher-order questions to offer a solution to a problem; and (6) organize information, using a graphic organizer, to determine properties of the materials and their specific purpose.	Lesson opens with a slide of a picture of a baby with the following on it, and students are asked to look at it: "Every child born will need 3.7 million pounds of minerals, metals, and fuels in their lifetime." Teacher asks, *What are minerals, metals, and fuels? Where do they come from? How are they alike? Different? Why do we need these materials? Why did the artist use a picture of a baby? What do you think the artist was trying to communicate in the picture? What is the artist's point of view?*
Explore	Students will (1) interact with materials (minerals) and use tools to guide their exploration; (2) use their observation and data collection skills; (3) communicate verbally with peers to confirm hypotheses, draw pictures, write descriptions, and label specimens drawn in the science notebooks; (4) begin to analyze information recorded; and (5) identify in writing common patterns, similarities, and differences.	Using trays of rock specimens, groups of students will (1) observe and identify properties and attributes, and categorize them; (2) describe and record their ideas in their science notebooks (if disagreements emerge, they use the written data in their notebooks to support or refute claims); (3) respond to the question, *Are there other attributes that were not mentioned (such as volume)?*; and (4) compare and contrast their ideas in their groups.
Explain	Based on student experiences during *explore,* the teacher will (1) introduce appropriate science vocabulary and content, using an anchor chart; (2) guide the students through an oral discussion to build science understanding over time; (3) encourage students to employ appropriate verbal, nonverbal, and listening skills to enhance interpersonal relationships; (4) ask questions to promote connections between the picture first presented and	Teacher will (1) encourage students to consult classroom resources available and their textbooks if they have questions; (2) ask, *What is meant by common properties or characteristics of a material (for example, color, streak, mass, volume, density)?*; (3) assist students in making the connections between the hands-on experiences during the *explore* phase and the points presented during the class discussion as they demonstrate appropriate

(Continued)

Figure 3.4 (Continued)

5E Phase	Student Science and Language Behaviors	Science and Language Lesson Presented
Explain (continued)	hands-on experiences; and (5) provide a learning environment that supports analyzing various types of information to determine the difference between facts and the big ideas (concepts).	communication skills; and (4) have a better understanding of science vocabulary, including the common properties of minerals, through analysis of different types of materials.
Elaborate	Students will (1) build relationships between variables identified during an experiment that relate to minerals; (2) use models (scientific and mathematical) to make connections between ideas and theories and to test their hypotheses; (3) become aware of connections involving cause and effect; (4) complete a data table and plot data on a graph; and (5) support their responses using various types of text evidence in their science notebooks.	Students have opportunities to test their ideas based on information gleaned from the discussions, the hands-on experiences, information written in their notebooks, and their textbooks. An example of a question posed: *What is the relationship between the mass and volume of the mineral (i.e., what is the density of the mineral)?* Students gain insight into the characteristics of density by conducting an experiment that looks at the relationship between the mass and volume of a mineral. This experiment stresses a relationship between variables, thereby providing a context for learning the big idea of density.
Evaluate	Students are assessed in a variety of ways: (1) entries in their science notebooks; (2) speaking and listening to their peers in their work groups and whole-class discussions; (3) questions they ask; (4) responses they give to questions; (5) reading their notebook entries and information on loop cards; and (6) matching activities of terms to definitions to identify their level of fundamental language skills, science vocabulary, and interpretations of graphics created so data can be interpreted and conclusions drawn.	For this lesson, students participate in the science loop: an oral exercise in which students read aloud the information on their card and listen attentively to what is being read so that they can respond with the definition so there is a match.

Source: Adapted and modified from "Teachers Fostering the Co-development of Science Literacy and Language Literacy With English Language Learners," by D. J. Carrejo and J. Reinhartz, 2014b, *Teacher Development*. Retrieved at http://dx.doi.org/10.1080/13664530.2014.914564. Reprinted by permission of Taylor & Francis Ltd, www.tandfonline.com on behalf of The Teacher Development.

explanations, and validate them based on gathered evidence. An anchor chart that might have been constructed during the earlier phases can be referred to now as a review. The goal of *explain* is to connect the experiences from *engage* and *explore,* and the students' roles include explaining, listening, questioning, and demonstrating their understanding.

Continuing with the lesson on minerals, the teacher introduces the science content relative to the grade and language levels—such as mineral, hardness, luster, color, crystal shape, cleavage and fracture, and streak—guiding the students through an oral discussion to build science understanding and again referring to the anchor chart prepared earlier. Students are encouraged to employ appropriate verbal, nonverbal, and listening skills as they contribute to group and/or class discussions. The teacher asks "rich" and "skinny" questions (see Chapter 4) to promote connections between the picture the students first viewed and the mineral specimens they examined in the *explore* phase. *What are common properties of minerals?* is a question that gets the ball rolling for students to analyze the information they have collected.

Elaborate

The *elaborate* phase differs from Bybee's (1997) in a few ways (see Figure 3.5). The emphasis is on conducting investigations that start with a "rich" question: *What is the relationship between . . . (the variables)?* Using this question frame, students test their ideas based on information previously gleaned from small-group and whole-class discussions. In addition, practices and crosscutting concepts from the NGSS are an integral part of the *elaborate* phase. *Elaborate,* as presented in this book, is an opportunity to have students learn the steps that are involved in solving problems and setting up investigations to come up with answers, which is central to inquiry learning. Figure 3.5 includes an expanded explanation of the phase, complete with steps for conducting an investigation, along with sentence frames, a "t" table and graph with sample numbers, and a scaffold for identifying claims and evidence.

Figure 3.5 uses popcorn as the unit of science study to provide a context for laying out the steps for a science investigation. Also included is a Claims and Evidence Scaffold that can be used to guide students in learning the importance of collecting data and using them to make claims or statements about what has been found out.

This approach to *elaborate* embeds the terms of variables, hypothesis, "t" table, and graphs with plotted data, and discusses results using terms such as *claim* and *evidence.* The Claims and Evidence

Figure 3.5 *Elaborate* Phase in Detail

Title of investigation:

Science and language skills/concepts:

Materials needed:

Elaborate

For our purposes, *elaborate* is the part of the science lesson where students come to know and understand the steps to an investigation. It starts with a question. In this experimental investigation, students use the question frame, *What is the relationship between ____ and ____?*

First, the word relationship should be discussed and defined, and examples provided and placed on the science word/phrase wall. A graphic organizer is constructed with the word relationship in the center, with lines radiating from the word to demonstrate what the students think the "relationship" means.

Using this frame—*What is the relationship between ____ and ____?*—opens the door to understanding *variables* (dependent and independent). For example, *What is the relationship between the brand of popcorn and the number of kernels popped?* The brand of popcorn is the independent variable, and the number of kernels popped is the dependent variable.

1. After coming up with a class *question* (using the *what is the relationship between ____ and ____?* question frame), take a minute to analyze the question for cause-and-effect phrases. For example, in the popcorn question, the brand of popcorn is the *cause*, and the number of kernels popped is the *effect*.
2. Students then formulate a hypothesis. It is an idea that can be tested.
3. Students design and conduct an experiment, make observations, and collect data and record them on the "t" data table.

***Brand of popcorn* is the *cause* (independent variable)**	***Number of kernels popped* is the *effect* (dependent variable)**
Brand A	
Brand B	
Brand C	

4. They *plot the data* from the data table to a graph (bar, line, circle), labeling each axis with the names of the variables.

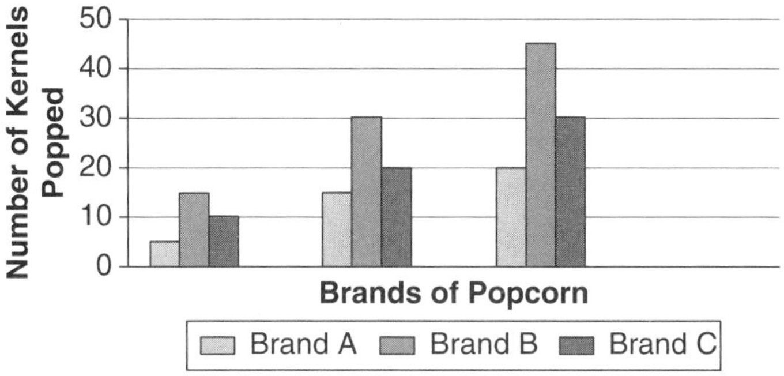

5. Now, students are ready to *analyze the data* they have collected. One place to begin is to review the information plotted—which brand has the most kernels that popped, the least that popped, and somewhere in between.

   Looking at the graph, decide which brand is the best to buy, based on the evidence they uncovered in this experiment. Ask, *Why do you think so?*

   If they need some support in coming up with answers, why do you think the Claims and Evidence Scaffold that follows may prove helpful?

   Students go back to the "t" table and the graph to fill in the Claims and Evidence Scaffold. They think about their "claims" or conclusions made about the popcorn brand—best, worst, in between. Once a *claim* has been identified, it must be supported with *evidence.* The key question is: *Is there evidence to support your claim of best, worst, in between?* If the answer is "yes," students go on to the second claim, finding evidence in the data collected and plotted on a graph.

Claims and Evidence Scaffold

Claims	Evidence

Taylor and Villanueva (2014) provide the following series of questions that teachers can ask to assist students in completing the Claims and Evidence Scaffold. The following question and sentence frames provide a template for student responses.

a. What do you *claim* to be true from your investigation?
b. How can you prove your claim? (How can you back up your claim?)

   I claim that when I did ____________, then ____________ happened.

   I know this is true because I observed ____________.

(Continued)

Figure 3.5 (Continued)

c. With the whole class, ask, *Who agrees with each group's claim?*

How many agree with ________ group's claim and evidence?

How many disagree with ________ group's claim and evidence?

Student response sentence frames might include:

I agree with________ claim because ________.

I disagree with ________ claim because ________.

d. Finally, ask, *Which of the following claims is most like yours [state the claim]? My claim is . . .*

- *similar to ________.*
- *somewhat similar to ________.*
- *completely different from my classmates.* (Taylor & Villanueva, 2014, p. 64)

6. Students in the upper grades will identify and then describe the variables in their investigation based on the question they posed and the data they collected.

7. In their science notebooks, students will do the following:

- Write the question and make a hypothesis, which is an idea that can be tested by an experiment or observation (*Sciencesaurus*, 2006).
- Sketch a "t" data table using the question and the variables they identified. Taking the popcorn question, *What is the relationship between the brand of the popcorn and the number of kernels popped?*
- Summarize the findings, looking at the information in the "t" table and drawing conclusions by using sentences following these frames: *In this investigation, I did________* or *I learned that ________*. They use the information from their Claims and Evidence Scaffold to respond. Emphasize that every claim must be supported by evidence.

Scaffold can assist students in where to look for their claims (i.e., in the "t" table where they recorded findings during the investigation) and their evidence (i.e., in the graph with plotted data collected, as patterns are more evident in graphic form). Taylor and Villanueva (2014) offer a series of question frames to get students to use the scaffold.

Evaluate

This phase checks to see what the students have learned and understood from the lesson. Teachers assess students in a variety of ways, as do students to determine their own progress. Rubrics listing performance criteria along with the task are insightful, providing both the teachers and students information about how they are progressing. Written entries in notebooks, responses to questions, student-formulated questions, the approaches that students take to build models and make changes to test their ideas, and reading the science loop cards are all viable opportunities for formatively assessing student science and language knowledge and skills. The loops have been developed to measure science learning and students' communication skills. Figure 3.6 includes an example of the answers for a science loop for earth science.

The loop is an oral exercise in which students read aloud the information that is on their card and the rest of the students listen to what is being read so that they can respond with the correct answer.

I have: core.	I have: sediment.
Who has: pieces of weathered rocks and minerals?	Who has: the breaking up of rocks by wind and water?

For example, each student receives a card that has the phrase, *I have* [science term—*core*], and another phrase, *Who has* [definition or picture of a different science term—*bits of weathered rocks and minerals*]? The process is then repeated until all terms have been matched with their respective definitions. The loop ends when the last definition matches the first term that was read. The science loop is also presented on the website in Word format so that the *I have* and *Who has* statements can be altered.

If you want even more information about each phase, refer to Figure 3.7, 5Es in the Science Classroom. This figure has three components: the first is a description of each phase, the second has a list of suggestions that teachers can use when planning, and the last provides suggestions for getting students involved in the science lesson. Figure 3.7 presents ways for teachers to differentiate science and language instruction for each phase of the 5Es. Last, the figure highlights how students use a variety of skills: cognitively—thinking about the science topic in a number of different ways, and kinesthetically—handling materials and discussing them with a partner or group members.

Figure 3.6 Science Loop Answer Key

1. I have cleavage.
   Who has the innermost layer of the Earth?

2. I have core.
   Who has bits of weathered rocks and minerals?

3. I have sediments.
   Who has the breaking up of rocks by wind and rain?

4. I have weathering.
   Who has the outer layer of the Earth?

5. I have crust.
   Who has the breaking down and carrying away of rock and soil by wind and moving water?

6. I have erosion.
   Who has a type of rock that forms from sediments?

7. I have sedimentary rock.
   Who has the property of a mineral that reflects light?

8. I have luster.
   Who has the process of change that rocks continually undergo?

9. I have rock cycle.
   Who has a solid element from the Earth's crust that has a definite chemical composition?

10. I have a mineral.
    Who has a rock that forms from melted rock, cools, and hardens?

11. I have igneous rock.
    Who has a layer of rock between the crust and the core of the Earth?

12. I have mantle.
    Who has the property that splits along flat surfaces of some materials?

Figure 3.7 5Es in the Science Classroom

Phase	Description: Involve students in activities that . . .	Teacher Role: Plan and implement experiences that . . .	Student Role: Active participation and involvement as students . . .
Engage	• Focus students' attention • Stimulate thinking • Generate interest • Access prior knowledge • Give students time to think and investigate, make decisions, solve problems, and collect information	• Create interest • Introduce a science topic using kinesthetic strategies • Motivate students • Ask for student input • Connect content to student interest • Tap prior knowledge • Raise questions and encourage responses • Use books or short articles on a science topic • Analyze a graphic organizer or completed anchor chart • Show, using examples of how to tell stories of science models that have been built • Have students assume roles and responsibilities (PI, MM, MD, RR) randomly • Accommodate all levels of language proficiency • Provide opportunities to use language	• Ask questions • Manipulate materials • Analyze illustrations • Participate in K-W-L, K-L-E-W • Brainstorm with partner or group members • Participate in class discussion to complete an anchor chart • Solve a problem • Construct models • Write stories of their models in their science notebook • Ask questions such as, *Why did ____ happen? What do I already know (or think I already know) about ____? What have I found out about ____?* • Show interest in the topic by asking questions, reviewing science literature books, checking the Internet, etc. • Follow directions and assume a group's roles and responsibilities

(Continued)

Figure 3.7 (Continued)

Phase	**Description:** Involve students in activities that . . .	**Teacher Role:** Plan and implement experiences that . . .	**Student Role:** Active participation and involvement as students . . .
Explore	• Develop inquiry skills (observing, predicting, investigating) • Get students to think, make decisions, and collect information; investigate and test their ideas; identify relationships; solve problems • Involve students in constructing models to explain their thinking	• Facilitate science learning • Accommodate all learning styles • Accommodate all levels of language proficiency • Provide opportunities to encourage language usage, listen as students interact with one another, ask "skinny" and "rich" questions, encourage cooperative learning	• Conduct investigations • Use observation skills while manipulating different objects • Construct models and tell their stories • Use observation skills while manipulating different objects • Record data on a "t" table • Analyze results (evidence) collected • Draw conclusions based on results • Participate in discussions • Cooperate with group members during the investigation
Explain	• Review tasks completed in the *engage* and *explore* phases • Model and use talk-aloud strategies for science terms that they encountered in previous phases • Clarify understanding of concepts, processes, and/or skills by using examples, pictures, and manipulatives • Explain and define terms and provide real-world examples • Allow students to analyze what they did when they carried out the *engage* and *explore* exercises	• Encourage the use of new words and concepts • Ask students to clarify and support their responses using evidence they collected • Use students' past experiences as a basis for explaining concepts and to address misconceptions • Encourage students to use their own words when defining, explaining, describing, and sharing their ideas • Use green/red cards to assess students' level of understanding	• Review the investigation by "walking through" it • Support their ideas with claims and evidence • Complete graphic organizers • Respond to "skinny" and "rich" questions • Use green/red cards to demonstrate they understand the teacher's explanation (red side up if they do not understand or green side up if they do understand) • Compare data gathered by each group and determine the group with the highest _____, the lowest _____, the most _____, the least _____, the best _____, the greatest _____, etc.

Phase	**Description:** **Involve students in activities that . . .**	**Teacher Role:** **Plan and implement experiences that . . .**	**Student Role:** **Active participation and involvement as students . . .**
Elaborate	• Connect learning to similar situations • Encourage students to communicate new understanding using science terms, etc. • Answer the question, *What is the relationship between ________ and ________?* • Get them to: ○ Identify the hypothesis ○ Identify variables ○ Create and test hypotheses ○ Record data collected on "t" tables ○ Plot data collected on graphs ○ Explain results ○ Draw conclusions	• Involve students in answering the *What is the relationship?* question • Get students to do the following steps: ○ State the question ○ Identify the hypothesis ○ Identify the variables ○ Conduct investigations ○ Collect data (three times to ensure consistent results) on "t" table ○ Plot data collected on a graph ○ Explain results ○ Draw conclusions	• Problem solve using a new situation • Make decisions • Write information in their science notebooks • Conduct investigations • Follow these steps for experiments: ○ Write the question ○ Write and test a hypothesis ○ Name the independent and dependent variables ○ Prepare "t" table ○ Conduct the investigation ○ Collect data ○ Record data on table ○ Construct a graph, label all parts, and plot the data collected ○ Explain results in their science notebooks ○ Draw conclusions and write them in their science notebooks ○ Write the story of the investigation starting with the question and ending with the conclusions in their science notebooks

(Continued)

Figure 3.7 (Continued)

Phase	**Description:** **Involve students in activities that . . .**	**Teacher Role:** **Plan and implement experiences that . . .**	**Student Role:** **Active participation and involvement as students . . .**
Evaluate	• Use measures to assess performance • Demonstrate the level of understanding of concepts, skills, processes, and their applications • Demonstrate understanding of new concepts by observing or responding to "rich" questions • Demonstrate that they know, understand, and can use what they have learned by telling, writing, showing, and/or doing • Use small groups so students can discuss cause-and-effect relationships, claims and evidence, variables, the significance of the data collected, and results recorded on the graph	• Involve the observation of students as they apply new concepts and skills in different real-world situations • Use a variety of formative assessment strategies • Provide opportunities to: ○ Assess students' knowledge and/or skills using a rubric of performance and knowledge measures ○ Review science notebook entries over time to identify changes in students' thinking and behaviors ○ Show that students are being cooperative by demonstrating respect, making good decisions, and solving problems	• Create products • Draw/write in their science notebooks to demonstrate their use of science language and show they understand the inquiry skills of observing, predicting, etc. • Respond to peers • Create and write stories using the steps to the investigation as a guide to sequence their writing or pictures • Take part in a science loop • Assess their science entries in their notebooks • Put information in graphic organizers, foldables, and K-W-L/K-L-E-W charts • List claims and evidence based on information collected during investigations and recorded on tables, graphics, etc. • Perform their roles and responsibilities within the small groups

Phase	Description: Involve students in activities that . . .	Teacher Role: Plan and implement experiences that . . .	Student Role: Active participation and involvement as students . . .
Evaluate (continued)	• Ask them to create write/tell the stories about: ○ the relationship between _____ and _____ in the investigation ○ their models ○ Complete two/three/four column foldable to respond to _____, _____, and _____. Also complete the wonderings column in K-L-E-W. • Get them to use oral language to communicate with their peers and to record information in their science notebooks	• Encourage students to assess their own learning • Ask "rich" questions, such as: ○ *Why do you think _____ happened when you _____?* ○ *What evidence have you collected regarding _____?* ○ *What claims do you have about _____?* ○ *What have you found out about _____?* ○ *How would you explain/describe _____?*	• Demonstrate that they are being cooperative by showing respect, making good decisions, and solving problems • Create and complete foldables, graphic organizers, and the wonderings column in K-L-E-W • Complete self-assessments

Available for download from **http://resources.corwin.com/ReinhartzGrowingLanguage**

Conclusion

The *Framework* sets a course for inquiry learning by laying out science and engineering practices, crosscutting concepts, and disciplinary core ideas. Often, teachers think they are implementing inquiry practices in their classrooms, but this may not always be the case. One way to determine if the principles of inquiry teaching and learning are being implemented is to pose and then answer three questions: (1) *What are teachers doing?* (2) *What are the students doing?* and (3) *How does the classroom support inquiry?* These questions and their subsequent answers shed light on how science inquiry supports language learning and are connected to the 5E instructional model. Also see the website, http://resources.corwin.com/ReinhartzGrowingLanguage, for additional resources and links.

Your Turn

1. What does inquiry science teaching mean to you?
2. In what ways and to what degree do you promote inquiry science teaching in your science classroom? Specifically, if an observer came into your classroom, what would he or she see you and your students doing?
3. On the continuum, Structured Inquiry → Guided Inquiry → Open Inquiry, where would you place yourself, and why? If you are at the left end, what can you do to move along the continuum? If you are at the opposite end, what can you do to support your colleagues in getting to this point in their teaching of science?
4. Use Figure 3.3 to plan your next lesson. What will be the topic of the lesson? How will you get the students' attention? What opportunities will be provided for exploring materials related to the topic? In what ways will the students investigate the topic further? What will you do to check the students' level of understanding?
5. You have been asked to be a mentor to new teachers joining the staff. Your first task is to get them on board with the new science standards and the 5Es. During your session with them, provide an overview of the three dimensions (science and engineering practices, crosscutting concepts, disciplinary core ideas) and ask them to take a moment to study them and to talk among themselves.

a. Next, ask them to select one or two items from each dimension. Once they have made their selections, have them use the 5E science lesson-planning template to plan a lesson on a topic that is part of their science curriculum.

b. Near the end of the session, ask each of the teachers to share their science lesson, and after their presentations you will have an opportunity to determine the extent to which they are familiar with the standards and how the dimensions can be applied in the planning process.

c. Based on the information from the formative assessment gathered during their short presentations, you will have areas on which to build for future whole-class and individual sessions.

PART II

Science and Language in the Science Classroom

A Good Pairing

4

The Power of Questions

© triloks/Thinkstock Photos

Good teaching is more a giving of right questions than a giving of right answers.

—Josef Albers

Introduction

Asking quality questions does not just happen: It is an acquired skill. Posing effective questions during instruction is often taken for granted, and many teachers think they can formulate them on the spot. Unfortunately, not all of us are that adept. Holding to such a myth often results in asking questions that require students merely to recall information, and in sacrificing the opportunities for them to apply, analyze, evaluate, and create something new from the science information presented. As the German-American art educator Josef Albers alludes to above, asking the right questions at the right time can be as important as knowing the right answer.

On average, teachers ask more low-level questions that often are referred to as "skinny" or "thin" questions. These questions serve to check on students' factual knowledge, in the hope that they have committed something to memory. Skinny questions usually require one-word or short-phrase responses to seek a fact or general information. For younger students in kindergarten and first grade, asking recall questions can be extremely helpful in determining the degree to which they have understood science information. For older students in grades 2–5, teachers should strive to add more high-level questions, sometimes referred to as "rich" questions, to their teaching repertoire. Across grade levels, striking a balance between skinny and rich questions is the ideal.

Teachers who do ask higher-order questions have greater learning gains, especially for upper primary and intermediate grade students (Rothstein & Santana, 2011). These types of questions challenge students' original understanding and alleviate misconceptions; they ensure that students comprehend the science information and that they have the skills to manipulate what has been learned in new ways.

Honing Questioning Skills

Prompting deeper levels of thinking is critical for the following:

1. Focusing students' attention on salient components in the lesson, which translates into improved comprehension.
2. Getting students ready for learning the next topic.

3. Stimulating interest in the upcoming topic.
4. Connecting previous information and materials to what is currently being presented.
5. Increasing student academic performance.
6. Responding successfully to questions on mandatory standardized tests.

To achieve these broad questioning goals, teachers should consider ways to enhance their questioning skills. First, they need to consider (1) the science and language objective(s) of the day's lesson, (2) what they will be teaching, and (3) what they want students to learn. Once these have been decided upon, it becomes important to write out the questions to be asked in advance. This may be viewed as a waste of time, but in the long run it is time well spent and leads to academic improvement.

Deciding on the total number of questions is also important. Consider writing 2–3 skinny questions using the information from the previous lesson to connect to the current science topic. As new information is presented, plan 2–3 skinny questions to assess learning levels and then intersperse 3–4 rich questions to further challenge students. This combination of skinny and rich questions will support students in accommodating and assimilating the new topic. The objective of asking a large number of questions is to gain insight into what students know and understand, what they still need to know to further their knowledge, and what they can do with it (Rosenshine, 2012).

After the questions have been written, the next step is to sequence them so that they are asked at the appropriate time during the science lesson. Timing can be everything. Finally, consider writing redirecting, reinforcing, and probing questions to get students to think more deeply. These can be standard questions that can be added to a teacher's questioning repertoire regardless of the science topic. Some examples: *So what evidence do you have to support your answer? How do you know that is the case? That is an interesting point you have made, but what are some other ways to think about it?*

How busy science teachers can take the time to write out questions for their lessons is a question that often arises. However, many science textbook series and/or district/state curriculum guides offer resources that can prove helpful. These resources may include objectives of the lesson/chapter, ideas for activities and investigations, and a series of questions to ask. Start here, but do not accept outright the questions presented. These resources always should be reviewed carefully.

Additional resources can be found in Figure 4.2, which includes useful verbs and question stems for each level of the cognitive domain. Once you decide on the set of questions to use, type them out and leave enough space between them so that the sheets can be printed, cut apart, and sorted. These ready-made question cards can be put in a folder and used again next year.

Response Strategies

For McTighe and Wiggins (2013), formulating questions is extremely important, but so are the follow-up questions to engage learners and extend their thinking and meaning-making. These are response strategies that are especially effective with rich questions that do not have expected answers.

Wait time is an important response strategy that refers to the period of teacher silence that follows a question (Wait Time I). Waiting at least 2 seconds for students to respond after a question is asked, and then waiting another 2 seconds after students respond before saying anything, is Wait Time II. Research has found that waiting at these two points in the questioning sequence has amazing results because it allows students time to process questions and formulate answers (Rowe, 1986; Tobin, 1987). In addition to stimulating thinking, Wait Time I and Wait Time II increase the following:

1. On-task student classroom behavior
2. Student responses beyond *yes/no* to include both phrases and complete sentences to explain their ideas
3. Student comments and questions that are relevant to the discussion
4. Student-to-student and student-to-teacher interactions
5. Teacher expectations of their students' abilities

Using Wait Time I and Wait Time II takes planning and practice. Teachers in their zeal to support students and to keep the lesson moving respond almost immediately once students offer responses to questions. Often, the end result is leaving many students behind. In contrast, Rowe (1986) notes that using wait times to slow down the pace of the lesson is actually a way to speed it up.

It takes patience to give students time to understand the question, formulate an answer, and respond. Slowing down the pace of the lesson gives students a chance to take a breath and get to the business of thinking and taking part in the discussion.

Implementing a wait time strategy has many benefits for teachers as well. Teachers are more relaxed; they have time to listen to student responses as they use science terms and explanations when remembering, applying, analyzing, and evaluating information; and they have opportunities to *assess what the students know and what they still need to know to understand the science topic.* Research also suggests that when using both forms of wait time, students behave better during discussions, think more creatively, and listen to one another's comments. This, of course, promotes the communication skills of listening and speaking that are so important for English learners.

Most teachers are pressed to "cover" the science content, but in doing so ELs lose out and fall behind because they are reluctant to participate, thereby assuming a more passive role in classroom interactions (Mohr & Mohr, 2007). They sometimes need time to adapt to the traditional question–answer sequence, and there is an initial silent period during which they receive the language as input before developing language-production skills (Krashen & Terrell, 1983; Saville-Troike, 1988).

Response protocol is another way to extend language learners' classroom interactions. English learners need a different type of support to develop their communication skills as part of teacher-led discussions (Mohr & Mohr, 2007). Asking rich questions yields rich teacher-to-student interactions. To entice students to participate in classroom discussions, teachers should consider using various response options that fall into six categories (Mohr & Mohr, 2007):

1. Responses that are correct. (*You are correct. Where can we go for more information about _____?*)
2. Responses that are partially correct. (*You are on the right track. Do you or your partner have more to add?*)
3. Responses in a language other than English. (*That is interesting. Can you ask your partner to tell us how we say that in English?*) Repeat the question and model the response in English.
4. Reponses that are questions. (*That is a good question; thank you for asking it. Would you like to call on one of your classmates for an answer?)*
5. Responses that are inappropriate or wrong. It is important to determine if the incorrect response is content- or language-based. (*What do you know about ____?*)

6. Silent responses. (*Can you show us, or draw it?*) Let the student know you will come back to it. (*Let me know when you are ready.*) Suggest that the student ask his or her partner.

The response protocol is especially important because it validates the students' responses and demonstrates the teachers' effort to scaffold opportunities for students to elaborate on their answers.

The wait time and response protocol are only two of many response strategies that teachers can use. Others include think-pair-share, class surveys involving the whole class with thumbs up and down, and having more than one answer to questions. What is not recommended is to call only on students who have their hands raised. McTighe and Wiggins (2013) suggest that over time, teachers should stop having students raise their hands at all, giving every student an equal chance of being invited to respond.

Different Types of Questions Call for Different Levels of Thinking

Different types of science experiences require different types of questions that lead to different levels of thinking. Achieving different levels of intellectual development means planning and asking questions that get students to recognize "that thinking is inevitably driven by . . . questions . . . that to answer questions we need information" to make inferences, and that in turn involves ideas (Elder & Paul, 2010, p. 4).

Bloom's Taxonomy

One of the eternal questions that face teachers is how to improve student thinking. We do not have to start anew. Benjamin S. Bloom contemplated the nature of thinking, and in 1948 spearheaded a group of educators to classify educational goals and objectives that would develop a method for classifying thinking behaviors that were important for learning (Forehand, 2005). The framework became a taxonomy with three domains—one of which was *cognitive,* which had six levels that originally included recall, comprehension, application, analysis, synthesis, and evaluation.

It was in 1956 that a handbook often referred to as *Bloom's Taxonomy* was published, and it has remained the standard for classifying thinking goals for more than half a century (Bloom, Engelhart, Furst, & Krathwohl, 1956). In 2001, Anderson and

Krathwohl published a revised version of the model of low to high thinking with changes in three broad categories: terminology, structure, and emphasis (Forehand, 2005). Figure 4.1 presents a concise comparison of the old (1956) and new (2001) versions of the cognitive domain. Note that *evaluating* moved down one level, and *synthesis*—now *creating*—moved to the top.

Bloom's Taxonomy is a multitiered, hierarchical framework of six cognitive levels of complexity in thinking. This means that students who function at the low level of *remembering* will be able to master content at the *understanding* level. Think of it as a staircase that teachers can use when they plan lessons and questions to encourage their students to "climb" to higher levels of thought. The lower part of the staircase includes the lowest three levels of *remembering, understanding,* and *applying*. The higher three levels now are *analyzing, evaluating,* and *creating.*

Bringing together *Bloom's Taxonomy* and the cognitive levels of thinking is crucial. Thinking is driven by questions—and through questioning, sound habits of thought are promoted and achieved. The information in Figure 4.2 takes the guesswork out of enhancing thinking and learning through questioning. The first column identifies the revised levels of *Bloom's Taxonomy,* along with key verbs that can be used in planning activities as well as when asking questions. The second column is critical because it sets up the tasks that students will be asked to perform to support them in moving up and

Figure 4.1 Comparison of Cognitive Domain in Old (1956) and New (2001)

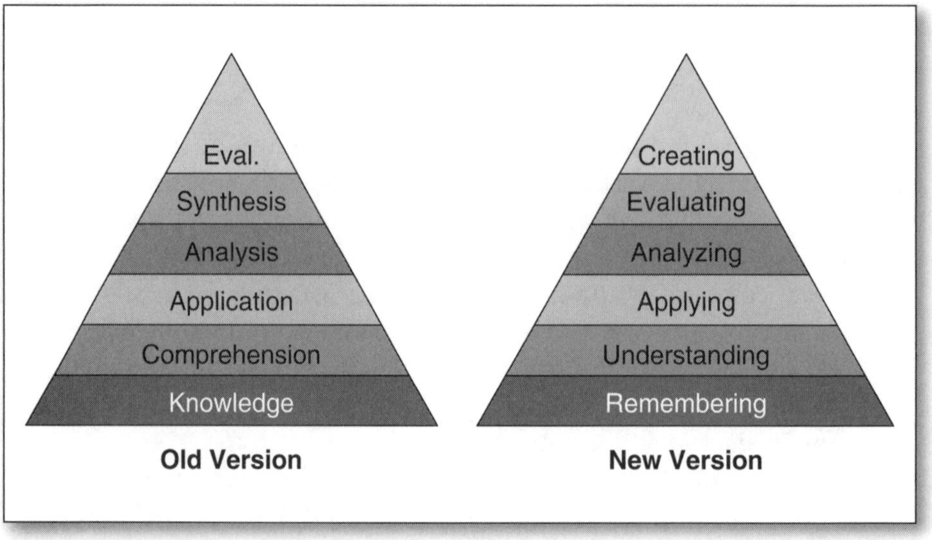

Source: R. Overbaugh and L. Schultz, http://ww2.odu.edu/educ/roverbau/Bloom/blooms_taxonomy.htm. Used with permission.

Figure 4.2 Asking Different Types of Questions

Bloom's Levels: Cognitive Domain Verbs to Consider	Teacher Strategies That Prompt Different Levels of Thinking	Question Stems That Activate Different Levels of Thinking
Remembering Recalling Recognizing Listing Describing Relating Locating Writing Saying Stating Naming	Teachers have the students retrieve relevant knowledge from memory by having them: • Recall the names of the _____. • List in order the steps to the investigation. • Construct a _____ of natural occurring events. • Tell all the information they remember from the lesson on an index card, or upon leaving on a sticky note attached to the doorframe. • State key points recorded on an anchor chart about _____. • Develop a graphic organizer to show what students did during _____ investigation. • Examine a box of _____ and identify what students see (patterns, textures, colors). • Complete a Venn diagram showing what they found after they conducted an investigation, what another group found, and what both groups found.	*How many _____ are similar and how many _____ are different?* *What was it that caused the change in _____?* *Can you name the parts to the _____?* *What happened when _____?* *What is the same and/or different from the other groups?* *Can you tell the difference between _____ and _____?* *What is the meaning of _____ found in the book?* *What is _____?* *What happened after you _____?* *What is related to _____ in the two investigations/exercises?* *What did you include in the Venn diagram? What is different for group A and for group B? What do they have in common?*
Understanding Classifying Summarizing Comparing Explaining Interpreting Outlining Discussing Distinguishing	Teachers have the students construct meaning from oral, written, and graphic information by having them: • Cut out or draw pictures of _____ to show the order _____ events took place. • Illustrate/draw what students think the independent and dependent variables were in the _____ investigation. • Create a cartoon strip showing the sequence of how _____ becomes a _____. • Write and sing a song based on the facts about _____.	*How will you begin your story about _____?* *From the pictures you have drawn, what is the sequence/order of the events?* *Why did you put them in that order? What system/criteria did you use?* *What results did you find after completing the investigation?* *Did you predict what happened in the investigation? Why? Why not?*

(Continued)

Figure 4.2 (Continued)

Bloom's Levels: Cognitive Domain Verbs to Consider	**Teacher Strategies That Prompt Different Levels of Thinking**	**Question Stems That Activate Different Levels of Thinking**
Understanding (continued) Predicting Restating Translating Comparing Describing	• Retell/restate the investigation in their own words, stressing what they found. • Paint a picture of the patterns they found in the _____ and tell its story. • Prepare a flow chart to distinguish one phase/stage from the next _____. • Make a coloring book to show what happened when _____. • Play the 20 Questions game. • Cut out word tiles that are synonyms or antonyms. • Manipulate materials such as a ruler to make a _____. • Fold a sheet of paper in two columns. Label one column _____ and the other _____, and write down the important information about each. • Write or tell a neighbor after a discussion what they learned.	*What do you think would happen next if you added _____ instead of _____?* *What was the science core idea when we did _____?* *What was the major point the author made in the _____ (book)? Why do you think so?* *What was the key factor that affected the _____?* *What distinguishes _____ from _____?* *What differences exist between _____ and _____?* *What is _____? What is an example of _____?* *What is a definition for _____?* *How does it feel? What if you used different materials?* *What sound do you hear?* *What mind map can be used to show key points for each topic?*
Applying Executing Implementing Distinguishing Examining Comparing Contrasting	Teachers have students carry out tasks by having them: • Design a questionnaire/survey to gather information about _____. • Write a commercial to sell a product. • Formulate questions and design and conduct an investigation to show information that supports _____ view. • Make an anchor chart to identify and show the stages of _____.	*Why do you think _____ occurred when _____ happened?* *If _____ had not happened, do you think you would have the same results? Different results? Why do you think so?* *How was this similar to _____? How was this different from _____?* *What was the underlying theme of _____?* *What is another possible outcome for _____?*

Bloom's Levels: Cognitive Domain Verbs to Consider	Teacher Strategies That Prompt Different Levels of Thinking	Question Stems That Activate Different Levels of Thinking
Applying (continued) Investigating Categorizing Identifying Explaining Separating Advertising	• Plot a graph to illustrate _____ information found in _____ investigation/recent newspaper article. • Use the science terms from _____ and make a game. • Make a class family tree, showing _____ traits. Make their own family tree, showing _____ traits the students inherited. • Plan and act out an advertisement about _____. • Write a biography of the _____ scientist, identifying his or her accomplishments and comparing these accomplishments to other scientists living at that time. • Pretend to be a reporter and contrast the problems/issues of _____ with _____.	*Why did _____ change occur when you _____?* *What is the same in today's lesson on _____ as compared to yesterday's lesson?* *What are some of the problems with having too much _____?* *What are the distinguishing contributions of _____?* *What was the turning point in the _____?* *What is your favorite _____, and why?*
Analyzing Differentiating Distinguishing Examining Comparing Contrasting Investigating Categorizing Identifying Explaining Separating Advertising	Teachers have students break apart material/information into parts and have them: • Conduct an investigation to produce information to support a _____ view. • Categorize pictures of _____ into different groups. • Identify the ingredients that make a _____. • Review a series of pictures of _____ and explain what is happening in one of the pictures they select. • Pick out the five most important items that they would need to _____. • Make a model of a _____ and explain why each of the parts is needed for the model to work. • Read a short article on _____ and have them identify the "bottom line" based on scientific evidence.	*What do you think happened when _____ happened?* *How was this similar to _____ compared to _____?* *Why do you like the _____ book?* *Why did _____ fit into the group?* *When making _____, what ingredients do you need?* *What if you left out _____, would it look/feel/act the same?* *When making a _____, what materials are most important for _____ to be a success?* *When making a _____, why are _____, _____, and _____ so essential to the model/picture/illustration?* *After reading an article on _____, what evidence do you think was provided to support _____ or to refute it?*

(Continued)

Figure 4.2 (Continued)

Bloom's Levels: Cognitive Domain Verbs to Consider	**Teacher Strategies That Prompt Different Levels of Thinking**	**Question Stems That Activate Different Levels of Thinking**
Analyzing (continued)	• Sort through a stack of cards and ask them to hold up the one that begins with the letter _____. • Analyze the panels on food boxes for _____ and _____. • Review advertisements and have students pick one and explain the main point to the advertisement on _____ and _____.	*What evidence was the "bottom line" based on in the article?* *What on the box of cereal tells you it contains _____?* *Does _____ advertisement tell you about its product? If yes, in what ways? If no, what is missing, and why do you think so?*
Evaluating Judging Selecting Critiquing Choosing Deciding Justifying Debating Verifying Arguing Recommending Assessing Discussing Rating Prioritizing Determining	Teachers have the students make judgments based on standards by having them: • Evaluate each standard in a rubric for a _____ science exercise/investigation. • Prepare a list of criteria to judge _____. • Rate the items for _____ by prioritizing them. • Conduct a debate on the _____ issue and have them write the information for each side of the issue. • Make a booklet recommending five rules on _____ that are important for a science class conducting investigations. • Convince others about _____ and why it should take place. • Participate in a panel discussion on _____, knowing each facet of the argument. • Write a letter to _____ with reasons for changing/adding _____ to the _____. • Write what they would like to add to _____ in their class/school with reasons and prioritize them beginning with the best one.	*Do you have a better solution for _____? If so, what is it, and in what ways is it better?* *What is the highest grade you can get on this exercise? What are you expected to do to succeed? What is a rubric? How does it work? Why is it important to _____?* *Do you think the _____ natural resources are valuable? Why do you think so? What value does it have to/for _____?* *Do you have evidence for your position on _____? What is it?* *Why do you think _____ is good? Why do you think _____ is bad?* *We are going to take a nature walk. What do you think we should do? What are three reasons for your choice?* *What "position" on the topic of _____ will you take in the panel discussion?* *In your letter to _____, what points will you make to support your ideas? Which one will you put first?*

Bloom's Levels: Cognitive Domain Verbs to Consider	Teacher Strategies That Prompt Different Levels of Thinking	Question Stems That Activate Different Levels of Thinking
Creating Inventing Composing Reorganizing Planning Constructing Designing Imagining Proposing Devising Formulating	Teachers have the students put together elements that form a whole in a way that is new by having them: • Design a _____ product that will house _____. • Create a new _____. Give a name and plan how to market it to their classmates and other customers. • Write a song/poem/chant/rap about _____ that they have been studying. • Imagine they are puppets trying to get students interested in _____. Write a script to show what they would do. • Take an existing cover of a book, CD, or magazine, and reimagine it with their ideas. Create a "prototype." • Participate in the Wheel of Ideas game. Design something that is new and test it out. • Devise a way to _____.	*Can you design a _____ to do _____?* *What words would you use in a _____ about _____?* *What would you like to create that is different from _____?* *What script would you write if you were the puppet?* *If you were given the cover of a book, a CD, or a magazine and asked to redesign it, what would you do? How would you change or modify it?* *Why?* *After studying about _____, what recipe would you come up with? Why? What ingredients would you use to promote _____?* *How would you sell a science idea about _____? How would you get started? What will you need?*

Source: Modified and adapted from *Bloom's Taxonomy* "Revised" Key Words, Model Questions, and Instructional Strategies, 2006; and *Toolbox for Planning Rigorous Instruction*, 2009.

Available for download from **http://resources.corwin.com/ReinhartzGrowingLanguage**

down the cognitive levels as outlined in the hierarchy. Last, sample question stems are presented that can be used to challenge students as they move back and forth from *remembering* to *creating*.

Hopefully, the ideas presented in Figure 4.2 will provide teachers with a jump-start on asking questions that promote different levels of thinking. This figure is available on the companion website, http://resources.corwin.com/ReinhartzGrowingLanguage, for easy access.

Cognitive Demand and Webb's Levels of Thinking

Academic rigor and thinking deeply about scientific concepts permeate the NGSS; there is an expectation that students engage in cognitively complex thinking and reasoning, getting them to persist when an answer is not obvious. They need to engage in tasks that demand interpretation and the construction of meaning (e.g., *cognitive demand*) rather than just simply verifying knowledge, following procedures, and/or carrying out exercises with weak conceptual understandings. That is why teachers need to be cognizant of the science exercises that can span from memorizing definitions to developing skills and constructing knowledge. The next step is to consider the level of thinking demanded of students to successfully participate in tasks (Kisa, Stein, & Schunn, 2013).

Cognitive demand as described by Webb (2002) includes four levels on which students interact with the science content:

1. Recall (students demonstrate a rote response, following a procedure with clearly defined steps)
2. Basic application of skills and concepts (students interpret information, organize and display data in tables or graphs, explain the purpose, and use experimental procedures to carry out an investigation)
3. Strategic thinking (students demonstrate more demanding reasoning, planning, and using evidence to draw conclusions, develop a logical argument, and explain events in terms of concepts)
4. Extended thinking (students use complex reasoning over time that makes connections within and among the science disciplines possible when they plan and conduct experiments, synthesize and combine ideas, and critique experimental designs)

Like Bloom, Webb developed a list of question stems and a list of verbs for depth of knowledge (DOK) levels. The information on these lists, along with a comparison of levels of thinking in *Bloom's Taxonomy,* can be accessed online by clicking on Levels of Thinking, DOK question stems, and Depth of Knowledge Levels (Common Core Standards: Overview—Depth of Knowledge), as well as on the companion website.

After analyzing what the students are expected to do (e.g., cognitive demands of the exercises), teachers are in a position to identify the types and degree of support and guidance that students will need to be successful. The information gleaned from this analysis will help to monitor the movement from structured inquiry to open inquiry and the types of questions that should be asked.

Webb's four cognitive demand levels and Bloom's cognitive demand categories have been used to describe different learning and assessment contexts (Hess, 2006). They represent cognitive actions based on the nature of the situation that could be high or low in cognitive demand. Their importance lies in getting teachers to consider what it takes to promote complex thinking about crosscutting concepts and reasoning about disciplinary core ideas and the use of science and engineering practices as outlined in the three dimensions in the science standards.

Getting Students Ready for Their Questioning and Responding Roles

Students Asking Questions

Teachers are not the only ones who ask questions in the science classroom; students do as well. In doing so, they become learners and thinkers who explore their world and build and integrate a deeper understanding of science topics (Chin & Chia, 2004). Thinking relies on the students' capacity to be seekers and integrators of knowledge. This capacity is nurtured by posing questions.

A good way to begin to develop this questioning capacity is to read Margaret Wise Brown's *The Important Book* (1999) to students. It offers a model for framing the question, *What is important about . . . ?* Once they use this question stem, students can explore things that interest them and find answers to their questions. Teachers may need to begin by defining the word *important.*

Once students begin asking questions that focus on everyday events and/or objects, they are ready to formulate questions and seek to find answers by exploring and investigating. Implementing this as a strategy boosts students' self-esteem and moves them along the path of inquiry. Their findings become a springboard for describing orally and in writing what they found. Compiling students' entries can result in "The Important Science Classroom Book," which can be taken home and shared with family members.

Giving students opportunities to ask questions is a central component to inquiry science. It places students in an active learning role as they investigate questions to seek new knowledge and integrate it into what they already know. Becoming skilled questioners has many benefits. These benefits include learning to structure a question; to gather, organize, and analyze information; and to come up with possible solutions to problems. The benefits do not stop there: Students learn to express themselves, make decisions, expand their understanding of science topics, seek and consider different points of view, and refine their understanding by accommodating relevant new information.

Students Responding to Questions

Becoming skilled responders is as important to students as learning to be skilled questioners. Scientists respond to questions all the time as they encounter new situations.

Modeling thinking strategies for the students plays an important role in answering questions. The goal in asking as well as in responding to questions is to have students see themselves as thinkers. As students practice good thinking skills, they develop sound habits of thought. The following seven-step process may prove helpful in teaching students how to sharpen their thinking skills to feel more comfortable in answering questions orally and in writing. Students must regularly do the following:

1. Listen carefully to the questions being asked.
2. Clarify the questions, if need be.
3. Ask themselves what science content is needed to answer the questions.
4. Formulate an answer in their minds by gathering and organizing information before answering or making comments.
5. Take into account comments and contributions made by other students and the teacher.

6. Take time to revise, and to make mental changes in their own answers that include this new information.
7. Learn to think in a different way as they respond to different types of questions.

Not all questions are the same, and they may require different types of thinking. For example, asking *yes/no* and *what if* questions requires students to use different thinking processes. The *yes/no* questions, for example, require dichotomous thinking—*it is or it is not?* Students have to choose depending on how much they know and remember about science topics to answer the questions. The *what if* questions require students to connect bits of information and to think more holistically as they formulate answers in their minds before sharing them with others. Taking time to teach and implement these steps before every lesson will help students realize that automatically raising their hands and/or blurting out something without thinking about it first are not acceptable response behaviors.

One place to begin developing response skills with students new to English is asking *yes/no* questions to review, assess what they already know, and determine what needs to happen in the next lesson(s). Using "Who Am I? 20 Questions" is another starting point. For example, 20 questions can begin with the teacher selecting an animal or plant for students to identify. Before the game starts, a few examples should be modeled involving all the students. The students will need time to practice, but once they get the hang of it they will be ready to start asking questions in their groups. One member of the group asks the others 20 questions that have *yes/no* answers: *Is it an animal? Is it a plant? Does it move? Does it need food? Does it look the same as an adult as it did as a baby (frog/tadpole, butterfly/caterpillar, etc.)? Does it eat other animals? Is it a tree?* If, after asking 20 questions, the questioner does not have the answer, it is time for a "lifeline," or clue. The group member responding to the questions provide the lifeline or clue, and it is in the form of a statement: *It is green in color all year round.*

By using this game-based strategy, students learn to ask broad questions first, followed by more specific ones. This lays the foundation for how living things are classified. The game can be modified to make it more complicated by asking questions that are more challenging—for example, *Does the animal live only in fresh water? Does the animal live only in salt water? Do the animals have skin (fur, scales, feathers)?* The questions should be developmentally and language-level appropriate. The goal is to have fun while using language to communicate the students' knowledge of the science topics. What is really great is that the activity does not require any special equipment or supplies.

Another way to give students opportunities to practice their response skills to questions is to participate in the Weather game. Give each group a stack of pictures of different places. Members of the group select one picture from the stack. Using this picture, they respond to the following questions:

1. What season is depicted in the picture?
2. What evidence do you have to support the season you selected?
3. What would this place look like in a different season of the year?
4. What three questions come to mind when you look at this picture? Write them in your science notebook under the title Weather game exercise (questions should start with who, what, where, when, or how), or tell your group members your three questions.

The next step is to have members of each group create a travel brochure advertising the location represented in the picture. The brochure should have four panels, one for each season of the year. Instruct students to hold their paper horizontally. In each panel, ask the students to describe the following: (1) the location during each of the four seasons, (2) the temperature in each season, (3) the type and amount of precipitation, and (4) the plants and animals that live there.

Once students work in small groups to have a dry run at participating in the Weather game, they gather for a whole-class discussion about each group's picture. It is at this time that teachers ask questions about their picture during each season and implement Wait Times I and II and the response protocol discussed earlier. Depending on the students' response, different questions are presented keeping the response in mind as well as focus on different levels of *Bloom's Taxonomy*. If the students respond in one of the six ways outlined, then follow-up questions have to be structured to accommodate different levels of language proficiency (Genesee, Lindholm-Leary, Saunders, & Christian, 2006), as well as on their levels of content understanding (Goldberg, 2008). In addition, teachers may opt to use aids that are tactile (green plant), visual (their brochures), and auditory (sound of howling winter winds) to make science more understandable to students (Samway & Taylor, 2008). These small-group and whole-class experiences not only offer a meaningful context for science learning, they also promote students' creative abilities as well as their communication skills.

Questions That Prompt Thinking at Various Levels

Achieving different levels of thinking means having students engage in different types of science investigative experiences to provide a context for talking about them. Posing skinny questions during an investigation, such as *What is the temperature of the water in the beaker?* or *How does a pendulum work?* results in students restating what they observed using a thermometer and/or in explaining the workings of a pendulum. These types of questions and responses often rely on observations, using science tools, and/or putting students' senses to work. These investigations get them to gather information by measuring the temperature of the water and by counting the number of times the bob goes back and forth before stopping.

Science investigations should not end there; they should be designed to get students to use the information stored in their memory and rearrange and extend it to the current situation. In doing so, students come to understand the science topic and have opportunities to put the knowledge gained to use in new ways.

With guidance in asking the question *If the length of the cord is changed, how many times will the bob swing back and forth until it stops?* students can move to the next cognitive level, of thinking hypothetically. *What if* questions provide a context for using the information collected and to speculate about the number of swings that occur when a change in the length of the cord is made in the model of the pendulum. In this situation, students mentally weigh all the information to come up with an answer. If the number of swings was 10, then shortening or lengthening the cord would mean the bob would go back and forth a different number of times. Engaging in these types of exercises not only challenges students but increases their confidence, laying the groundwork for them to think at higher levels.

Asking relationship questions during the *elaborate* phase gets students to process information at higher levels. Continuing with the pendulum example, asking a question about the relationship between the length of the cord and the number of times the bob swings back and forth gets students to think about two variables—the length of the cord and the number of swings. As they record information on the "t" table during an investigation, responses to this question unfold. In examining the table, students ask themselves, *Is there a pattern?* The number of swings of a 6-inch cord is greater than the number of swings of a 12-inch or 18-inch cord. There is indeed a pattern.

Length of the Cord **(Independent Variable)**	Number of Swings **(Dependent Variable)**

In this example, students are gathering evidence to answer the relationship question based on the information collected and recorded in the number of swings column. In doing so, they begin to recognize a cause-and-effect relationship between the length of the cord and the number of swings. The cause is the length of the cord (the *independent* variable) and the effect is the number of swings (the *dependent* variable).

There are other examples of rich questions that are generally open-ended, require more time to think, and serve as the connective tissue between previously learned information and the current science event. They are "bright idea" questions and serve as "mental starters." Here are three exercises to trigger bright ideas and to get the mental starters going with students.

The first, *Which one is out (which one does not belong, and why?)*, begins with a set of pictures on a science topic—for example, the solar system—projected on the wall for the whole class to view. Models or other objects can be used in place of pictures.

There are no right or wrong answers, just ways to evoke student thinking at different levels within the cognitive domain—getting them to compare, observe, speculate, sequence, classify, distinguish, and decide. It can begin with *Which picture is out?* or *Which picture*

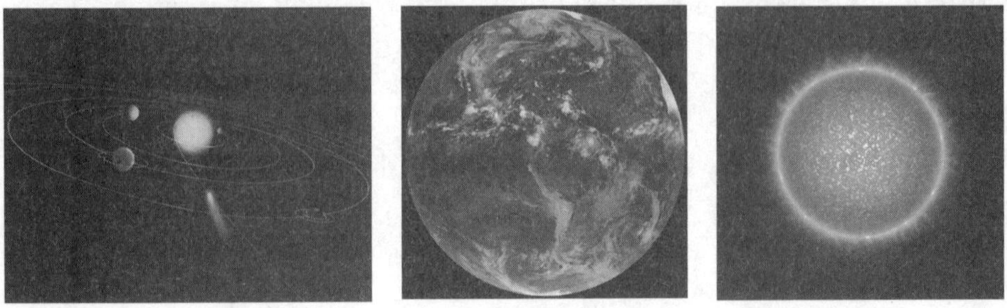

© Digital Vision/Thinkstock Photos © Stocktrek Images/Thinkstock Photos © pialhovik/Thinkstock Photos *does not belong, and why?* Teachers model examples, for instance, by showing three pictures of the solar system as presented—one is the solar system with planets, one is the Earth, and one is the sun. In this example, students might pick *the sun as the picture that is out or does not belong* because it is the only one that has a ring around the circle or because in color it would be yellow. It may be helpful to use a sentence frame: *I pick the picture in the middle because it is the only that has ____,* or, *I pick the picture on the left because it is the only one that ____.* So students can pick any picture they think is out or does not belong as long as they can support their choice with evidence.

This questioning strategy certainly provides opportunities for students to use descriptive and academic science terms as they make their choices and express their reasons for them. In addition, their level of thinking moves from describing (remembering and understanding) to making decisions (evaluating) and developing a scenario (creating).

A second exercise—Positive, Minus, and Interesting (PMI)—has four steps (*Sources of Insight*, p. 1). For example, in a lesson on energy, the exercise can start with the question, *What would the world be like without electricity?*

Positive student statements might be:

1. There would be more time to spend with family.
2. There would be no need for coal to make electricity.
3. You would go to bed earlier after the sun goes down and get more rest.
4. There would be more wind-up toys.

Minus (negative) student statements might be:

1. It would be scary at night without bright streetlights.
2. There would be no public transportation.
3. There would be no TV, videos, or iPads.

Interesting student statements might be:

1. You would be more creative finding ways to spend your time.
2. Torches might become more fashionable.
3. People would be fitter because they would walk more.

This questioning exercise begins by working with students to do the following:

- Write a question on a specific science topic.
- Write three positive statements.
- Write three minus statements.
- Then write three interesting statements.

As students come up with each statement, the PMI exercise gets them to think. Their thinking expands as they generate responses.

A third rich questioning exercise that requires higher levels of thinking is the *big science question* (e.g., *Why is the sky blue?*) that gets students to wonder. These are questions that often stump students, but they also stimulate their curiosity and imagination.

These three questioning exercises ask students to function at the high end of the cognitive domain. Using them on a regular basis can generate a sense of excitement and communicate to them that there still is a lot to be discovered. They can become the scientists who confront many of the mysteries in our world. "Through science we ask questions, collect data, and acquire new knowledge that contributes to our growing understanding of the natural world" (*Doing Science*, p. 3).

Conclusion

Daily, science teachers strive to find ways to promote student thinking. Increasing and sustaining students' thinking about their world begins with asking questions and finding viable answers. Inquiry teaching provides the context for students to ask questions to satisfy their natural curiosity as they conduct investigations that have a purpose, as they gather information, and as they discover new things on their own (Annenberg Learner, nd).

Asking quality questions is an important first step in getting students to think, but it does not just happen. It takes a commitment and a willingness on the part of teachers to prepare different types of questions that have different cognitive demands and tap all six levels of the cognitive domain using both skinny and rich questions. Preparing and asking a combination of low (skinny) and high (rich)–level questions during a science lesson or series of lessons have positive academic consequences for students. Getting started is often the hardest part.

The second aspect to asking quality questions deals with implementing different response options. There are six categories, which are a part of response protocol for teachers to be aware of as they structure the classroom environment and organize the science content. Implementing these options has important implications for English learners as they assimilate information presented and discussed.

Different types of questions target different levels of thinking. Figure 4.2, for example, offers an extensive list of useful verbs, teaching strategies, and stems for asking questions that build students' thinking skills. Without quality questions, students engage in science without paying much attention to the hows and the whys of it.

Your Turn

1. Have would you rate your questioning skills? Take a moment and respond to the following questions. Place a check in the box that best describes your questioning behavior. You can download a copy of the survey from the companion website, http://resources.corwin.com/ReinhartzGrowingLanguage.

To what extent do you . . .	To a great degree	To some degree	Not very often	Never
1. Plan questions to ask in your science class?				
2. Encourage students to expand or elaborate on their answers?				
3. Ask questions that reveal prior knowledge?				
4. Ask skinny questions?				
5. Ask rich questions?				
6. Differentiate your responses to match those of the students?				
7. Use Wait Time I?				
8. Use Wait Time II?				
9. Ask students to pose their own questions?				
10. Ask questions that result in instructional conversation?				
11. Use scaffolds to support student responses?				
12. Respond to students who remain silent when asked a question?				
13. Use the response protocol?				

Source: Adapted and modified from *Asking More Effective Questions*, by W. F. McComas and L. Abraham.

- Summarize your responses: What are you doing well and what are some things that you may want to change?
- Based on this information, how would you describe your questioning skills to a preservice teacher you will be mentoring during the next semester?

2. To get students involved in a class discussion, it is helpful to have questions to prompt them to take part and that also get them to elaborate on their contributions. These prompts may include questions such as the following:
   - What is another example of _____?
   - What material is the best (worst) to use for _____, and why?
   - Now it is your turn to come up with questions that prompt students to expand their answers and/or to encourage them to participate.
3. During a lesson on animals, students working in groups are given a deck of cards with pictures/words of different foods on each one, and they are to sort the cards according to the kind of animal (herbivore, carnivore, omnivore) that would most likely eat that food. Have students share their results with the whole class.
   - What questions would you ask to get the activity started or back on track if the answer is not totally correct, if a language other than English is used, if the answers are questions, if the answers are incorrect, or if there are no responses? Come up with several questions for each of these scenarios and then practice using them in your class.
4. Figure 4.2 offers several ways to get students to think at different levels. Pick a verb from each level and formulate questions that could be used during the science lesson(s) you will be teaching. Challenge your students to come up with questions for each level, write them on an anchor, and have them vote (evaluate) on which ones they think are best, just OK, or not so good.
5. I get pushback from teachers when I ask them to plan lessons—and, specifically, to write out questions—because they are extremely busy. I continue to support the idea that we can accomplish more if we do these things. Think about planning science lessons and questions using Revell and Norman's quote, "Whenever you feel like saying 'Yes, but . . . , try saying instead 'Yes, and . . .'," and generate ways that will get us all to "work smarter" and longer.

5

Doing Science

© Catherine Yeulet/Thinkstock Photos

The most incomprehensible thing about the world is that it is comprehensible.

—Albert Einstein

Introduction

What is most important about conducting investigations is to have students think and see themselves as scientists who are actively engaged in "doing science." Students readily accept the invitation to learn and develop a plan to verify, extend, and/or discard ideas that they have generated. In science, students can take advantage of their natural curiosity. Additionally, investigations involve a whole host of communicative language as students employ a variety of methods to gain insight when proposing explanations and finding solutions to questions, and when critiquing their own science practices. During the investigative process, teachers can gauge students' knowledge and how they are thinking by observing and listening to them and asking them questions (Ash & Kluger-Bell, 2000). Science investigations begin with students exploring phenomena, which is a basic tenet of the science standards. Investigations are at the center of inquiry teaching, which establishes a context for interactive experiences involving both teachers and their students (National Research Council [NRC], 2013).

Investigations Come in Many Different Forms

So what are science investigations? They are opportunities for students to interact with phenomena; to collect data using scientific tools in their classrooms, laboratory settings, and/or in the field; and to uncover solutions to problems (Texas Education Agency [TEA], 2010). Many state standards suggest specific percentages of time during science instruction for laboratory and field investigations. There seems to be general agreement among science educators that in grades K–1, 80% of the time should be devoted to classroom and outdoor investigations. For the other grades, the division of exploratory time is 60% for grades 2–3, and 50% for grades 4–5. These percentages are only recommendations, but if followed, science practices shift from relying on direct teacher instruction to supporting students in the construction of their own science knowledge (Bencze, 2010).

As the percentage of time devoted to investigations decreases when ascending the grades, formal science content expands and plays a greater role. In the 5Es, the *explain* phase is a time for introducing scientific labels, terms, and explanations to clarify further what was encountered during the earlier experiences. For example, according to the percentage recommendations, fourth graders should experience a balance between science content instruction (50%) and laboratory investigations (50%).

As they participate in investigative experiences, upper elementary students are better prepared cognitively to accommodate and assimilate science topics and crosscutting concepts. Building on their investigative experiences, they are ready for sense making of these concepts, such as patterns, cause and effect, scale, systems, energy and matter, structure and function, and stability and change in science. Investigations serve as the foundation for comprehending how facts fit into the bigger science picture. It is helpful for teachers to plan investigations that get students engaged in experiences that call for varying levels of thinking. Three types of science investigations—descriptive, comparative, and experimental—are presented.

Descriptive Investigations

These focus on collecting information and drawing conclusions about what is uncovered, and they are propelled by questions. Students spend much of their time observing and recording what they see based on questions. By asking well-defined questions, information is generated from which students can draw inferences and analyze. No comparisons are made and no hypothesis is generated; nor are there variables to manipulate (TEA, 2010).

Figure 5.1 provides an example of a descriptive investigation using "energy beads" whose colors change in the presence of ultraviolet light (see the companion website, http://resources.corwin.com/ReinhartzGrowingLanguage, for a color version of the photos below that show that when the energy bead bracelet is exposed to light, the beads change color). Several descriptive investigations are included to get students to think about the role of sunlight in causing the beads to change color (Steve Spangler Science, 2000).

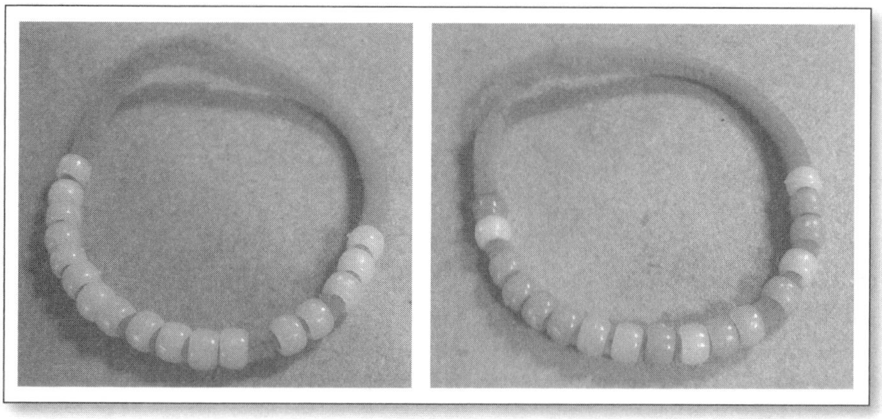

Figure 5.1 Descriptive Investigation: Energy Beads

I. The Science Behind Energy Beads

1. Energy beads are beads that change color when exposed to sunlight because they contain different pigments that change in the presence of ultraviolet light (UV).
2. The beads will remain white indoors but will change color when exposed to UV light. Often, the term *light* is used to describe many different forms of light (incandescent light, fluorescent light, or sunlight). But not all light is made up of the same energy.
3. Energy beads uncover an invisible form of light energy called ultraviolet light, which is not visible to the naked eye. As there are different colors of wavelengths in the visible spectrum (red, yellow, green, blue), so too are there different wavelengths of ultraviolet light.
4. Energy beads help us understand how solar radiation can be harmful and how to reduce the risks associated with exposure to sunlight. UV radiation wavelengths are short enough to break the chemical bonds in skin tissue, which contributes to wrinkles or skin cancer.

II. Descriptive Investigations

A. On a Sunny Day

1. Place a handful of energy beads near a fluorescent light.
2. What do you notice? Did any of the beads change color? Why? Why not?
3. Describe to a group member at least one thing you noticed.
4. Can you get a sunburn or a tan by sitting next to a fluorescent light? Why? Why not?
5. Observe the beads when the sun is out at different times of the day.

   Morning: ____________

   Noon: ______________

   Afternoon: ___________
6. According to the data collected, at what time of day does the sun give off its most intense UV light? How do you know? What evidence is there to support your claim for the time of day?

B. On a Cloudy Day

1. See if the beads change color on a cloudy day.
2. If they change color, why do you think doctors warn people to wear sunscreen even on a cloudy day?

C. The Sunglasses Test

1. Test to see if your sunglasses block out ultraviolet light. Take a few beads and cover them with the lens of the sunglasses.
2. What happened? Tell a group member, or write in your science notebook at least two things you observed before and after covering the beads with the sunglasses. Students share what they wrote with group members about your observations.
3. If the beads changed color, why do you think that happened?
4. If the beads did not change color, explain why.
5. What can you conclude about sunglasses and sunlight? (Sunglasses are constructed to block out harmful ultraviolet light from our eyes. If not, the UV coating is not working and the sunglasses cost too much!)

D. UV Filter Tests

1. Collect a variety of glass and plastic containers/products to find out which materials block out UV light. There are materials that have built-in UV protection such as the front windshield of a car, while the side windows do not. Check it out to see if this is true.
2. Test these materials one at a time by placing them between a UV light source and the beads.

   What do you see? Did anything happen? Did the material/container absorb UV rays?
3. What evidence do you have to support your conclusions/claims about these materials?
4. Describe what you observed in your science notebook and share your findings with the class.

E. Make an Energy Bead Bracelet

1. Thread a few beads onto a piece of pipe cleaner/string/yarn to make a bracelet. See the website for the color change in the energy beads in the bracelet.
2. When your bracelet is complete, tie it around your wrist, at first cover the bracelet with your other hand, and walk outside into the sunlight. Then uncover it.
3. Keep your eyes on the beads. Did anything happen to them during your walk? If so, what? What can you conclude about the energy beads that make up your bracelet?
4. What does your bracelet look like out in the sunlight? Inside the classroom?

Source: Adapted and modified from Steve Spangler Science, 2000, http://www.stevespanglerscience.com/lab/experiments/uv-reactive-beads. Used with permission.

When students wear their bead bracelets, there are many opportunities for them to describe what happens to the pigment in the beads indoors and outdoors. Ultimately, students make meaningful connections between sunlight and its impact on human skin, resulting in wrinkles and contributing to cancer. They can also investigate this topic further.

Comparative Investigations

Like descriptive investigations, the bedrock of comparative investigations is collecting information emanating from questions—for example, different living and nonliving organisms and related phenomena. Students follow a sequence of steps to compare the data they have collected.

Figure 5.2 offers several ideas for conducting comparative investigations.

By analyzing the temperatures during different seasons or the frequency of the same animals or plants in different locations, students begin to recognize patterns. For example, during winter months it is colder than in the fall and much colder than in the summer. When comparing the same animal or plant population data, students also detect relationships and discover reasons that explain the data collected. As the term *comparative investigation* implies, students make predictions and conduct fair tests to measure relationships and collect comparative data about them.

Figure 5.2 Conducting Comparative Investigations

Questions	Ideas for Investigations: Compare Two or More Things
What will the students be doing?	• Compare two or more objects: Which ball bounces higher, a tennis ball or a racket ball? Which container holds more sand, the plastic box or the plastic jar? Which container evaporates water faster, the basin or the beaker? • Compare two or more organisms: Which insect jumps higher, a beetle or a grasshopper? Which is attracted to light the fastest, an earthworm or pill bug? Which grows faster, a bean plant or a corn plant? • Compare two or more conditions: Will plants grow best in warm places (near a heat source) or cold (in a cooler/refrigerator)? Do earthworms prefer to live in light or dark places? Do marbles move farther distances when rolled on a rough surface (carpet) or smooth (tile)?
How is a comparative investigation different from the other types?	1. There is no list of variables. 2. The investigation is done one time—no need for three trials. 3. Students compare the information they collected (using an advance organizer). 4. Students explain how the information is alike or different.
Where do comparative investigations take place?	1. In the classroom, outside on the school grounds, or at home. For example, plant a seed in soil and place it in the refrigerator at home and students record their data over a specific period of time; it grew 5 cm, while the plant on the counter grew 10 cm. Two of the earthworms went to the light in the box; three of the earthworms went to the dark side of the box. 2. The results can be displayed using a tripanel board to share with the class.

Source: Adapted and modified from Denton ISD, Comparative investigations, McNair Elementary School, Denton, TX. Used with permission.

Experimental Investigations

These are analogous to comparative investigations. There is one key difference, however: the control. A control is used to measure a relationship between two variables. In this type of investigation, students manipulate variables.

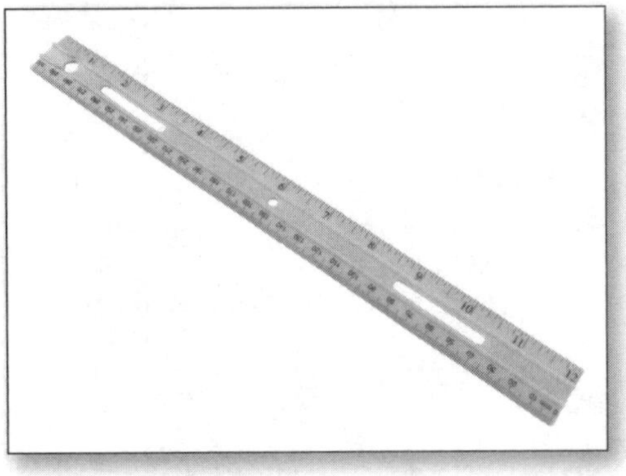

© Ryan McVay/Thinkstock Photos

For example, in rolling a marble down a ramp (e.g., a grooved ruler), the students determine the relationship between the angle of the ramp and how far the marble travels. To conduct a fair test, the surface that the marble travels and the size and type of the marble remain the same for all trials. Keeping the surface and size and type the same is the control. Now, students are ready to collect data from changing the angle of the ramp, putting it in three different positions (e.g., using stacked books). Three runs are made at each position, and students take the average distance the marble travels for each position. Once the averages for each of the three different angles of the ramp are recorded, the students plot these three numbers on a graph.

A guide for conducting experimental investigations can be found in Figure 3.5 (see page 70). It describes the *elaborate* phase, which includes an experiment in great detail.

In an experimental investigation, students ask testable questions and deliberately change the independent variable to determine the type and extent of the relationship existing with the dependent variable. These investigations involve a fair test in which the independent variable (the ramp angle) is manipulated to measure if a change has occurred (the distance traveled by the marble).

Figure 5.3, Experimental Investigation: And the Beat Goes On, is an example of an experimental investigation in which students take their pulse at rest and then again after three different activities—slow walking, fast walking, and jogging in place. This investigation has been uploaded to the companion website, http://resources.corwin.com/ReinhartzGrowingLanguage, in Word format so that it can be modified to meet individual student and grade-level needs.

In experimental investigations, students encounter measuring words and superlative terms. The measuring words include *length*,

Figure 5.3 Experimental Investigation: And the Beat Goes On

A. Question: What is the relationship between ____________________
__________ and ______________________________?

B. Hypothesis: I think ______________________________

C. Variables: Independent and Dependent

Independent Variable (IV)	Dependent Variable (DV)
______________________	______________________

D. Directions

1. Work with a partner. Be sure to have a watch with a second hand, and a copy of this worksheet to record data.
2. Count the number of heartbeats for 1 minute after each activity. Take your pulse at your wrist or throat.
3. Fill in the information on the "t" table for you and your partner.

Types of Activity	**Pulse at rest**	**Pulse after slow walking**	**Pulse after quick walking in place**	**Pulse after jogging in place**
Number of heartbeats per minute	Trial no. 1 = Trial no. 1 = Trial no. 1 = __________ Average =	Trial no. 1 = Trial no. 1 = Trial no. 1 = __________ Average =	Trial no. 1 = Trial no. 1 = Trial no. 1 = __________ Average =	Trial no. 1 = Trial no. 1 = Trial no. 1 = __________ Average =

E. Graph the results from the "t" table by plotting the averages for each activity. Label the *x*-axis and *y*-axis.

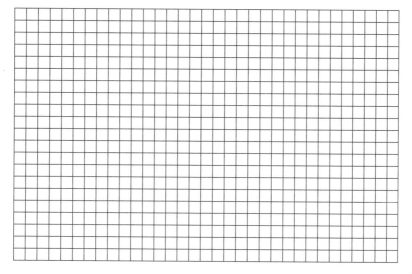

(Continued)

Figure 5.3 (Continued)

F. Describe the results (three sentences)

1. Write (or orally share) what you did.
2. Look at the graph, describe in writing (orally) what it says, tell its story.
3. Describe what you found out about the relationship between _____ and _____.
4. Describe the relationship between the IV and DV.

G. Write the conclusion (three sentences)

1. Restate the question and describe the relationship between the IV and DV.
2. Restate the hypothesis and what was found.
3. Explain the outcome of the experiment.

height, and *width*, for example, as well as the superlatives *longest*, *highest*, and *widest*. These words often appear in questions on standardized tests. The superlative word forms present a particular challenge to English learners; consequently, teachers should model what each form of the word means using concrete objects.

In the examples presented for each investigative form, students follow a thread of inquiry, albeit with different purposes in mind. In a descriptive investigation, the objective is to describe something; in a comparative investigation, the objective is to compare and contrast something with something else; and in an experimental investigation, the objective is to achieve measurable results. There is no best investigation; all three are important. Each nevertheless serves to accomplish a different end, but oftentimes they complement one another, giving students a variety of opportunities to experience investigative-based learning and to talk and to write about it. Students continue to expand the skills of application, analysis, evaluation, and creativity as they solidify their conceptual understanding when engaging in more cognitively demanding investigations. Such experiences, according to Drapeau (2014), promote and encourage students to use creative and divergent thinking to generate ideas.

It is the totality of these investigative exercises that fosters different levels of thinking driven by questions that students attempt to answer. Investigations are all about students having ideas and using them to formulate new ones. In this cycle of thinking, students assimilate and accommodate new ideas as they clarify old ones.

Name That Investigation

It is through asking and answering questions that students construct their own knowledge. Figures 5.4 and 5.5 challenge students to identify which type of investigations—descriptive (D), comparative (C), or experimental (E)—are being exemplified.

By reading the descriptions and the questions, the students also become familiar with ways to investigate ideas that they may have and want to test.

Enhancing Investigative Skills

For students to be successful investigators, they need several ways to develop their inquiry skills. These practices should be varied and frequent. Teachers become mentors and facilitators as students over time take on more active roles in their learning. Their objective is to guide students to take more responsibility for asking questions and designing plans for answering them. There are several instructional strategies available to help students build their investigative capacities as they work toward gaining independence as "scientists."

Think Aloud

One such strategy is "think aloud." Teachers may choose to read a short science book to spark curiosity, and as they read the book, they ask questions and talk through how the character in the story, for example, wants an answer to a question. In the children's book *And Everyone Shouted "Pull!": A First Look at Forces and Motion,* by C. Llewellyn (2004), questioning is used to find out how the load was moved up the hill to take the produce to market. *Dr. Xargle's Book of Earthlets,* by J. Willis (2003), is another book that can be used to show how Dr. Xargle, a green alien, instructs his class about human babies (Earthlets). Teachers can use the humorous, incorrect information about humans to discuss the difference between observations and inferences (Ansberry & Morgan, nd).

Teachers also can model for students how to explore an area of interest from the character's point of view. Through verbalization, students become aware of the steps involved in thinking to formulate a question and outline a plan for collecting data. Teachers can use cartoons, objects, or covered boxes that students examine; each

Figure 5.4 Name That Investigation From Descriptions

Directions: Based on the following descriptions, determine which type of science investigation the student is performing/executing.

Descriptions	**Name That Investigation: D, C, E**
1. This investigation was part of a study on plants. A student placed a stalk of celery in a container of colored water and left it in the water overnight. The next day she saw that the stalk had developed colored tubes at the bottom. She cut off a slice of celery, looked at it with a magnifying glass, described it, and made a sketch of what she saw in her science notebook.	
2. This investigation was done during a unit on plants and, specifically, photosynthesis. To find out where CO_2 enters and O_2 exits the leaf, the student painted the back of the leaf of a Wandering Jew plant (scientific name: *Tradescantia fluminensis*) with clear nail polish. When the polish dried, he pushed his fingernail into the edge where the nail polish dried; then he pulled. A clear sheet with the impression of the leaf came off. The student prepared a glass slide and placed the clear sheet on it. He looked at it under a microscope and saw the stomata, which he proceeded to count, and he drew what he saw in his science notebook.	
3. In a science lesson focusing on the role of heat in changing matter, a student was given three clear plastic tumblers, nine chocolate chips, three small clear medicine cups, and three clothespins. Using the clothespins, she attached the medicine cups to the inside of each of the plaster tumblers. She added three chips to each medicine cup; filled each of the tumblers with water at different temperatures to the bottom of the medicine cups; added cold water from the tap to tumbler no. 1, warm water from the tap to tumbler no. 2; and, under the supervision of her teacher, hot water from the tap into tumbler no. 3. She studied the chips under three different conditions and explained to her partner what occurred, and why.	
4. After listening to *The Diary of a Worm* by D. Cronin (2003), a student designed an investigation that focused on the topic of stimulus and response. He decided to work with earthworms to see if they are sensitive to light. He put them in a covered box and left them there for 15 minutes. Then, he opened the box and noticed that the earthworms did not move. Next, he used a flashlight, shining it on them for 15 minutes. He watched them during this time and took notes. After that time, the student measured how far the earthworms moved (the distance), using cm.	

Source: Adapted and modified from Project Share: Knowledge Knows No Boundaries. Used with permission.

Figure 5.5 Name That Investigation From the Question

Questions	Name That Investigation: D, C, E
1. *What is the average temperature in _______ and _______ during the month of June?*	
2. *Why does the pH in the water change as it travels?*	
3. *How many _______ are on the school grounds?*	
4. *What is in the _______?*	
5. *What is the relationship between _______ and _______?*	
6. *Why is _______ better than _______?*	
7. *Is there a difference in _______ and _______?*	
8. *When _______ changes, how does _______ change?*	
9. *Under what conditions does _______ melt?*	
10. *What type of _______ reaction occurs when you add _______?*	

Source: Modified from Project Share: Knowledge Knows No Boundaries. Used with permission.

of these items stimulates students to get ideas about the world around them. After teachers ask questions and involve their students in constructing anchor charts, demonstrations, and discussions, they follow suit by setting up investigations propelled by questions.

Visual Mapping

This is a second strategy that can be used to guide students in clarifying their ideas, asking investigative questions, and designing plans for answering them. Toni Krasnic's book *Mind Mapping for Kids* (2012) is an easy-to-follow guide to implementing visual thinking in the elementary classroom while improving reading comprehension.

The terms *graphic organizers* and *concept maps* are often used interchangeably because they involve visual formats. When students use these visual representations, they develop skills in organizing and representing ideas, and in building connections between them

(Graphic Organizers/Concept Maps—http://www.temple.edu/studentaffairs/disability/faculty-resources.html).

Visual mapping uses colors, pictures, and/or words to encourage students to start thinking about their ideas by recording them on paper in random ways. A central idea is written in the center, and then students brainstorm to come up with other ideas. The representation moves outward to subareas, connected with lines. This network of hierarchical information provides a visual representation of an idea, concept, or problem under study that students can see. This strategy is open-ended and fosters divergent thinking that can be mapped, making relationships and connections more evident.

Figure 5.6 presents several graphic organizers for brainstorming and comparing and contrasting ideas along with sample images. The spider map, web, PMI, and K-L-E-W can get students off to great starts in developing new ideas. The second set of graphic organizers in Figure 5.6 is designed to get students to compare and contrast things, places, events, and people.

Graphic organizers can be used before, during, and after instruction with the whole class, small groups, and individually.

Investigations and Inquiry: How the Two Are Linked

Inquiry is commonly defined as seeking knowledge through questioning. *Questioning* is at the epicenter of all investigations. It is not a matter of finding the "right" question or getting the "right" answer. Rather, it is a matter of asking questions to find solutions to current problems (e.g., Ebola disease).

By conducting investigations, students are inquiring—and that in turn supports their ideas about the world around them. These experiences are *means* and not ends; they are ways to develop inquiry skills. These skills will serve students well as they systematically and objectively sift through all the information that bombards them throughout their lives. Using graphic organizers provides ways to organize and sort this information.

Planting the seeds for ongoing learning and developing an inquiring attitude should be the goals toward which teachers work in their science classrooms. Immersing students in investigations that involve recognizing patterns and meanings is a way for them to approach knowledge in ways that make it accessible, useful,

Figure 5.6 Building Investigative Skills Using Graphic Organizers

Examples	Descriptions and Uses
Brainstorm graphic organizers	• The graphic organizers help students communicate their ideas as they brainstorm, make decisions, and solve specific problems to amass information in an open-ended way (http://www.writedesignonline.com/organizers/analyze.html#spider). The goal is to stimulate creative thinking in order to develop new ideas. Using spider maps and webs helps students generate ideas as they examine different issues. The PMI and K-L-E-W charts encourage students to pull from their prior experiences as they think and wonder about new ideas.

PMI

P+	
M-	
I?	

K	L	E	W

Examples	Descriptions and Uses
Compare and contrast graphic organizers	• The goal of these organizers is to investigate two or more things to identify similarities and differences. The Venn diagram (one thing in each circle and what they share in the middle), compare/contrast matrix (begins with the questions, *What is being compared? How similar or different are they?*), and the two t-charts (comparing similarities and differences by labeling the individual characteristics on either the right or left sections (http://www.writedesignonline.com/organizers/comparecontrast.html#ccmatrix).

Venn Diagram

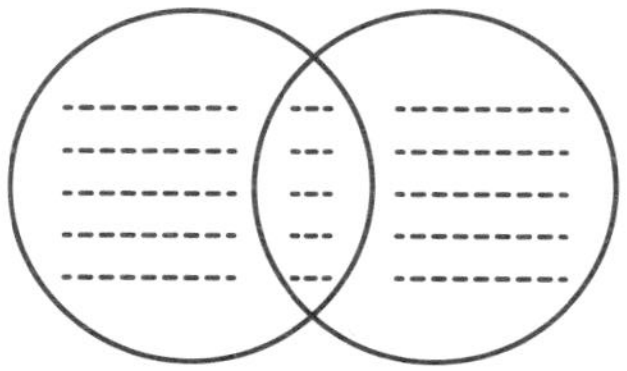

T-Chart

+ item	– item
+ item	– item
+ item	– item

Compare/Contrast Matrix

	Name 1	Name 2
Attribute 1		
Attribute 1		
Attribute 1		

T-Chart

Looks Like	Sounds Like

Source: Adapted from http://www.writedesignonline.com/organizers/analyze.html#spider and http://www.writedesignonline.com/organizers/comparecontrast.html#ccmatrix.

transferable, and applicable to many situations. These are the qualities of effective inquiry teaching and learning as well (Concept to Classroom, 2004).

If these attributes are present in science classrooms, teachers are striving to achieve a *balance* between the "how" we know and the "what" we know paradigm. It is a balanced approach that is crucial to learning science. Asking questions and searching for answers are extremely important components to inquiry, and students who learn to work from this conceptual framework are more likely to see the interrelatedness of knowledge and appreciate where knowledge comes from and how to put it to use in productive ways.

Levels of Inquiry

An overview of three levels of inquiry (structured, guided, and open) was presented as a continuum in Figure 3.2 (see page 57) that shows one form leading to another. Banchi and Bell (2008) take a somewhat different view in their article "The Many Levels of Inquiry," with the same goal of getting students ready to conduct more open-ended inquiry investigations. They too use similar descriptions for structured, guided, and open inquiry, but they add another one upfront, which they call confirmation inquiry.

According to Banchi and Bell, in the first level, *confirmation inquiry*, students participate in an investigation that confirms a known scientific principle. For example, students observe a cup of club soda with a few raisins in it. They see the raisins bobbing up and down, and they ask why this is occurring. Students make their observations and record them in their science notebooks and/or share them with their partner. And it is from the interplay of doing and observing that other questions arise and that students move closer to understanding what is going on (Steve Spangler Science, "Dancing Raisins").

In the second level, *structured inquiry*, students investigate a question posed by their teachers and follow the prescribed procedures for answering it. For example, they are given two unopened, same-size cans of the same brand of cola—one diet and one regular—and a tub of water. Before placing the cans in the tub to see what will happen, the students make predictions. Once the predictions have been recorded or shared, they place both cans in the water and watch what happens. The can of regular cola sinks while the can of diet cola floats. Students brainstorm reasons why this is happening. In this investigation, students followed the procedures laid out to answer a

teacher-scripted question: *Which one will sink and why, and which one will float and why do you think so?* The third level, *guided inquiry*, differs from structured inquiry in that students still use a teacher-presented question, but they now are ready to design the plan and procedures for carrying it out.

And last, in *open inquiry*, students do both—they ask the question and design the steps to answer it. After the sink and float investigation, students are now ready to explore the concept of sink and float using different objects that have the same volume but different masses—a wooden cube and a medal cube, for example. Their question might be, *What is the relationship between the object and the amount of water it displaces?* Then, they must decide on the procedures to answer that question. One way might be to do what Archimedes did over 2 millennia ago—measure the displacement, this time in a graduated cylinder. The students have now arrived at the level of open inquiry.

Conclusion

Inquiry is at the heart of science learning. When students describe objects and events, ask questions, construct and test explanations, communicate their ideas to others, employ critical thinking, and consider alternatives, they are engaging in science inquiry (Just Science Now, np). In an inquiry-based science classroom, students work as scientists. At first, they work from teacher-posed questions and procedures, and then they gradually proceed on their own. Like scientists, students have opportunities to follow leads derived from their questions. It takes planning and the implementation of strategies that support inquiry teaching and learning to get students to this point.

While each type of investigation has its own characteristics and serves a slightly different purpose, it is the totality of these experiences that benefits students. The graphic organizers offer teachers and students a starting point for connecting the dots when engaging in investigations. In an inquiry-based science classroom, students move from being followers to becoming leaders.

The companion website offers several links to lesson plans that explore the science standards by topics, as well as ideas for a project-based engineering curriculum for grades K–5. In addition, there are lessons on dozens of science topics for kindergarten, with some relating to ways to keep students healthy at school and at home.

Your Turn

1. Return to Figures 5.2 and 5.3 and test your knowledge of the type of investigations that are presented based on the descriptions and questions. Now it is your turn to stump your students. Develop a few investigative descriptions and questions to challenge them. Groups of students read your sets of descriptions and questions and identify them as either descriptive (D), comparative (C), or experimental (E). The group that makes the most matches, gets (*you decide*).
2. Plan inquiry lessons (structured, guided, open) using the following science/language objectives as a starting point:
   - Students will observe the picture below.

   - Students will describe to their partners what is taking place in the picture.
   - Students will describe in writing, orally, or by drawing pictures how temperature causes water to change.
   - Determine the grade level for the lesson.
   - Use a graphic organizer that promotes brainstorming for ideas and strategies to teach the science lesson.
   - Now "explain" to your grade-level team members the lesson(s) that you developed and ask them to "evaluate" it.
3. Locate a copy of Krasnic's book (there is a Kindle edition). Organize a small group of teachers to meet and read through the 158 pages;

then collaboratively identify five ways that the mind-mapping strategies can be used in your classrooms.

- What will you need?
- How will you get started using this strategy in your science classroom?
- According to Linus Pauling, "The best way to have a good idea is to have lots of them." What do you think he meant, and how can you apply it in your science classroom?
- How can graphic organizers play a role in generating lots of ideas?

6

Navigating Through the Practices, Crosscutting Concepts, and Core Ideas

Physical Sciences and Earth and Space Sciences

When you make the finding yourself—even if you're the last person on Earth to see the light— you'll never forget it.

—Carl Sagan

Introduction

The new science standards initiate a conceptual shift that impacts the way teachers teach and students learn. This shift reflects the interconnectedness of the science disciplines as they are experienced and practiced in the real world and provides a unifying approach to the teaching and learning of science in grades K–5.

The core ideas span the science disciplines as they align with the science and engineering practices in the standards. It is with the *Framework* in mind that the science topics for the exercises and investigations in Chapters 6 and 7 were chosen. These different exercises demonstrate how the core ideas spiral throughout the elementary science curriculum, and generally include science and language objectives, the science focus, materials needed, and instructional procedures. These exercises also follow the 5E instructional model.

Overview of the Standards by Grade Levels

It is important to note that the Next Generation Science Standards (NGSS) are a set of student performance expectations, rather than a curriculum to follow. The elementary science standards for grades K–5 are in narrative form. The goal is to build on foundational knowledge that becomes progressively more abstract in higher grades. It is through the implementation of the eight science and engineering practices that students gain an understanding of the core ideas in the physical sciences (PS); life sciences (LS); earth and space sciences (ESS); and engineering, technology, and the applications of science (ETS).

Learning Science in Grades K–5

Science learning progresses through the grades, and with each succeeding year the science and engineering practices and core ideas are revisited, but at a higher developmental level. In the primary grades, students learn to recognize patterns and formulate questions. By the end of the fifth grade, they are gathering, describing, and using information about their world in ways that demonstrate grade-level expectations. These practices vary slightly from grade to grade in their implementation and when studying specific science concepts. Students are expected to continue to develop an understanding of the crosscutting concepts because they are critical to organizing facts and other bits of information into big science ideas. For example, the science topics of forces—particularly push and pull, the general introduction to weather, and the survival needs of plants and animals—form the basis of what kindergarteners learn.

The figure below, excerpted from the larger Figure 6.1, presents these topics along with the disciplinary corresponding core ideas of PS 2 (forces), PS 3 (energy), ETS 1 (engineering design), ESS 2 (Earth's systems), ESS 3 (Earth and human activity), and LS 1 (from molecules to organisms).

Topics	Disciplinary Core Ideas	Student Performance Expectations
• Forces: push or pull	• **PS 2:** Motion and stability: forces and interactions • **PS 3:** Energy • **ETS 1:** Engineering design	• Understand the effects of different strengths or different directions of pushes and pulls on the motion of an object • Understand transferring energy between objects • Analyze the design solution
• Weather	• **ESS 2:** Earth's systems	• Weather ○ Understand the patterns and variations in local weather ○ Understand the purpose of weather forecasting ○ Be prepared for and respond to severe weather
• Needs of plants and animals (including humans) to survive	• **ESS 3:** Earth and human activity • **LS 1:** From molecules to organisms: structures and processes	• Plants and animals ○ Understand what organisms need to survive ○ Understand the relationship between the needs of living things and where they live

The building blocks in the primary grades for learning about forces, weather, and the needs of plants and animals include understanding and using the organizing concepts of patterns, cause and effect, systems, etc. During the school year, teachers work to support students in formulating and responding to questions:

- *What happens when you push or pull an object?*
- *Where do animals live? Why do they live there?*
- *What is the weather like outside today? What was the weather like yesterday?*
- *Was it different from today?*

These and other questions get students to recognize patterns of pushing and pulling objects with varying degrees of force; the needs of plants and animals to survive; and the day-to-day temperatures, types of precipitation, and responses to severe weather.

In addition to formulating questions and answering them, primary grade students are also expected to develop and use models, plan and carry out investigations, analyze and interpret data, come up with solutions, use evidence to support their claims, and communicate information they have collected. Kindergarteners are not the only ones who learn about forces and weather. Third, fourth, and fifth graders study these topics as well. The intent is to construct new knowledge on the groundwork that has been laid in the lower grades and to ratchet up science learning seamlessly. For example, in the third grade the emphasis shifts from knowing what weather is to addressing weather hazards such as hurricanes or drought, and to identify ways to minimize their impact.

In the standards, the narratives for grades K–5 are packed with extremely important information that can be confusing to sort out. To make the standards more user-friendly, I have developed a figure for all grade levels. By listing the organizing concepts for the disciplinary core ideas, along with the general topics and core ideas for that grade, in Figure 6.1 teachers have a visual reference map to consult. Additionally, student performance expectations are included and are aligned with the science topics and core ideas for easy access, giving an overview of the major science emphasis for each grade level. Figure 6.1 shows that the standards view science learning as cumulative and moving to higher conceptual levels and different foci as students ascend the grades.

Figure 6.2, Breaking Down Science by Grade Levels, offers a quick synopsis of the science focus for each grade using the core idea codes (e.g., PS 3).

The rest of the chapter offers glimpses into disciplinary core ideas, beginning with physical science topics and followed by earth and space science topics. Life science topics will be included in the next chapter. The engineering design core ideas are integrated throughout these disciplines for grades K–5.

Physical Sciences Across the Grades

Forces

Force, specifically pushing and pulling, is the first big idea that young students learn. In Figure 6.3, kindergarteners move objects

(Text continued on page 137)

Figure 6.1 Overview of Crosscutting Concepts, Topics, Disciplinary Core Ideas, and Student Performance Expectations for Grades K–5

Grade Level	Crosscutting Concepts for Disciplinary Core Ideas	Topics	Disciplinary Core Ideas	Student Performance Expectations
K	• Patterns • Cause and effect • Scale, proportion, and quantity • Systems and system models • Energy and matter • Structure and function • Stability and change	• Forces: push or pull • Weather • Needs of plants and animals (including humans) to survive	• **PS 2:** Motion and stability: forces and interactions • **PS 3:** Energy • **ETS 1:** Engineering design • **ESS 2:** Earth's systems • **ESS 3:** Earth and human activity • **LS 1:** From molecules to organisms: structures and processes	• Understand the effects of different strengths or different directions of pushes and pulls on the motion of an object • Understand transferring energy between objects • Analyze the design solution • Weather ○ Understand the patterns and variations in local weather ○ Understand the purpose of weather forecasting ○ Be prepared for and respond to severe weather • Plants and animals ○ Understand what organisms need to survive ○ Understand the relationship between the needs of living things and where they live • Help students to formulate questions to answer questions (for example, *"What happens if you push or pull an object hard(er)? Where do animals live?, Why? What is the weather today? How is it different from yesterday?"*) • To demonstrate grade-appropriate proficiency in understanding core ideas, students are expected to: ○ ask grade-level appropriate questions ○ develop and use models ○ plan and carry out investigations ○ analyze and interpret data ○ design solutions ○ engage in argument from evidence ○ obtain, evaluate, and communicate information and use these practices to demonstrate understanding of the core ideas.

Grade Level	Crosscutting Concepts for Disciplinary Core Ideas	Topics	Disciplinary Core Ideas	Student Performance Expectations
1	• Patterns • Cause and effect • Scale, proportion, and quantity • Systems and system models • Energy and matter • Structure and function • Stability and change	• Sound and light waves • Plant and animal external parts • Parents and their offspring • Inherited traits from parent to offspring • Solar system	• **PS 4:** Waves and their applications in technologies for information transfer • **LS 1:** From molecules to organisms: structures and processes • **LS 2:** Ecosystems: interactions, energy, and dynamics • **LS 3:** Heredity: inheritance and variations of traits • **ESS 1:** Earth's place in the Universe	• Understand the relationship between sound and vibrating materials ○ Light travels from place to place and students understand this idea by having objects made of different materials placed in the path of a light beam • Understand how plants and animals use external parts to help them survive and meet their needs to grow • Understand the behaviors of parents with their offspring to help them survive • Understand that young plants and animals are similar, but not exactly the same as their parents • Understand through observing, describing, and predicting some patterns of moving objects in the sky • Formulate questions to answer questions that are based on observations, speculative thinking, and comparisons (for example, *What happens when objects vibrate? What happens when the lights go out?*) • To demonstrate grade-appropriate proficiency in understanding core ideas, students are expected to: ○ Plan and carry out investigations ○ Analyze and interpret data ○ Construct explanations and design solutions ○ Obtain, evaluate, and communicate information. and use these practices to demonstrate understanding of the core ideas.

(Continued)

Figure 6.1 (Continued)

Grade Level	Crosscutting Concepts for Disciplinary Core Ideas	Topics	Disciplinary Core Ideas	Student Performance Expectations
2	• Patterns • Cause and effect • Scale, proportion, and quantity • Systems and system models • Energy and matter • Structure and function • Stability and change	• Plants and animals • Wind and water erosion	• **LS 2:** Ecosystems: interactions, energy, and dynamics • **LS 4:** Biological evolution: unity and diversity • **ESS 2:** Earth's systems • **ETS 1:** Engineering design • **PS 1:** Matter and its interactions	• Develop an understanding of ○ what plants need to grow ○ how plants depend on animals for seed dispersal and pollination • Compare the diversity of life in different habitats • Understand that wind and water change the shape of the land and design solutions to slow or prevent such change • Use information and models to identify the shapes and kinds of *land* on Earth • Use information and models to identify the shapes and kinds of *bodies of water* on Earth • Formulate questions to answer questions that address changes in the land and what causes it to change (for example, *How does the land change? What are different bodies of water? How do the properties of materials relate to their use?*) • Understand properties of materials based on observations through analysis and classification of different materials • To demonstrate grade-appropriate proficiency in understanding core ideas, students are expected to: ○ Develop and use models ○ Plan and carry out investigations ○ Analyze and interpret data ○ Construct explanations and design solutions ○ Engage in argument using evidence ○ Obtain, evaluate, and communicate information and use these practices to demonstrate understanding of the core ideas.

Grade Level	Crosscutting Concepts for Disciplinary Core Ideas	Topics	Disciplinary Core Ideas	Student Performance Expectations
3	• Patterns • Cause and effect • Scale, proportion, and quantity • Systems and system models • Energy and matter • Structure and function • Stability and change	• Weather ○ Impact of weather-related hazards; ways to reduce them	• **ESS 2:** Earth's systems • **ESS 3:** Earth and human activity	• Organize information and use information about weather conductions by seasons • Make claims about ways to reduce weather hazards
		• Organisms and their traits ○ Comparison of animals, plants, and environments today and in the past ○ Organisms in a changing environment: what happens?	• **LS 1:** From molecules to organisms: structures and processes • **LS 2:** Ecosystems: interactions, energy, and dynamics • **LS 3:** Heredity: inheritance and variation of traits • **LS 4:** Biological evolution: unity and diversity	• Develop an understanding that ○ organisms' life cycles are similar and different ○ organisms have different inherited traits ○ the environment can affect trait development • Use evidence to construct explanations of how individuals of the same species have variations that may contribute to survival, finding mates, and reproducing • Develop an understanding of organisms that lived long ago and their environments • Develop an understanding that when the environment changes some organisms survive and reproduce, others move to new places, others move to transformed environments, and others die
		• Forces: equal and unequal on an object • Magnets and their uses	• **PS 2:** Motion and stability: forces and interactions	• Can determine the ○ effect of balanced and unbalanced forces on the motion of an object ○ cause-and -effect relationship of electric or magnetic interactions between two objects not in contact with one another • Apply their understanding of magnetic interactions to design and solve a problem with magnets • Help students to formulate questions to answer questions (for example, *What is typical weather in different parts of the world during different times of the year? How can the impact of weather-related hazards be reduced? How do organisms vary in their traits? What happens to plants and animals when their environment changes?*) • To demonstrate grade-appropriate proficiency in understanding core ideas, students are expected to: ○ Plan and carry out investigations ○ Analyze and interpret data ○ Construct explanations and design solutions ○ Obtain, evaluate, and communicate information and use these practices to demonstrate understanding of the core ideas.

(Continued)

Figure 6.1 (Continued)

Grade Level	Crosscutting Concepts for Disciplinary Core Ideas	Topics	Disciplinary Core Ideas	Student Performance Expectations
4	• Patterns • Cause and effect • Scale, proportion, and quantity • Systems and system models • Energy and matter • Structure and function • Stability and change	• Waves—patterns of waves	• **PS 4:** Waves and their applications in technologies for information transfer	• Use a model of waves to ○ describe patterns of wave amplitude and wave length ○ show that waves can cause objects to move
		• Weathering and erosion	• **ESS 1:** Earth's place in the universe	• Develop an understanding of the effects of weathering or rate of erosion by water, ice, wind, or vegetation
		• Patterns of Earth's features	• **ESS 3:** Earth and human activity	• Apply their knowledge of natural Earth processes to generate and compare multiple solutions to reduce the impacts of such processes on humans • Describe patterns of Earth's features, students analyze and interpret data from maps
		• Plants and animals that support survival, growth, behavior, and reproduction	• **LS 1:** From molecules to organisms	• Develop an understanding that plants and animals have internal and external structures that function to support survival, growth, behavior, and reproduction
		• Energy • Forms of energy: Sound, light, heat, and electric currents	• **PS 3:** Energy • **ETS 1:** Engineering design	• Define energy, conservation of energy, and transferring energy between objects or system • Use a model to describe how an object can be seen when light is reflected from its surface and enters the eye • Use evidence to construct an explanation of the relationship between the speed of an object and the energy of that object • Understand that energy can be transferred from place to place by sound, light, heat, and electric currents or from object to object through collisions • Demonstrate their understanding of energy by designing, testing, and refining a device that converts energy from one form to another • Help students to formulate questions to answer questions (for example, *What are waves? What are some things they can do? How can water, ice, wind, and vegetation change the land? How do internal and external structures support the survival, growth, behavior, and reproduction of plants and animals? What is energy? How is energy related to motion? How is energy transformed?*) • To demonstrate grade-appropriate proficiency in understanding core ideas, students are expected to ○ Ask questions ○ Develop and use models ○ Plan and carry out investigations ○ Analyze and interpret data ○ Construct explanations and design solutions ○ Engage in argument from evidence ○ Obtain, evaluate, and communicate information and use these practices to demonstrate understanding of the core ideas.

Grade Level	Crosscutting Concepts for Disciplinary Core Ideas	Topics	Disciplinary Core Ideas	Student Performance Expectations
5	• Patterns • Cause and effect • Scale, proportion, and quantity • Systems and system models • Energy and matter • Structure and function • Stability and change	• Matter	• **PS 1:** Matter and its interactions • **ETS 1:** Engineering design • **PS 3:** Energy	• Describe that matter is made of particles too small to be seen except through the development of a model • Understand that regardless of the type of change that matter undergoes, the weight of matter is conserved ○ Mix two or more substances to determine if new substances result • Define energy, conservation of energy, and transferring energy within systems • Know that energy in animals' food was once energy from the sun.
		• Brightness of the sun and stars • Patterns of shadows in the day and night and different seasons • The interaction of geosphere, biosphere, hydrosphere, and/or atmosphere. • Earth's resources	• **ESS 1:** Earth's place in the universe • **ESS 2:** Earth's systems • **ETS 1:** Engineering design • **ESS 3:** Earth and human activity	• Understand the patterns of daily changes ○ in length and direction of shadows, day and night ○ the seasonal appearance of some stars in the night sky • Develop a model to describe ways the geosphere, biosphere, hydrosphere, and/or atmosphere interact • Describe and graph percentages of water and in various reservoirs to provide evidence about the distribution of water on Earth
		• Plant and animal needs obtained from air and water • Food chain and web • Food sources for plants (food chain and webs)	• **LS 1:** From molecules to organisms • **LS 2:** Ecosystems: interactions, energy, and dynamics • **ETS 1:** Engineering design	• Understand that plants get materials they need for growth chiefly from air and water • Use models to describe ○ the movement of matter among plants, animals, decomposers, and environment • Formulate questions to answer questions (for example, *When matter changes, does its weight change? Can new substances be created by combining other substances? How does matter cycle through ecosystems? Where does energy in food come from? How do lengths and directions of shadows change? How does the appearance of some stars change in different seasons?*) • To demonstrate grade-appropriate proficiency in understanding core ideas, students are expected to: ○ Develop and use models ○ Plan and carry out investigations ○ Analyze and interpret data ○ Use mathematics and computational thinking ○ Engage in argument from evidence ○ Obtain, evaluate, and communicate information and use these practices to demonstrate understanding of the core ideas.

Source: Adapted and modified from *A Framework for K–12 Science Education: Practices, Crosscutting Concepts, and Core Ideas*, by National Research Council, 2013. Washington, DC: National Academies Press.

Figure 6.2 Breaking Down Science by Grade Levels

K	1	2	3	4	5
Physical Sciences **PS2:** Motion and stability: forces and interactions **PS 3:** Energy	**Physical Sciences** **PS 4:** Waves and their applications in technologies for information transfer	**Physical Sciences** **PS 1:** Matter and its interactions	**Physical Sciences** **PS 2:** Motion and stability: forces and interactions	**Physical Sciences** **PS 3:** Energy **PS 4:** Waves and their applications in technologies for information transfer	**Physical Sciences** **PS 1:** Matter and its interactions **PS 2:** Motion and stability: forces and interactions **PS 3:** Energy
Life Sciences **LS 1:** From molecules to organisms: structures and processes	**Life Sciences** **LS 1:** From molecules to organisms: structures and processes **LS 3:** Heredity: inheritance and variation of traits	**Life Sciences** **LS 2:** Ecosystems: interactions, energy, and dynamics **LS 4:** Biological evolution: unity and diversity	**Life Sciences** **LS 1:** From molecules to organisms: structures and processes **LS 2:** Ecosystems: interactions, energy, and dynamics **LS 3:** Heredity: inheritance and variations of traits **LS 4:** Biological evolution: unity and diversity	**Life Sciences** **LS 1:** From molecules to organisms: structures and processes	**Life Sciences** **LS 1:** From molecules to organisms: structures and processes **LS 2:** Ecosystems: interactions, energy, and dynamics
Earth and Space Sciences **ESS 2:** Earth's systems **ESS 3:** Earth and human activity	**Earth and Space Sciences** **ESS 1:** Earth's place in the universe	**Earth and Space Sciences** **ESS 1:** Earth's place in the universe **ESS 2:** Earth's systems	**Earth and Space Sciences** **ESS 2:** Earth's systems **ESS 3:** Earth and human activity	**Earth and Space Sciences** **ESS 1:** Earth's place in the universe **ESS 2:** Earth's systems **ESS 3:** Earth and human activity	**Earth and Space Sciences** **ESS 1:** Earth's place in the universe **ESS 2:** Earth's systems **ESS 3:** Earth and human activity
ETS 1 Engineering Design K–2			**ETS 1 Engineering Design** 3–5		

Source: A Framework for K–12 Science Education: Practices, Crosscutting Concepts, and Core Ideas, by National Research Council, 2013. Washington, DC: National Academies Press.

(Text continued from page 129)

from one place to another in as many different ways as possible. The Science Focus section offers teachers background information that includes several science terms such as *force, push, pull,* and *friction* that they can introduce using "think aloud" strategies to acquaint students with them. This information will be followed up in other grades. In the 5E lesson in Figure 6.3, students investigate using an assortment of balls and what happens when cardboard tubes and ramps are used to move them. The Make It Move exercise in *explore* asks students to name the object they used, how they made it move, and how they would move it again. This information is shared orally. An adult in the room can record it on an anchor chart, or students can do so by drawing pictures in their science notebooks.

The information recorded on anchor charts can be revisited as students continue to explore the topic of push and pull with different materials. The following are sample questions that teachers can ask to initiate the brainstorming segment of the lesson:

- *What objects roll?*
- *What do these objects have in common?*
- *How did you start the object rolling?*
- *What did you do to stop it?*

Another exercise focusing on force is Figure 6.4, Analyzing the Movement of Objects. It is designed to get students to build on earlier push/pull experiences, but this time exploring the use of different amounts of force to see what happens. Patterns begin to emerge—the more gently an object is pushed or pulled, the shorter the distance it moves; the harder it is pushed or pulled, the farther it moves.

In the 5E lesson presented in Figure 6.4, students listen to the story *Duck in the Truck,* by J. Alborough (2002). The book is about a duck's truck that gets stuck in some muck. The key question is: *Will the duck's three friends be able to get the truck out of the muck, and how?* Teachers pose questions throughout the reading of the book to involve their students in this dilemma, which includes the topic of force.

Also, students participate in a discussion about "Is it a push or is it a pull word?" exercises. Students identify words that are associated with push and pull that begin with specific letters in the alphabet (e.g., *bounce* for the letter *b*). Teachers write these words in the alphaboxes sketched on chart paper large enough for students to see the letters and the respective words. The details are described in *explain.* By recording students' push/pull words, they can read them later, when they reference them for other tasks in *elaborate* and *evaluate.*

Figure 6.3 Investigating Forces: Pushing and Pulling

I. **Science Objective:** Students will move objects in as many different ways as possible by pushing and pulling them.

Students will use science terms that will demonstrate when they share and report out in writing that they understand force.

Language Objective: Students will describe orally what happens when the teacher uses a ramp and drops a ball from the top and when they push or pull different objects.

Students will complete in writing the sentence frames on the Make It Move sheet twice.

Students will share orally with group members what they observed and did to get the objects to move.

Students will use words and phrases on index cards and construct a sentence using science information from the lesson.

II. **The Science Focus:**

A. *Force* is a *push* or *pull* that produces a change in the motion of an object.

B. The position and motion of objects can change by pushing or pulling them.

C. An unbalanced force makes a resting object move, brings the moving object to rest, or changes its direction.

D. Changing the surface on which an object moves can make it easier or harder for the object to move because of *friction*, a force that acts when two surfaces rub against each other.

E. The steepness of a ramp affects how far a ball rolls.

III. **Materials:**

- Assortment of objects: balls, cardboard tubes, ramps, blocks. (This exercise could take place in the block center so students can investigate using these materials.)
- Meter sticks (you can put them end to end and count the number of meter sticks the object rolled).
- Chart paper and book, *Move It!*
- 2 copies of the Make It Move sheet for each group.

IV. **Engage**

Instructional Procedures:

A. Review the previous day's work by having students observe as some of the balls and other materials are pushed and pulled.

B. Students describe orally what they think (predict) will happen when the teacher uses a ramp and drops the ball from the top.

C. Read the beginning of the book, *Move It!* (2005) by A. Mason, to get students interested.

V. **Explore**

Instructional Procedures:

A. Each group has an assortment of balls, cardboard tubes, ramps, blocks, and meter sticks.

B. Students explore as many different ways as possible to make a marble (object) move from one place to another.

C. Give groups of students the Make It Move sheet with sentence frames like the ones below.

They respond orally or in writing:

1. *I used* ________________________________ *object.*
2. *I made the object move by* ________________________.
3. *Another way I made it move:* ______________________.

VI. Explain

Instructional Procedures:

A. Have students share with group members what they did and observed before working with the whole class.

B. Bring the students together to brainstorm what they discovered and learned about pushing and pulling during their investigations.

C. Use an anchor chart to record the group ideas/comments. To get the brainstorming started, here are some questions to ask:

1. *What objects rolled?*
2. *What do these objects have in common?*
3. *How did you get an object to roll?*
4. *Did you stop an object from rolling? How did you stop it?*
5. *What questions can we ask to guide our investigations?*

D. Continue to read the book *Move It!* to add to the discussion on force.

VII. Elaborate

Instructional Procedures:

A. Return to the anchor chart, where group comments were recorded.

B. Have students ask questions before they continue to investigate.

C. Have each group try out the ideas from another group to see if they get the same results.

D. Have each group complete a *new* Make It Move sheet.

E. Have each group report out again and with a different color pen; the teacher records their responses on the anchor chart.

VIII. Evaluation

Instructional Procedures:

A. Take the pushing and pulling ideas from the anchor chart.

B. Have the students pick out words (adjectives, nouns, verbs) and phrases and write (draw) them on 5 × 7 index cards or cut sentence strips.

C. In working in groups, students use a chart like the one below and put the cards in the appropriate column. (Previously, teachers worked with students on adjectives, nouns, verbs, and phrases, and used a chart like the following.)

Adjectives	Nouns	Verbs	Phrases
round	marble	rolled	down the ramp
rubber	ball	bounced	on the floor

D. Once students have placed the cards in the specific column, they are ready to construct sentences using the information from the chart. They read their sentences to the whole class. Then the whole class reads the sentence composed by each group.

Figure 6.4 Analyzing the Movement of Objects

I. **Science Objectives:** Students will explain how a push or pull affects how an object moves, the difference between a push and pull, and the way to change how something is moving when it is given a push or a pull.

Students will analyze changes in the movement of objects.

Students will respond to the questions, *Is it push? or Is it a pull?* for the alpha-boxes.

Language Objectives: Students will respond orally to questions during the reading of a book .

Students will orally retell the story.

Students will respond orally to the *Is it a pull or push?* questions.

Students will read the information in the pull and push alpha-boxes.

II. **The Science Focus:**

A. When a force is exerted, things move. Students may be unaware that a force affects the motion of an object.

B. A force has a direction. A direction may be back and forth, straight, fast or slow, or in a circle, zigzag, or curve.

C. By pushing or pulling, an object moves.

III. **Materials:**

- Books: *Duck in the Truck* by J. Alborough or *Push and Pull* by H. J. Endres.
- Paper for the anchor chart and different color markers. (First use one color, then change the color of the marker for new information; for corrections, add a third color.)
- Chart paper for two alpha-boxes (one for push and one for pull).

IV. **Engage**

Instructional Procedures:

A. Read *Duck in the Truck* or *Push and Pull*, by Nelson or Endres to stimulate interest in the topic.

B. Ask students questions as you read to get them to think about the topic of forces.

C. To build on prior science knowledge of force and motion, have objects to jog their memories about ramps, marbles, trucks, cars, etc.

D. In groups, students retell the story that was just read to them, either orally or in writing in their science notebooks.

V. **Explore**

Instructional Procedures:

A. Point to a truck or another object and ask *What is a push?* and *What is a pull?* Have these objects available for students to use.

B. Follow up if students are having difficulty and continue to brainstorm answers to these questions. They should understand that pushes and pulls are ways to use force to move an object. During this discussion, record what the students say on an anchor chart.

C. Continue the discussion by focusing on the amount of force that is needed to move different objects.

D. Ask the students, *Did you use push or pull forces when you got up off the floor to stand? Are there other ways to use your bodies to push or pull?*

VI. Explain

Instructional Procedures:

A. Construct two alpha-boxes on chart paper. Each should look like the following. Be sure to have two charts. Use the alpha-boxes when students respond to the questions *Is it a push?* or *Is it a pull?*

a	b	c	d
e	f	g	h
i	j	k	l
m	n	o	p
q	r	s	t
u	v	w/x	y/z

B. Ask students to think of things that can be pushed. When they mention something, write its name in the alpha-box that begins with the same letter. See the chart below for an example. This activity can continue for several days, serving to activate prior knowledge when students read the words on the chart, but also to introduce new ones.

Push Words

a	b bike	c coin	d
e	f	g	h
i	j	k	l
m	n	o	p
q	r remote	s swing	t
u	v	w/x	y/z

Pull Words

a	b	c	d
e	f	g	h handle
i	j	k knob	l
m	n	o	p
q	r rope	s	t
u	v	w/x	y/z

VII. Elaborate

Instructional Procedures:

A. The students return to the alpha charts once there are examples in the boxes.

B. After the students have generated a variety of words that have been placed in the boxes, they read the words.

C. Students in groups to ensure that the words are in the correct boxes use a variety of materials to test their ideas.

D. Students use the claims and evidence scaffold to support their reasons for any changes that are made.

VIII. Evaluate

Instructional Procedures:

A. Students come together and the recorder reporters from the groups take turns to share the changes, if any, that their group made in the alpha-boxes.

B. They share their reasons (claims and evidence) if they think a word was not in the correct box; the teacher draws a line through the word and adds it to the appropriate box with a different color.

Source: Adapted and modified from *Let's Use Force*, by M. L. Damjanovich, 2011. Used with permission.

In the 5E lessons on forces, students may be asked to conduct both descriptive and comparative investigations when they use different balls (tennis ball and a basketball) to determine which one rolls the fastest or farthest with the same push. The Investigating Forces lesson (Figure 6.5) provides the context for making comparisons using ping-pong, golf, and rubber balls. Students using a flicking motion with their finger use the same amount of force (soft/hard) to explore how far each ball moves to determine the effect of a force on each of them.

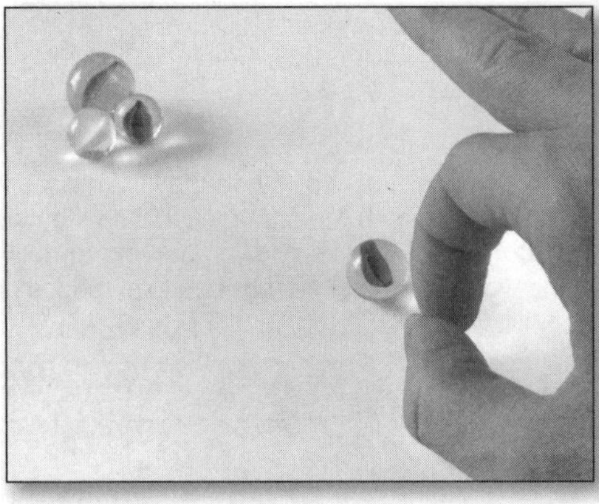

© Emmeci74/Thinkstock Photos

In this lesson, students working in pairs or small groups take part in a series of guided inquiry investigations to continue their study of forces. One involves using three different balls and recording the results. They compare, analyze, and draw conclusions by interpreting the data they collect; they then complete the following sentences in their science notebooks or complete them orally with their partner or an adult who may be in the room: ________________ *happened when I* ________________. *I conclude that* ________________ *happened because* ________________. Teachers move around the room and listen to student-talk to determine their level of understanding about the topic.

If misconceptions about forces are evident, teachers bring students together to brainstorm what they have uncovered about this topic. Some of the questions that will help to clarify students' thinking include: *What did you find out about the ping-pong, golf, and rubber balls when you used the same amount of force to move each ball? Which ball traveled the greatest distance using a soft flick? A hard flick? Why?*

Once they complete the investigation using a flicking motion, they use other objects and formulate a question to guide their exploration. They complete the following sentences as they did before: ________________ *happened when I* ________________. *I conclude that* ________________ *happened because* ________________. Once these sentences are complete, students come together again, but this time they share the questions they asked that guided their investigations, as well as respond to teacher-posed questions.

Figure 6.5 Investigating Forces

I. **Science Objectives:** Students will work with balls that have different properties to investigate what happens when force is applied to an object and demonstrate that the greater the force applied to an object, the greater the change in motion.

Language Objectives: Students will write predictions, observations, and conclusions based on their analysis in their science notebooks using sentence frames or orally respond to questions and sharing information with group members.

Students will record information on the Data Recording and Investigation sheets.

II. **The Science Focus:**

A. Force is anything that tends to change the state of rest or motion of an object.

B. Forces cause changes in the speed or direction of the motion of an object.

C. The greater the force placed on an object, the greater the change in motion.

D. Students develop working definitions of science terms. As students gain more experience with and understanding of the core idea, their definitions become more accurate. The advantage of using working definitions is that they are indicators of students' understanding and can be used as formative assessments that guide future planning.

III. **Materials:** For each group:

- One ping-pong ball, golf ball, rubber ball
- One ruler (may need a meter stick)
- Safety goggles
- Spherical objects with varying properties (such as a tennis ball or racket ball)
- Chart to record operational definitions
- Data Recording Sheet
- Investigation Form, if used

IV. **Engage**

Instructional Procedures:

A. Each group receives one ping-pong ball, one golf ball, one rubber ball, one ruler/meter stick, and safety goggles.

B. The students make predictions about what they think will happen as they roll, drop, etc. these balls, and record them in their science notebook or share them with group members before they begin.

C. They observe what happens when force is applied to each ball.

D. They then *compare* the relative effects of a force using the same strength on the balls of different mass.

E. Ask students how they would describe or define the key science terms.

F. Write their working definitions on a chart, and students write them in their science notebooks.

V. **Explore**

Instructional Procedures:

A. Students work with a ping-pong ball.

B. Students use a gentle, flicking motion with one finger to make the ping-pong ball move, then the golf ball, and finally the rubber ball. They repeat the activity using a hard flicking motion.

C. Students measure the distance each ball moved using the ruler/meter stick.

(Continued)

Figure 6.5 (Continued)

D. After group members complete the flicking (soft/hard) for each ball, the recorder reporter completes the first two columns on the Data Recording Sheet below:

Balls	Distance Moved Using a Soft Flick	Distance Moved Using a Hard Flick	Conclusions
Ping-pong ball			
Golf ball			
Rubber ball			

E. Students analyze the data recorded in the table and make comparisons and draw conclusions about the force applied to these balls. They construct explanations for what happened and include them in their science notebook:

_______________ *happened when I* _______________.
I conclude that _______________ *happened because* _______________.

VI. Explain

Instructional Procedures:

A. Students come together to brainstorm what they uncovered about the topic of force in their investigations and if there were any differences from what they experienced in *explore.*

Ask the following questions to get the brainstorming going:

- *What did you find out about the ping-pong ball/golf ball/rubber ball as a force in motion?*
- *Which ball traveled the greatest distance? Why do you think so?*
- *Did the balls move the greatest distance when a greater force was applied to the balls? If so why did that happen? If not, why?*

B. During this phase, any misconceptions are addressed and students review the operational definitions recorded on the chart. Any changes are recorded using a second color pen, and a line is drawn through information that is omitted.

VII. Elaborate

Instructional Procedures:

A. Students plan and carry out an investigation to explore applying a force to other objects.

B. They formulate their own questions that will guide them in carrying out the investigation and get them to think about variables, hypotheses, collecting data, etc.

C. Students can follow the steps presented in Figure 6.6 as a guide.

D. Students in their science notebooks record information related to planning, executing, and conclusions about the investigation they carried out.

VIII. Evaluate

Instructional Procedures:

A. Group members share the questions that guided their investigations and report on the results they found.

B. Direct the students' attention to the chart again and review the definitions shared during *engage* and modified during *explain,* and ask them if they want to make any additional changes. These changes are recorded in a third color pen, and again a line is drawn through information that is eliminated.

C. Science notebook entries are reviewed to determine if the students grasped the science core idea and completed the data sheets and sentence frames.

Source: Adapted and modified from *Flicking With Force*, by T. Hislop and H. Green, 2003. Utah Education Network. Used with permission.

Last, students complete a homework assignment with family members. Together, they list forces that they experience every day, from pushing a carriage, to swinging a bat, to kicking a soccer ball, etc. Students can share with their parents the information on forces recorded in their notebooks, and together they can walk around their residence and find forces to list. Also as a family project, they can design a ping-pong paddle. The criteria would be to use what they know now about force and outcomes and construct the best tournament-winning paddle they can.

The next logical step is to conduct an experiment. They can test the effects of a force on an object and use the guide included in Figure 6.6. It provides a scaffold for formulating a relationship question, identifying the independent and dependent variables, recording information on a "t" table, and plotting the results on a graph and telling its "story." Their stories explain the variables involved in the experiment and what each data point on the graph represents. The students also write three complete sentences to summarize the results from the experiment that include the title, question, hypothesis, and variables. Then they are ready to state their conclusions. They also are ready to use evidence they have collected and recorded on the "t" table and plotted on a graph to support their claims. These claims and the evidence form the basis for the conclusions.

As part of *evaluate*, students can play the Science Cube game. They roll two cubes, one with a term on each face and the other with directions for what to do. They then "act out" the word, "use it in a sentence," etc. They roll both cubes at the same time. The "force words" and the directions cubes can be found in Figures 6.7a and 6.7b. A $2 \times 2 \times 2$ wooden block also can be used with the words taped or written on each face, and this can be done for the directions as well. The templates for both cubes are on the companion website, http://resources.corwin.com/ReinhartzGrowingLanguage, in Word so that the science words and directions can be changed to reflect the science topic.

Before students play the Science Cube game, teachers should make clear how to get started and what each of the actions are on the direction cube: for example, what students are expected to do when the side marked "give an example" comes up. Students can play the game in pairs, in small groups, and then even with the whole class. By playing it prior to doing it with the whole class, students have opportunities to practice and to get ideas from one another about how to act the word out, give a synonym or antonym for it, etc. The Science Cube game has elements both of charades, discussed in Chapter 2, and role-play, discussed in Chapter 8.

Figure 6.6 Investigation Form

Name: ____________________ Date: __________ Page in SN: _______

I. Question: *What is the relationship between* ______________________________ *and* ____?

II. Variables:

Independent Variable: _____________ Dependent Variable: _______________

III. Hypothesis: *I think* ____
____

IV. Data Table (create a "t" table for you and your partner and record the information collected):

V. Graph the average of the trials:

VI. Results (write three complete sentences telling the story of the graph):

A. ____

B. ____

C. ____

VII. Conclusions Based on Evidence (three complete sentences):

A. ____

B. ____

C. ____

Figure 6.7a Science Cube With Science Terms

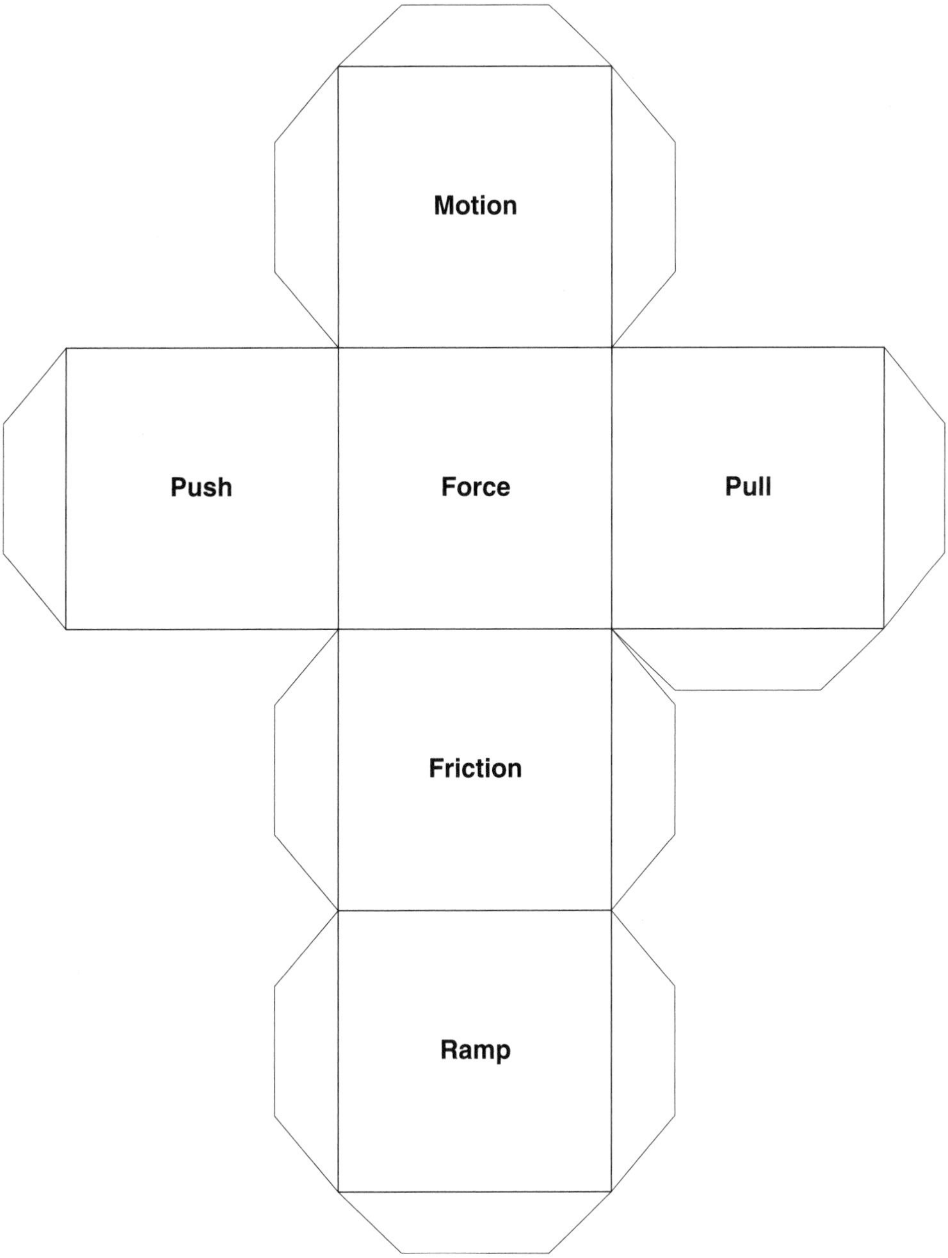

Available for download from **http://resources.corwin.com/ReinhartzGrowingLanguage**

Figure 6.7b Directions for the Science Cube Game

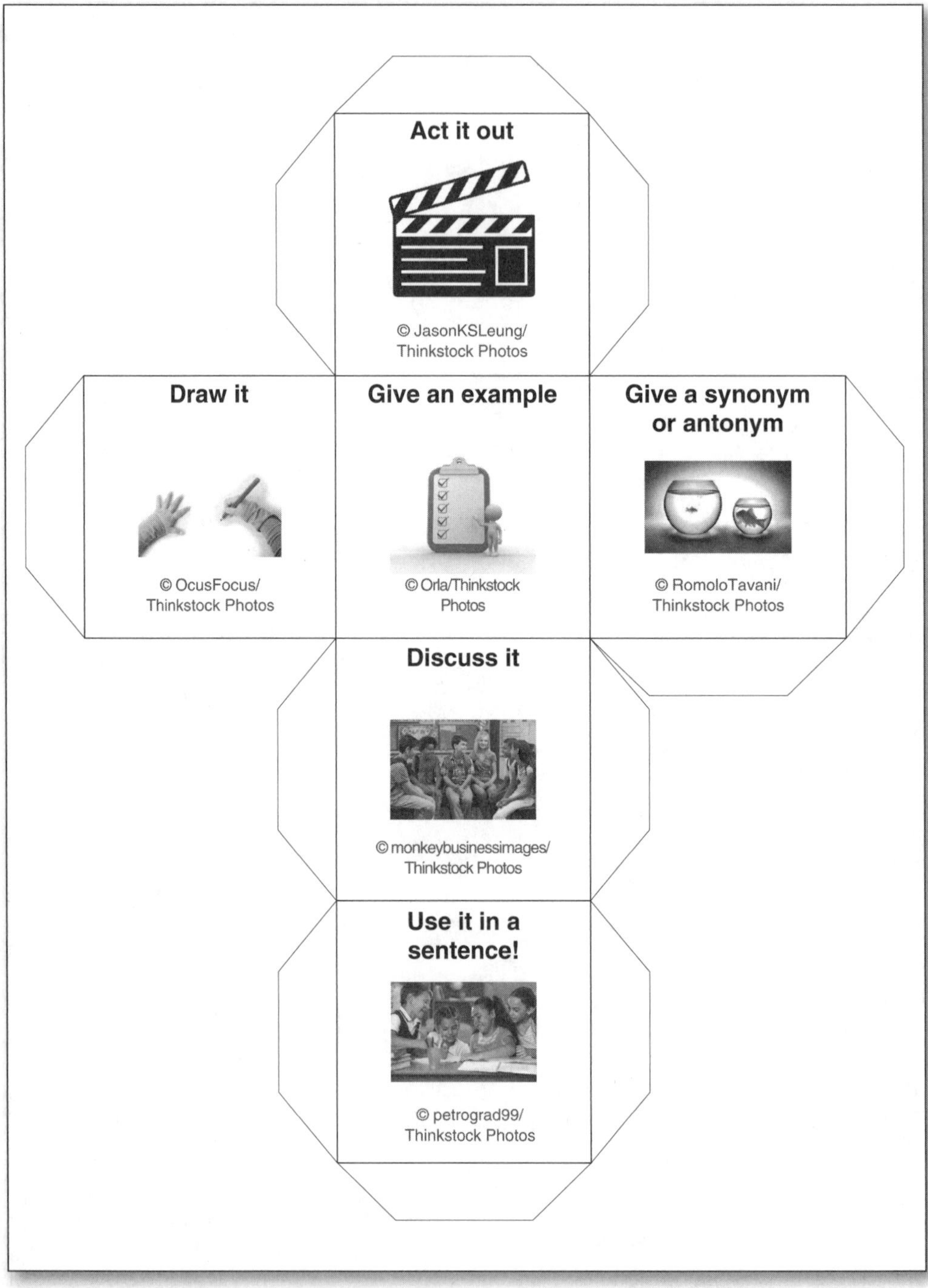

Playing the game benefits both the students and the teachers. Students are placed in situations in which they get to express what they know in different ways. Teachers have a chance to assess the depth of the students' understanding by not solely relying on what they say, draw, and/or write. There are many opportunities for formative assessment to take place.

Forces That Shape the Earth Around Us

In the fourth grade, students study the earth science core idea of the planet Earth's place in the universe, specifically the effects of weathering and erosion by the forces of wind, water, ice, and vegetation. Students connect previous experiences on forces to the study of the earth and space science core idea (Earth systems). Before students investigate wind action on "sand dunes" by blowing on a small pile of sand in the center of a sheet of newspaper, they all should put on safety goggles. To produce a stronger wind, a fan can be used during a class discussion about natural forces that shape the Earth.

In addition, students investigate the effect of the force of water on soil. They pick a spot outside and draw a picture of the site. Then they pour a cup of water on the spot from a short distance off the ground and draw another picture of the site. They repeat this action by pouring a cup of water from as high as they can stretch. They make a sketch of the ground again. They compare their drawings. What do they notice? Is there a difference? If "yes," what do they think caused the change to the site?

The next step can be to use maps, and for students to identify regions of the United States that are more vulnerable to the natural forces of wind and water than are other parts of the country. They can also determine if there are similar patterns across the globe, such as in Latin America or Africa. Maps are additional tools that can be used to connect the topic with several of the crosscutting concepts of patterns, cause and effect, scale, and stability and change. Students can compare the impact of wind and water on the Atlantic and Pacific coasts with coastlines in other countries and continents. Are there any similarities? Differences? Having students complete a graphic organizer such as a Venn diagram assists them in organizing their ideas and gets them to recognize the underlying causes that can lead them to identify patterns. By looking at coastlines on maps, students gather data to support their claims about the existence of patterns.

© Anthony Harris/Thinkstock Photos

Energy

K. B. Bradley's book *Energy Makes Things Happen* (2003) is a great nonfiction introduction to the core idea of energy. The book opens with pictures of young children playing ball, flying kites, and cooking hot dogs. It presents a continuum of different aspects of the topic of energy by showcasing the ways stored energy is converted into moving energy using objects from everyday life. This book is unique because it covers the complex core idea of energy without using complex scientific terms such as *potential* and *kinetic,* but it does include *fuel, transfer,* and the phrase *gives off.* It can easily be incorporated into science lessons. The book offers ideas for simple exercises in the Find Out More About Energy section. It can be used with kindergarteners as well as fourth and fifth graders, all of whom are required to learn about some aspect of energy under PS 3. Integrating books such as *Energy Makes Things Happen* is a great way to enhance the study of science topics.

Figure 6.8 offers a format for following the 5Es when using literature in science. The guide suggests a variety of ideas, such as using sticky notes to conceal information that may be on the front

Figure 6.8 Using Science Literature Books Following the 5Es

Grade Level: ______________________________

Book Title: ______________________________

Phase	Teacher and Student Behaviors
Engage	• Begin the lesson by examining the book title and cover. (Cover the book with sticky notes to conceal the contents and remove them one at a time as students predict what they think the book is about.) • Use cues/clues/questions to support students as they make predictions about what happens in the story. • Draw a Venn diagram on an anchor chart. In the first circle, record the students' predictions, and in the second circle what was in the book. In the middle circle show what the predictions and the book's content have in common. • Engage students in a discussion about their experiences as they relate to the story. • Return to the Venn diagram and add any new information about the book in the second large circle. • Have students record information or make drawings in their science notebooks, depending on their learning/language levels.
Explore	• Have objects and materials relevant to the book's content if appropriate for the students to explore. • Encourage students to focus on the different forms that illustrations can take as the book is read. • Continue to ask questions regarding the book's science content. • Point out key science information (terms or definitions; pictures that illustrate, for example, states of matter, different animals, etc.). • Involve students by having them come up and point to information/illustrations in the book. • Leave a copy in the classroom library for students to peruse during their free time.
Explain	• Model how to examine different features presented in the text, such as bold print, pictures, etc. • Describe how the science information unfolds from the beginning to the end of the book. • Ask students to describe some of these changes. • Model ways to deconstruct or "interpret" any science diagrams or other visuals in the book. • Return to the Venn diagram to review and possibly add more information.

(Continued)

Figure 6.8 (Continued)

Phase	Teacher and Student Behaviors
Explain (continued)	• Review with the student if the predictions were accurate, based on the information presented in the book. • Use sticky notes to mark pages that can be revisited. Ask students to find pictures and/or objects provided that relate to the science topic presented in the book. • Ask them to hold the picture/object up when they hear the signal word of the day presented in the book.
Elaborate	• Provide a variety of materials for students to use to create pictures of the main points and/or characters in the book. • Have students describe the science content in the book in their own words. • Students develop their own stories based on the science content presented in the book. See ideas for telling "science tall tales" in Chapter 2. • Students design an investigation to learn more about the science topic in a science book—for example, *Energy Makes Things Happen,* by K. B. Bradley (2003). There are many ideas about energy that students can investigate.
Evaluate	• Assess student stories when telling their science tall tales—including the main features of the book and their creative ideas. This can be done orally, in writing, and/or with drawings or pictures cut out from magazines. • Review student science notebook entries, if appropriate, respond in writing to their most interesting, exciting, and/or challenging aspects of the story and the reasons why they thought so. • Observe students as they point to the following features in a book: 1. Title 2. Front and back covers 3. Table of contents, if there is one 4. The glossary, if there is one • Listen to students as they ask and answer questions, such as: *What do these books have in common with the one the teacher is reading? What is the science topic? What do you know now about the topic that you did not know before*?

Source: Modified from "Storybook Science," by M. Enfield and E. Mathew, 2012, *Science and Children. 50*(2), 46–49.

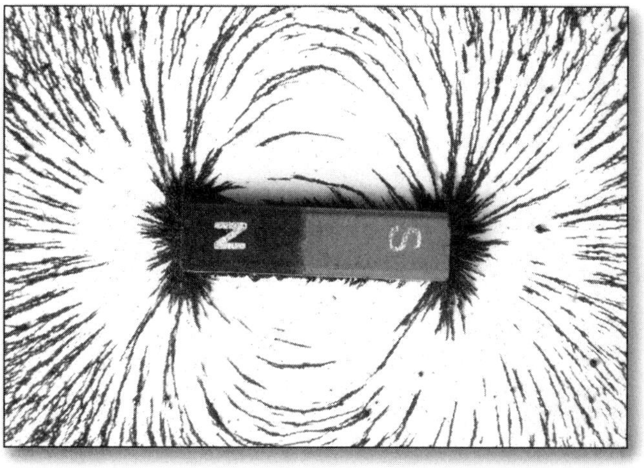

© Matthew Cole/Thinkstock Photos

and/or back covers (to keep students in suspense). Or using graphic organizers (e.g., Venn diagrams) to record student predictions in the first circle, what is in the book in the second, and what both circles have in common in the middle. Or having relevant materials available so students have opportunities to examine and "play" with them. Different types of children's literature focusing on science should be integral parts of K–5 classrooms.

Magnets

The study of magnets is sprinkled throughout the elementary grades. Students learn about the magnetic properties of objects, make predictions about objects that are attracted to magnets, and verify predictions by engaging in a variety of investigations. The 5E lesson on magnets presented in Figure 6.9 is adaptable for any grade by selecting grade-level appropriate investigations and reading materials that are suitable for individual levels of language proficiency.

Figure 6.9 offers an array of ideas for students to review as well as learn more about magnets as they explore books, participate in investigations, read or listen to the Magnet Poem, and spell out vocabulary words using magnetic letters. Using the "magic glove" begins the lesson about magnets on a mysterious note; then, building on this experience, students work through five stations that accommodate different learning styles.

Another way to engage students in magnets is to show them a glass jar filled with sand in which a large metal paper clip and a large plastic paper clip are buried. Teachers ask the students how they can get the paper clips to move in the capped jar. A magnet will move the metal one, but not the plastic one. Why? This easily assembled exercise stimulates students' thinking about magnetism.

Figure 6.9 Magnets: It Is All About Attraction

I. Overall Objectives:

A. Science Objective: To learn about magnets

B. Language Objective: To use communicative language

© lovin-you/Thinkstock Photos

II. The 5Es

Engage

A. Objectives:

Science Objective: The students will begin to explore the topic of magnets and magnetic properties.

Language Objective: The students will orally explain why they think the nails are moving.

B. Materials:

- Adult- and student-sized gloves
- Nails in a box
- Magnets (U-shaped, bar magnets)

C. Instructional Procedures:

1. Before students enter the classroom, put a magnet inside the adult glove so it cannot be seen.
2. When the science lesson begins, show the students the box with nails in it.
3. Ask them how they can move the nails *without* touching the box.
4. After a short amount of time, put the adult glove on with the magnet inside on and move your hand with the glove over the box to move the nails. Ask, *What do you think is causing the nails to move?*
5. If the students mention the glove, have them put on the smaller glove and wave it over the nails.
6. Continue to ask questions to get students thinking about what caused the nails to move.

Explore

A. Objectives:

Science Objective: The students will explore magnetic properties of different objects.

Language Objective: The students will respond orally to questions about objects on their desk.

The students will write observations in their science notebooks.

B. Materials per Group:

- At least three different magnets
- Two pieces of chalk
- Rubber bands
- Nails (may want to put tape on the tips)
- Coins: pennies, dimes
- Plastic spoons, iron filings
- Students have their science notebooks

C. Instructional Procedures:

1. Write a set of questions on the white/chalk board or on chart paper:
   - *What do you think will happen when you hold the magnet near the objects on your desk?*
   - *Do you think all the magnets will respond in the same way to the same objects? Why do you think so? Why not?*
   - *Do all the objects respond in the same way?*
   - *Which ones move toward the magnet? Why do you think this happened? Did you try all the magnets provided?*
2. Time is provided for students to "play" (investigate) with the magnets and the objects on their desks.
3. The recorder reporter writes down the observations made by group members.
4. At the end of the *explore* phase, bring the class together and have the students share their findings.

Explain

A. Objectives:

Science Objective: The students will use several terms from the word/phrase wall: *Magnet*, different magnets for example: ring magnet, bar magnet, attract, repel,and property.

Language Objective: The students will listen to the story and respond to questions about the book.

B. Instructional Procedures:

Read one of the following books, *Magnets Push, Magnets Pull* by M. Weakland (2011), *Magnets* by J. Cooper (1992), *What Magnets Can Do* by A. Fowler (1995), or *Amazing Magnetism* by R. Carmi and J. B. Stamper (2002), emphasizing the points and pictures that are relevant to the lesson.

C. Ask questions to stimulate interest in the book and have students point to the relevant pictures and illustrations.

Elaborate

A. Objectives:

Science Objectives: The students will make observations and discuss them with group members.

The students conduct an experiment after formulating a question to guide their investigation. For example, they determine the relationship between the type of magnet and its strength to pick up the most paper clips. For example: *What is the relationship between ________________ and __________________?*

Language Objectives: The students will make predictions orally and discuss them with group members and record them in their science notebooks.

The students will draw pictures of the investigation they plan and complete the "t" table, graph, etc. in their science notebooks.

B. Instructional Procedures:

1. **Materials per Group**: Bag of paper clips, different magnets (horseshoe/U-shaped, bar, circle, etc.), science notebooks (SN)

(Continued)

Figure 6.9 (Continued)

2. The students will (a) make predictions before beginning their investigation and write them in their SN; (b) discuss with group members what they observed after using different magnets to pick up the paper clips; (c) draw a picture after each magnet is used in their SN; (d) complete a "t" table; (e) plot data on a graph; (f) discuss with group members the results they found and write/draw them; and (g) write their conclusions in their SN.

"t" Table

The question:	
Type of magnet	**Number of paper clips picked up**

Graph points recorded in the table above.

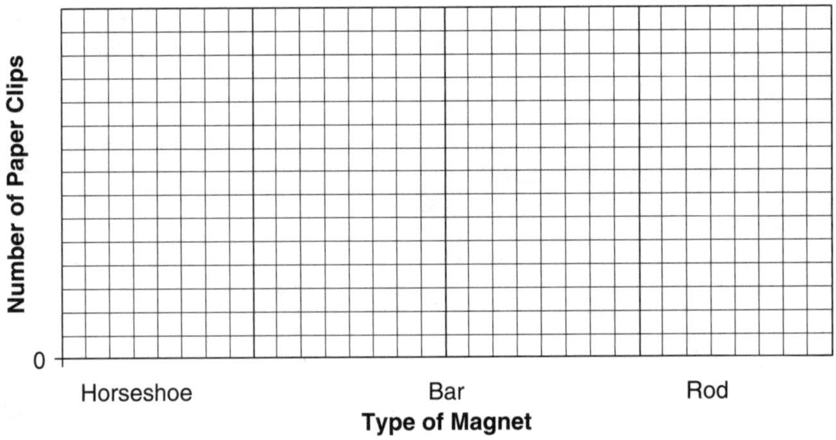

Results: Students explain (tell the story of) the graph in their SN by writing three sentences or drawing pictures to depict the results.

Conclusions: Students write or draw in their SN what they conclude about the magnets they used and the number of paper clips picked up.

Evaluate

A. Objectives:

Science Objective: The students will participate in each of the stations set up to promote their understanding of magnets.

Language Objectives: The students will talk in their groups at each station.

The students will use magnetic letters to spell out words in the lesson.

The students will listen and read the Magnetic Poem.

The students write a Magnetic Me story.

The students will read/peruse a book in the Scientist's Corner.

B. Instructional Procedures:

1. Set up a series of science stations that focus on different aspects of magnets.
2. Some ideas for science stations might be:

   Station 1: Making predictions and testing different materials using a magnet to identify which materials have a magnetic property. Then they check their predictions by testing the materials using the magnet to see if their predictions were correct.

   Station 2: Students use magnetic letters to spell at least three words learned in the lesson. (They can use the word/phrase wall if they need help.)

   Station 3: Listen to the students read (or tape them reading) the Magnet Poem by Mr. R's World of Math and Science Poems at http://sciencepoems.net/index.html#physics (if students are struggling readers, have science buddies read the poem to them and have them point to the read object and the word on the word/phrase wall when the terms come up in the poem).

Magnet Poem

I ate a magnet,

© lovin-you/Thinkstock Photos

Tasted good,
Mom got mad,
I knew she would . . .
"Get that magnet out!" she cried,
"Magnets aren't good inside!"
Tried to fish it out with wood,

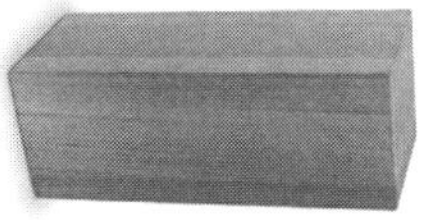

© prapann/Thinkstock Photos

But magnet didn't stick too good . . .
Tried to fish it out with rubber,

© ajt/Thinkstock Photos

Then I tried
Some whale's blubber,

(Continued)

Figure 6.9 (Continued)

Tried to fish it out with glass,
Then I tried
Some green crab grass,

© Jupiterimages/Thinkstock Photos

Tried to fish it out with plastic,
Things were getting pretty drastic,
Paper, onions, basketball,

© koosen/Thinkstock Photos

Nothing pulled it out at all!
Dad saw and said,
"Here's the trick,
To certain things,
Will magnets stick!
Things with iron,
Are the key,
Try one, son, I think you'll see . . ."
So I went, and found
An iron nail,

© koosen/Thinkstock Photos

Now I'll really
End this tale . . .
Tied the nail,
To a string,
Dropped it down my mouth,
That thing,
And when I pulled that nail out
The magnet was attached no doubt . . .
Don't eat magnets,
And in fact,
Stick to food,
That won't attract!

Source: Poem used with permission from Mr. R's World of Math and Science Poems at http://sciencepoems.net/index.html#physics

Station 4—"Magnetic Me"

The students write a book about themselves using the idea of what they are "attracted" to: food, TV shows, video games, cartoons, songs, etc. Teachers provide a template for the students to follow, starting with a cover page, a biography, and pictures and drawings of what they like.

Station 5—The "Scientist's Reading Chair"

Students will pick a book from the "scientist's corner," sit in the chair, and read the book or flip through it looking at the pictures. At the end of the week, ask students (scientists) what they learned about magnets that they did not know before.

Earth and Space Sciences Across the Grades

© Rainer Claus/Thinkstock Photos

Weather

Weather is a fun topic to teach at any time of the year. Studying weather in the spring, for example—when flowers bloom, leaves appear on trees, and animals are born—is a great time to talk about the sun, clouds, and spring rains. Studying weather can be as playful as picking clothes for paper dolls for specific seasons, or making weather headbands that symbolize sunny, rainy, cloudy, and windy weather. This art-related science project gets students thinking about ways to communicate the types of weather without words. For sunny weather, the headband can have yellow triangles emanating from it, representing the rays of the sun. For cloudy weather, paper cutouts of clouds with streamers hanging down represent rain. And when the wearer of the rain headband runs, the streamers move, portraying wind.

A lesson on weather can begin with a poem such as "Rainy Day Safari" in J. F. Hauser's *Science Play* (1998, p. 58), where pictures are substituted for words. It begins with, "Grab your , rain coat, and a willing grown up. Now go out for. . . ." Students can explore wind directions by making wind vanes showing the four cardinal directions—north, south, east, and west. They also can make windsocks out of brown paper lunchbags and decorate them with pictures from magazines and newspapers, or draw on them. These are only some of the tools students can use to study weather; others include rain gauges, thermometers, barometers, and weather maps.

After participating in several weather-related exercises in the primary grades, and when the dust settles, it is essential that students know that by observing local weather conditions they should be able to describe the patterns of sunny, cloudy, rainy, warm, and cold not

Umbrella photo: © Leoshoot/Thinkstock

only from day to day, but quantitatively by counting the number of days where they live that have each of these patterns. They also should note that it is cooler in the morning than in the afternoon; that each season has different amounts of sunlight, wind, and precipitation in the forms of rain, snow, hail, or sleet; and that these seasonal patterns can be described along with their impact on living things and the land (NGSS, 2013).

In the upper grades, weather and climate should be presented so that students have opportunities to describe how the ocean influences ecosystems and landforms, and how landforms influence the winds and cloud formations. Individually, geosphere (solid and molten rock, soil, and sediment), biosphere (living things including humans), hydrosphere (water and ice), and atmosphere (air) are systems, and when they interact the impact can be observed and measured (NGSS, 2013).

Studying weather at different grade levels brings into play the need for making observations, constructing models, graphing data, and developing arguments to show that organisms adapt to their environments to meet the demands of daily life. In the final analysis, weather is learning about the basic features of temperature, wind speed and direction, and different forms of precipitation. The Climate Kids, NASA's Eyes on the Earth, website offers an array of ideas, games, videos, and questions for addressing this extremely important topic (http://climatekids.nasa.gov/menu/keep-up/).

© Claudio Divizia/Thinkstock Photos

Whether it is telling the story of a water droplet and tracing its adventure down a mountain side to when it finally reaches the ocean, completing a chart of the current season with family members employing their senses, looking at weather maps in the daily newspaper and predicting weather patterns from them, or reading *What Will the Weather Be?* by L. DeWitt (1993), each activity encourages students to expand their vocabulary of weather words as well as use their literacy skills. There are so many books, such as *My Favorite Time of Year* by S. Pearson (1988) and *Weather* by S. Simon (2006), that can be borrowed from the school library and readily displayed and made available in the classroom. These books can be used throughout the grades with different purposes, because they offer many oral and written opportunities for students to share what is important to them about weather at specific times of the year.

Conclusion

Becoming familiar with the three dimensions and how they fit together across grade levels is key to implementing them when planning and teaching. The science standards form the backbone for teaching the core ideas within the physical sciences and earth and space sciences. The student expectations offer the big picture of what students will learn. The disciplinary core ideas spiral through grades K–5, demonstrating that learning of these ideas at each grade level is addressed in more cognitively demanding ways. Teachers also are afforded a myriad of strategies for incorporating science literature into teaching topics on the physical sciences and earth and space sciences.

Here, the goal is to see how the core ideas and student expectations fit into the whole of implementing the science standards. Additionally, the information in Figures 6.1 and 6.2 serves as a visual for mapping K–5 science learning. The 5E lessons show that students learn science not only by manipulating objects to identify patterns and cause-and-effect relationships, or by listening to or reading(or perusing) literature books; they also learn science by getting new ideas so that, in the words of an anonymous fourth grader, they discover things that they never thought they could discover.

Your Turn

1. Find your grade level in Figure 6.1 (page 130).
   a. Select one of the physical science (PS) ideas and the corresponding student expectations.

b. How will you teach this topic? Jot down your ideas and strategies, and work with a colleague to brainstorm further.

c. Use the 5Es to organize what you have come up with as well as a framework for implementing these ideas and strategies in your science classrooms.

d. Consider team teaching with this colleague what you have planned together, so that changes can be made if needed. In addition, by teaming you model for the students what it means to work with a partner and demonstrate how it enriches the end results.

2. Using Figure 6.8 as a guide, pick one of the books suggested in this chapter (or another that you have not used before), and follow these steps:

   a. Title of book: ______________________________

   b. Make a copy of the guide from the companion website, http://resources.corwin.com/ReinhartzGrowingLanguage, and circle the specific activities that you would like to use within each phase. Using the book, how will you engage the students?

   c. Try out what you have planned. What would you add or modify the next time you use a book to teach this science topic?

3. In what way can you implement the science cube exercise into what you plan to teach next (or use the science cube in conjunction with the book you read)?

   a. Lesson objectives:

      Science:

      Language:

      Construct the science cube based on this information. The direction cube does not necessarily change unless you would like to change the words or the graphics to better meet the needs of your students.

   b. Directions: How will you prepare your students for using the science cubes? (E.g., review the directions to ensure students understand what the graphics and words mean before beginning.)

4. Even if your science curriculum does not include the topic of energy, review the three 5E lessons based on it:
   a. How can you use at least two of the ideas in your classroom with another science topic?
   b. How can you make your classroom more science-focused using ideas in this chapter?
   c. How can you promote science and language learning using the ideas that you have selected?

7

Life Sciences Across the Grades

© Ingram Publishing/Thinkstock Photos

One must learn by doing the thing; for though you think you know it, you have no certainty, until you try.

—Sophocles

Introduction

The study of plants and animals, including humans, is interspersed through the grades. The range of study is wide, from laying the groundwork for what is living and nonliving; the basic needs of organisms, where they live, and what they eat or how they get their food; to the diversity of life and the transmission of traits from one generation to the next. In addition, when focusing on plants and animals, the crosscutting concepts become a part of the study. For example, students examine the following:

1. The *structure and function* of plants and animals
2. Different habitats within an ecosystem and the factors that influence why plants and animals live there
3. How plants and animals get food and use *energy* from it to grow and develop
4. The movement of animals and their tracks
5. The coverings on animals
6. Multigenerational inherited traits passed on and how they contribute to the *diversity* of life
7. *Cycles* in nature
8. The *size and quantity* of different plants and animals
9. Plant and animal behaviors
10. Plant and animal cells and how they form tissues, organs, and systems

Living or Nonliving? That Is the Question

An introduction to studying the difference between living and nonliving things can begin by showing students a toy car and a goldfish in a bowl and asking them to describe what they see. Teachers record what the students say about each on a blank piece of chart paper. Then, on a large two-column chart—with one column labeled Living (L) and the other column Nonliving (NL), like the one in Figure 7.1—the teachers return to the students' observations and ask them to place each in the appropriate L or NL column.

Figure 7.1 Living (L) and Nonliving (NL)

Living (L)	Nonliving (NL)

Teachers can take this activity outside, giving students practice in classifying objects as living or nonliving. Teachers place a hula-hoop on the ground for each group of students, and the groups decide if the objects in the circle are living or nonliving, and record them in the appropriate column on a similar chart in their science notebooks. By going outside, students can see things in a natural setting where there is sediment, rocks, grass, weeds, and possibly even trash.

In another exercise, to determine the differences between living and nonliving things, students are given five bean seeds, five pieces of gravel, two plastic sandwich bags, six cotton balls, water, push-pins, and a marker to label one bag *A* and the other *B*. Students have to decide which are alive—the bean seeds or the pieces of gravel. Students place three cotton balls on the bottom of each bag and wet them using the same amount of water. The beans are poured into bag A and the gravel into bag B. The students pin their bags (A and B) on the bulletin board for 24 hours, making notes in their science notebooks when they come to class, before lunch, and before they go home, to see if any changes might have occurred in the bags. Students continue to observe their bags for another 24 hours. If the bean seeds begin to sprout, the students can measure the stems and roots. The teacher makes a list of student responses to the question, *How do you know it is alive (growth, movement, transpiration, etc.)?* At a later time, teachers return to the lists of responses and, together with the students, cross off statements that do not apply. On the website Kinderg arten . . . Kindergarten, http://crisscrossapplesauce.typepad.com/files/is-it-living-recording-sheet.pdf, there is a downloadable recording sheet, along with pictures for students to use to answer the question, *Is it alive?* In addition, there are living and nonliving flashcards ready to download from kindergartenkindergarten.com, and for students to cut out and sort.

Last, students can practice distinguishing between living and nonliving things by observing their physical characteristics when viewing video clips and/or still pictures. There are several multimedia resources and ideas to use on this topic for grades K–5 (e.g., https://www.youtube.com/watch?v=cPiNTkCmmv0). During the viewing, students are encouraged to gather evidence to support how they define what is living and nonliving.

The Biosphere

To better understand what the biosphere is, it is helpful to begin with how it is organized. The biosphere supports life and is where humans, animals, and plants live. Within the biosphere, there are several levels featured in Figure 7.2, beginning with biomes and ascending to individual organisms.

A *biome* is a set of ecosystems in which organisms live. There are many biomes on Earth, including tundra, taigas, temperate forests, tropical rain forests, grasslands, and deserts, among others, that are presented in Figure 7.3. The figure presents overviews of six major biomes that include information about the amount of water each receives, general temperatures, conditions of the soils, names of common plants and animals that live there, and lists of books to be used when studying about each of these areas on Earth.

The next level includes *ecosystems*. Ecosystems are communities of organisms that interact with their environments. *Communities* include different populations of organisms that live in given areas. A *population*

Figure 7.2 The Organization of the Biosphere

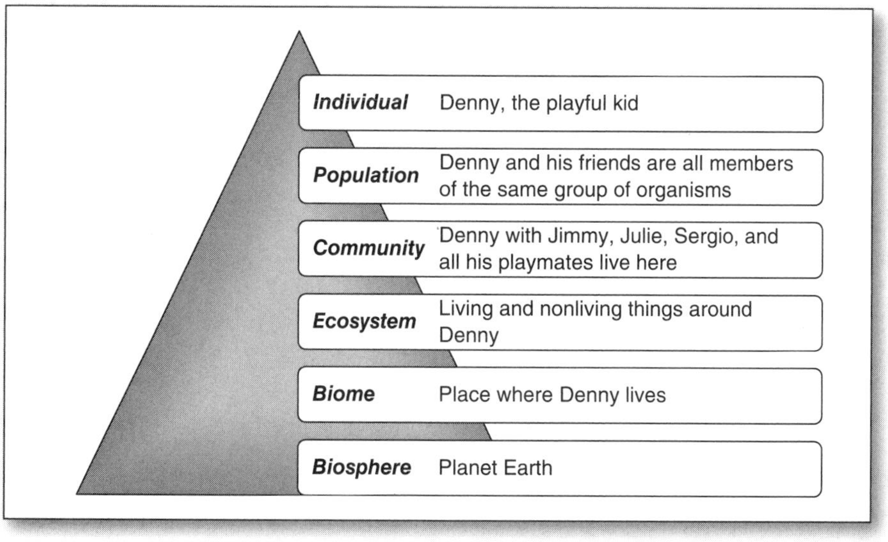

Figure 7.3 Biomes of the World

Biome	Water	Temperature	Soil Condition	Plant	Animal	Books
Desert	Limited	Hot during the day and colder at night	Generally poor	Sparse: succulents (cactus), sage brush, creosote bush, desert ironwood, Joshua tree, Mojave, ocotillo, soap tree, yucca	Sparse: reptiles, insects, arachnids, reptiles, birds, chipmunk, centipede, rattle snake, kangaroo rat, sand cat, gecko, bat, black-footed cat, bearded dragon	*A Desert Habitat* (2006) by K. Macaulay and B. Kalman *Desert Animal Adaptations* (2011) by J. Murphy *Cactus Hotel* (1993) by B. Z. Guiberson
Tundra	Dry	Cold	Area covered with ice—permafrost	Lichens, mosses, bearberry, Labrador tea, pasque flower, arctic willow, cotton grass	Migrating animals—polar bear, caribou, arctic fox, snowy owl, musk ox, ermine, harlequin duck, lemming	*Arctic Tundra: Land With No Trees* (1997) by A. Fowler *What If There Were No Lemmings?* (2010) by S. Slade
Taiga (coniferous forest)	Adequate	Cool year-round	Poor, rocky soil	Conifers—pine, spruce, fir, juniper, cedar	Mammals, birds, insects, arachnids—bald eagle, black bear, bobcat, lynx, grizzly bear, long-eared owl, red fox, snowshoe rabbit, wolverine	*Counting in the Taiga* (2009) by F. McKissack and L. McKissack *The Forested Taiga: A Web of Life* (2004) by P. Johanson

Biome	Water	Temperature	Soil Condition	Plant	Animal	Books
Temperate deciduous	Sufficient	Cool season and warm season	Fertile soil	Deciduous trees—oak, maple, fruit trees, dogwood, horse chestnut, magnolia	Mammals, birds, reptiles, insects, arachnids—bat, boa, bison, eagle, deer, ladybug, grouse, turtle, woodchuck, elk	*Exploring the Deciduous Forest* (2006) by L. Tagliaferro *Temperate Forests* (2011) by P. Benoit
Grassland	Wet season, dry season	Warm to hot (often with a cold season)	Fertile soil	Grasses—windmill grass, kangaroo grass, native spear grass, feather-heads, slender rice-flower, plains flax lily, creamy candles, chocolate lily	Mammals, birds, insects, arachnids—aardvark, cobra, dingo, death adder, cotton rat, dhole, echidna, clouded leopard	*Grasslands (Habitat Survival)* (2012) by B. Silverman *Grasslands* (2000) by D. R. Stille
Tropical rain forest	Extremely wet	Always warm and humid	Poor, thin soil layer	Banana, orchid, coffee, Brazil nut tree, poinsettia, cacao, rubber tree, heliconia, sapodilla, bromeliad (pineapple)	Bee, anteater, bird-of-paradise, anaconda, anoa, bandicoot, bettong, babirusa, eye-aye	*The Great Kapok Tree* (2000) by L. Cherry *Nature's Green Umbrella* (1997) by G. Gibbons

Source: Adapted and modified from Enchanted Learning, http://www.enchantedlearning.com/biomes. Used with permission.

is a group of similar individuals that live in a specific geographic area at a given time. The final level of the biosphere is the *individual,* and is defined as any living thing or organism.

Telling Biosphere Stories

In the organization of the biosphere depicted in Figure 7.2, two features are prominent: the ascending levels and the story of an individual, "Denny," and his ascent through them. "Denny" is used as an example of how an organism fits into each level. Students demonstrate their understanding of the organization of the biosphere by using pictures or in writing, telling the story of an organism (fluffy white rabbit, twiggy apple tree, a family member, etc.) that they have selected.

Plants and Animals

After reviewing the "biomes of the world" in Figure 7.3, it is evident that there are many different groups of plants and animals living on Earth. But before focusing on one or the other, it seems appropriate to discuss what plants and animals have in common and how they differ. Using a Venn diagram in Figure 7.4, students begin to think about

Figure 7.4 Venn Diagram of Plants and Animals

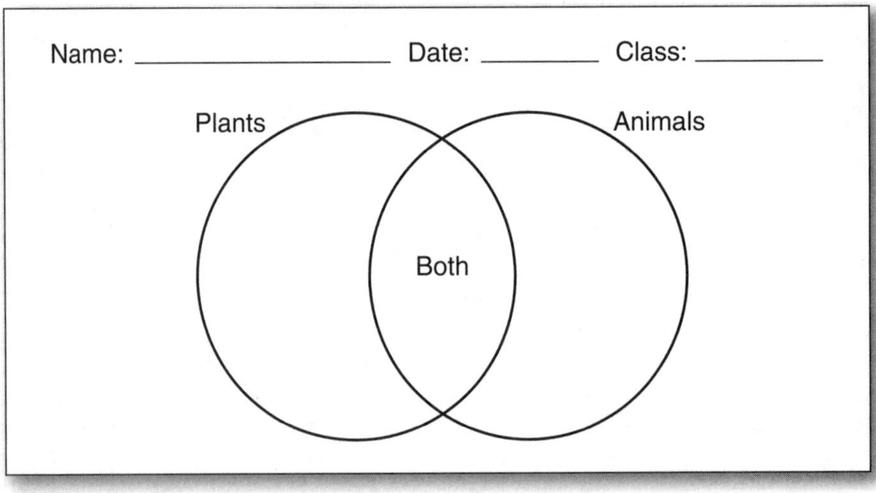

these questions and to fill in the information. Copies of the diagram, which can be accessed on the companion website, are passed out to students for them to complete individually or in groups, using cutout pictures from discarded magazines from the school library, or words on index cards from their word boxes on plants and animals. These items are placed in the circles or in the middle.

When the students have done as much as they can, the teacher brings the class together and asks them to share what they have placed, drawn, and/or written on their diagrams. Their individual contributions are then entered on a chart-sized diagram for the whole class to see. Once class members have shared what is on their diagrams, they go back and put a line through what is not accurate on theirs and add what others have contributed. By participating in this multistep exercise, students have several ways to test and expand what they know and what they need to know about plants and animals.

Plants and animals are two of the major groups or *kingdoms* of living things. They share the "needs" of air, space, water, and food for them to survive. To address the issues of what plants and animals have in common and the differences between them, Figure 7.5 may prove helpful.

The differences between plants and animals have contributed to each kingdom's diversity. Yet plants and animals need one another, and this *interdependence* forms the web of life. Before moving on, teachers should return to the class Venn diagram and review it with the students in light of the information included in Figure 7.5.

Getting in Touch With Nature

Students deepen their understanding of the web of life by getting in touch with nature. Taking students on a "science safari" on the school grounds gets them more in tune with their local environment. A "color walk" is a good beginning for the science safari. Students take a box of crayons on a walk on the school grounds. They also wear their energy bead bracelets that were described in Figure 5.1 and observe the color changes in and out of the sunlight. On the color walk, students hunt for materials that are safe, such as twigs, leaves, and/or flower petals that are on the ground. When students return to the classroom, they sort the found objects according to color, using individual sheets of paper. Then they place the appropriate-color crayon on the respective sheet. Which crayon has the most matches? The totality of matches reflects the colors in their local environment.

Figure 7.5 Needs of Plants and Animals

Needs	Plants	Animals
Light	Plants use sunlight to make their own food (photosynthesis). 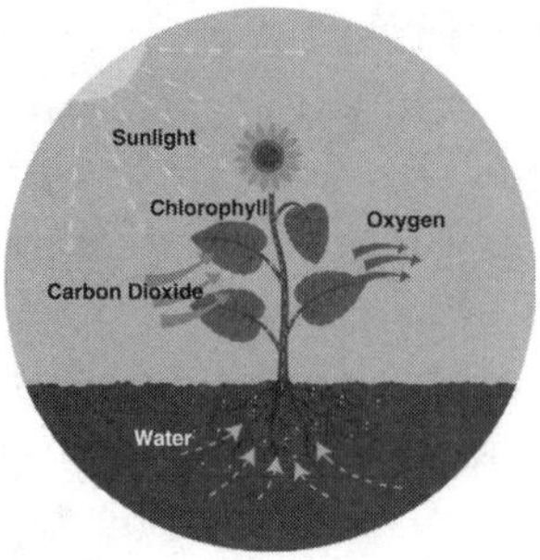 © mervin07/Thinkstock Photos	Animals do not use light to make their food, nor do they need light to survive. Moles, for example, live underground in the dark.
Food	Green plants have chlorophyll and can make their own food.	Animals cannot make their own food and are dependent on plants as well as other animals for food.
Air	During the process of photosynthesis—using sunlight for energy and chlorophyll, water, and carbon dioxide (given off by animals)—plants produce food and give off oxygen.	Animals exhale carbon dioxide, which plants use to make food during photosynthesis. In order to live, animals breathe in the oxygen produced by plants.
Water	Plants need water.  © amenic181/Thinkstock Photos	Animals need water.  © Linda More/Thinkstock Photos
Movement	Plants generally are rooted in one location and do not have the ability to move from place to place.  © feellife/Thinkstock Photos	Most animals have the ability to move from place to place.  © Petr Sterba/Thinkstock Photos

Needs	Plants	Animals
Living space	Plants need a space in which to live and grow and to acquire the resources to survive.	Animals need a space in which to live and grow and to acquire the resources to survive.
Basic cell structure	Plant cells have different structures (e.g. cell walls) and have a different shape than animal cells. 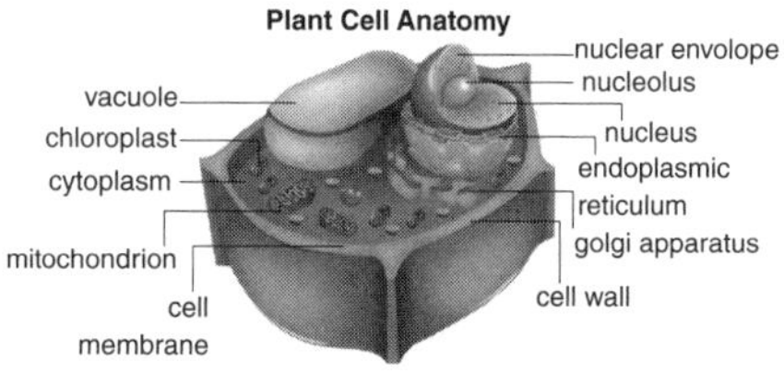 © blueringmedia/Thinkstock Photos	Animal cells do not have cell walls and have a different shape than plant cells. 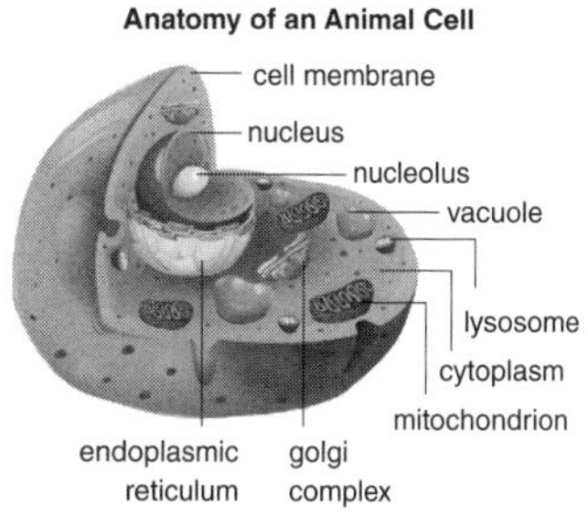 © blueringmedia/Thinkstock Photos

Taking color walks and repeating the exercise four times a year offer insights into the changes that take place during each season of the year, which can be compared, described, and explained.

Students on their walk also can look for different shapes in nature—leaves, branches, twigs, flowers, rocks, etc. Upon returning to the classroom, students draw these shapes on construction paper and cut them out. They punch holes in them and thread them on a pipe cleaner that is bent to form a bracelet. This bracelet is worn on their wrist so that they are reminded of the shapes they saw on their walk, providing yet another avenue for using science terms in a meaningful context.

Students may come across the fruit of plants in which seeds are encased. These may include pinecones, horse chestnut, mesquite or mimosa tree pods, etc. When the students return to the classroom, there is an apple, orange, avocado, or other fruit cut open on paper plates on their desks. They examine the fruit and take note of the number and shape of the seed(s) in each. Students can make tables listing or drawing each fruit and the number and shape of its seeds. They also can compare these seeds with those found on their safari.

This may be an appropriate time to have students look at different types of seeds and do a seed sort, using the dichotomous classification system in Figure 7.6.

Additional piles may be created within the categories of "big" and "small." The students also will note that seeds come in a variety of shapes, colors, and textures: Some are large or small, smooth or rough, flat or thick, etc.

Figure 7.6 Dichotomous Classification System

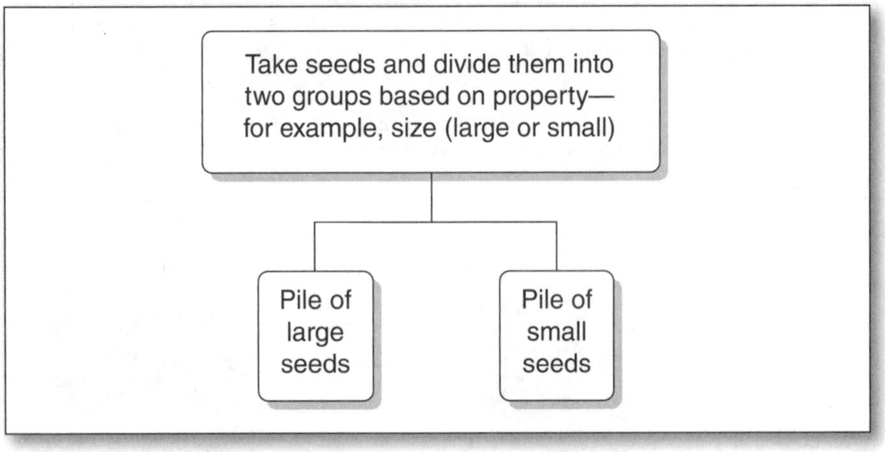

The students can be given a small plastic bag with a variety of seeds (wild bird mix, 15-bean soup mix, etc.), with a brief note and a foldable with six to eight sections to take home, encouraging family members to observe the seeds together and to have students share their knowledge about them. At home, students label the sections of the foldable to match the different types of seeds according to size, shape, etc., and glue them down in the appropriate sections of the foldable. Reading *Plants and Seeds* by C. H. Walker (1992) or *A Seed Is Sleepy* by D. Aston (2014) can be another way to expand on the topic of seeds and to move into learning about other plant parts.

Plants in the Web of Life

Learning about plants means putting students' senses to work. Take, for example, observing different seedlings such as marigolds. Each group of students is given two different types of young marigold plants that have flowers and roots, newspaper or paper plates for the plants, a ruler, and a wooden Popsicle stick to examine the parts of the plants. Students should use Figure 7.7 to guide their comparative observations of the marigold plants as they become acquainted with their main parts. Figure 7.7 is on the website and can be copied and distributed to the students.

Reading *Planting a Rainbow* by L. Ehlert (1992) reinforces colors and shapes and makes students aware of how flowers are planted and how they bloom. At first glance, this book may appear to be more appropriate for young students, but it can be adapted in many different ways for older students, depending on the science lesson. First and foremost, it is packed with beautiful color illustrations that appeal immediately to the senses that teachers at all grade levels can use

Figure 7.7 Marigold Grid

	Marigold no. 1	Marigold no. 2	They are alike because . . .	They are different because . . .
Stem shape (round or square)				
Leaf color				
Leaf texture (rough, smooth, hairy)				
Number of petals per flower (few, many)				
Smell (sweet, stinky)				
Length of the stem (in cm)				
Length of the roots (in cm)				

when planning science lessons that focus on the physical structures, variation of traits, and diversity of plants.

Students can make their own garden collages or construct their own flowers (making sure that they have all their parts) by using different colored construction and tissue papers that are glued onto 8 × 10 sheets of card stock. These collages then become a part of the "class community garden." Students can share with visitors their class garden and tell them about all the plants that live there. The class garden also can serve as an inspiration for writing limericks, songs, and stories.

Students can interview a local master gardener for tips and suggestions about growing plants in different climates. As a guest speaker, the master gardener comes to talk with the students about plants that grow best in their location. Before the interview takes place, the teacher should prepare the students in how to interview guest speakers, including modeling how to ask questions and listening to what is being said. The speaker should be informed about the age of the students. Finally, the teacher brainstorms with students on how the pictures and illustrations in *Planting a Rainbow* come together, and to take note of the students' creative ideas that emerge.

Along their science safari walk, students "search for sounds"—rustling leaves, birds singing, twigs crunching, and wind blowing—and record them in their science notebooks using words or drawings. Check out the Calmsound Nature Sounds website (www.calmsound.com), which offers free sounds of nature, including country gardens, rain, thunderstorms, etc. The students also should stop and take deep breaths to determine if there are smells from fragrant flowers, newly mowed grass, or animals.

At the end of their safari, students participate in a "touch walk." They work with a partner using materials provided (blindfold, sheet of paper, pair of socks, pencil, crayons) to explore the different textures in the area. One member puts on the blindfold and the other guides his or her partner around to touch different safe, natural materials—rough tree bark, smooth leaves, wet grass, etc. Then they switch roles. Last, the students learn about seed dispersal by putting on a pair of socks over their shoes, and they walk about in a 5 × 5 meter area. Then they take off the socks and examine what is sticking to them. They make sketches of these materials in their science notebooks. This may be a suitable time to introduce how seeds travel from place to place—on the fur of animals (simulated by using the socks) and through animal excretion containing seeds from the fruit that they have eaten. Humans also disperse seeds—for example, when seeds attach themselves to clothing, or when humans eat fruit (e.g., watermelon) and discard the seeds.

At the conclusion of studying plants and completing these exercises, it is important that students share what they have learned; they also need to demonstrate that they have an understanding of the role of plants in the web of life. Answering the following questions will stimulate students' thinking about plants: (1) *What do all plants have in common?* (2) *What are some ways plants are different from one another?* (3) *How do plants change with the seasons of the year?* (4) *What happens in the winter?* (5) *How do plants adapt to living in biomes with limited water? Or in cold temperatures?* (6) *How do orchids (epiphytes) survive? What adaptations have they developed?* (7) *Why are plants different colors?* (8) *What would happen to a cactus plant if transplanted into a tropical rain forest?*

Animals in the Web of Life

In the animal kingdom, physical characteristics matter, particularly size and color. Some animals are large, like elephants, moose, horses, or whales, while others are small, like ants, hummingbirds, mice, or tree frogs. Still other animals are very colorful, like sea horses, parrots, skunks, or ladybugs. Some animals have external patterns, like snakes, giraffes, zebras, or tigers. What a wondrous assortment of animals live on land, in water, or somewhere in between!

Using a double bubble map (Figure 7.8), discuss with students the animals that live on land and those that live in water. For younger students use pictures of animals for them to place on the map, and for older students have them write in the names of the animals. Animals such as crabs, frogs, turtles, and birds form a bridge between the two groups. This exercise affords ample opportunities to use language as students name animals that fit into these two major categories, make comparisons, and explain their reasons for including an animal in one group or the other.

Figure 7.8 Double Bubble Map

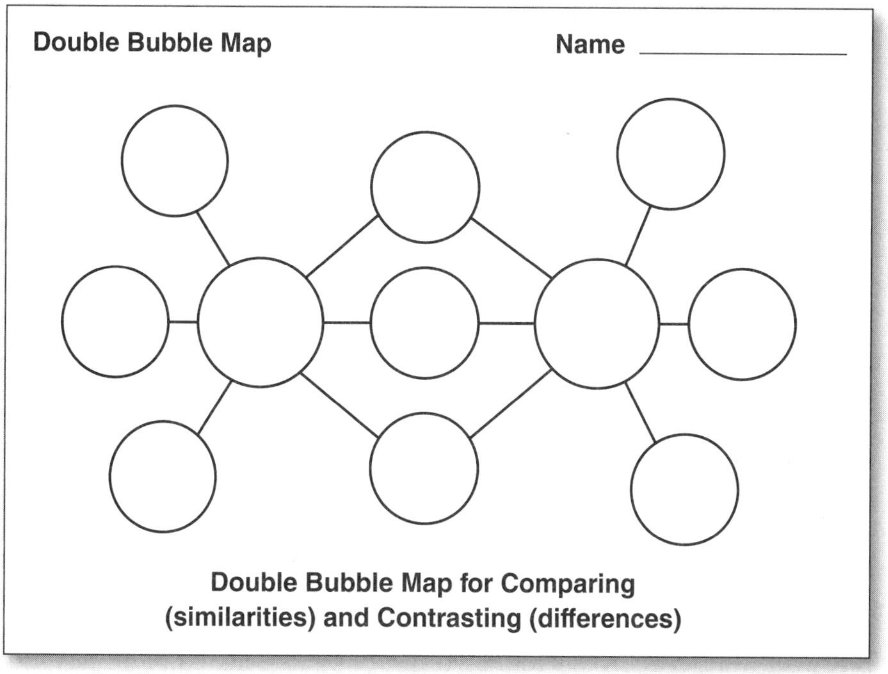

Teachers can read the counting rhyme "Over in the Meadow" by Olive A. Wadsworth (1800s), which includes different animals in different settings. The beginning of the rhyme is presented below in Figure 7.9a with words, and with pictures in Figure 7.9b. Links to the complete versions of both, and Figure 7.9b in full color, are on the website. Currently, there are many books on the market that feature this rhyme by different illustrators.

The Never-Ending Search for Food. This is the number one activity for animals. Food gathering by animals, as illustrated in food

Figure 7.9a "Over in the Meadow" With Words

Written by Olive A. Wadsworth (1800s)

Over in the meadow,
In the sand in the sun
Lived an old mother toadie
And her little toadie one.
"Wink!" said the mother;
"I wink!" said the one,
So they winked and they blinked
In the sand in the sun.

Over in the meadow,
Where the stream runs blue
Lived an old mother fish
And her little fishes two. . . .

To see an illustrated version of this poem in its entirety, please visit http://www.isd622.org/cms/lib07/MN01001375/Centricity/Domain/33/OverintheMedowBook.pdf

chains and webs, is complicated. Food chains tend to be linear, whereas food webs tend to spread in many different directions, as shown in Figure 7.10.

If organisms lower in a chain disappear, it impacts organisms at the higher levels and makes their search for food even more challenging. For example, if there is a severe drought followed by a forest fire that burns trees and low-lying plants, the food supply is already compromised. Then, if heavy rains follow, the land is stripped of organisms at the lower end of the food chain. Consequently, larger animals face the prospect of starvation or are forced to migrate in search of other food sources. Organisms in a more complex food web—for example, in an ocean environment—are all connected. If there is a disruption of the food web, such as from an oil spill that kills many life forms, the surviving animals are also driven to find alternative food sources.

Some animals in food chains and webs are *herbivores*, such as caribou, lemmings, and rabbits, and eat only plants. Other animals are *carnivores*, such as foxes and lions, and eat only meat. *Omnivores*, such as humans, eat both plants and animals. In the case of a wolf in the arctic, its food source is caribou, musk oxen, hares, lemmings, and foxes. In this

Figure 7.9b "Over in the Meadow" With Words and Pictures

Written by Olive A. Wadsworth (1800s)

Over in the meadow,

© givaga/Thinkstock Photos

In the sand in the sun

© Gabriele Maltinti/Thinkstock Photos

Lived an old mother toadie

© WhippinDog/Thinkstock Photos

And her little toadie one.

© TheLionRoar/Thinkstock Photos

"Wink!" said the mother;

© WhippinDog/Thinkstock Photos

"I wink!" said the one,

© TheLionRoar/Thinkstock Photos

So they winked and they blinked

© givaga/Thinkstock Photos

In the sand in the sun.

© Gabriele Maltinti/Thinkstock Photos

Over in the meadow,
Where the stream runs blue
Lived an old mother fish

© smontgom65/Thinkstock Photos

And her little fishes two . . . .

To see an illustrated version of this poem in its entirety, please visit http://www.isd622.org/cms/lib07/MN01001375/Centricity/Domain/33/OverintheMedowBook.pdf

Figure 7.10 Sample Food Chain and Food Web

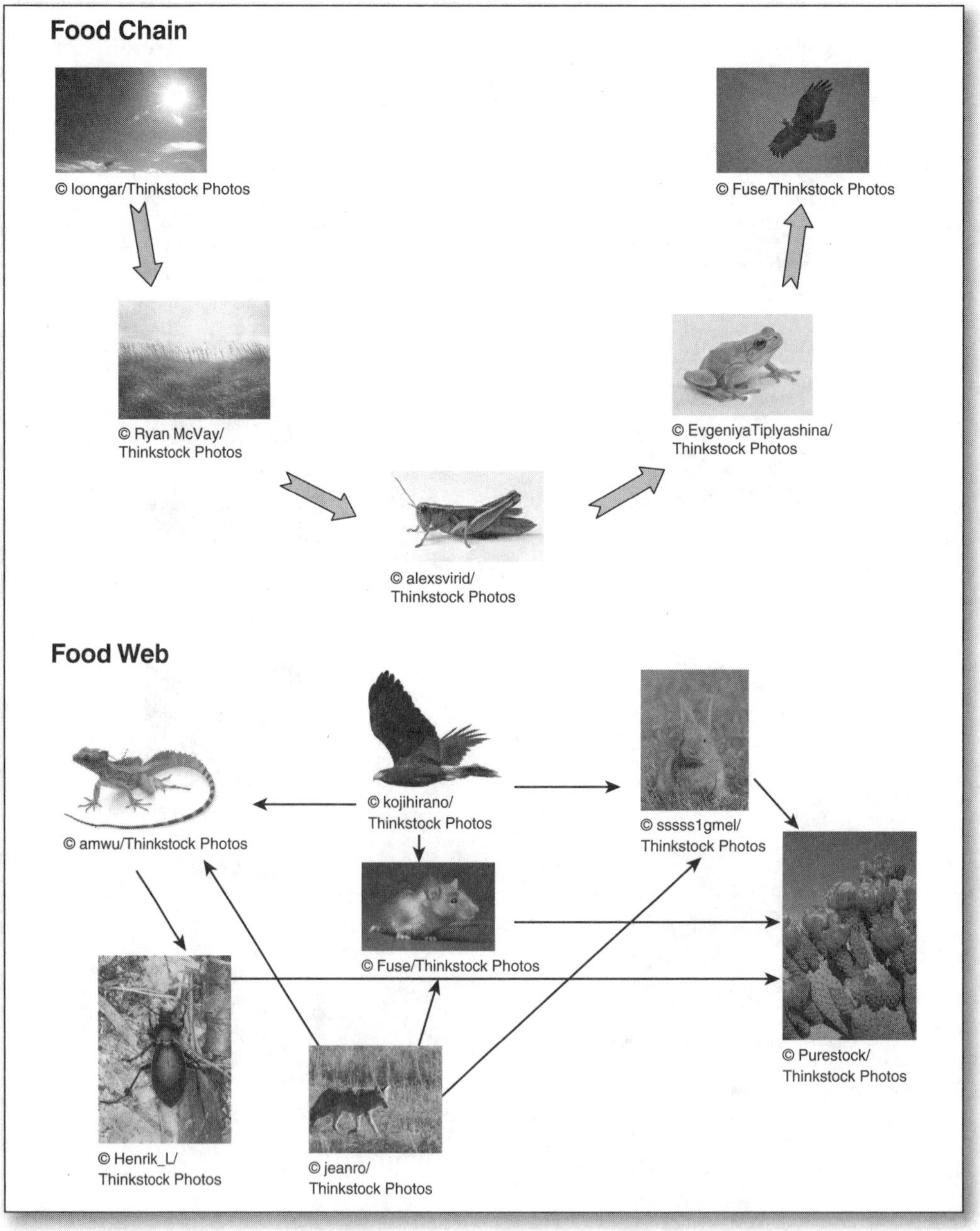

feeding pattern, the wolf preys on other animals that eat plants. Plants must be available for the herbivores so that carnivores have meat to eat.

To explore a specific ecosystem and the food chains and webs in it, students are given a stack of pictures of animals and plants and characteristics of different ecosystems. They are also provided a set of cutout arrows. Using the pictures, the students design and build a food chain or web and place the arrows to connect them. They first sketch their designs in their science notebooks. Finally, they tell the story of the food chain or web and explain how each works.

Working with *owl pellets* is another way that students learn how a food chain works, as well as about skeletal structures of the prey (i.e., rodents) that have been eaten by the owls. R. Manna presents a lesson on "Dissecting Owl Pellets," along with where to get them (http://www.scholastic.com/teachers/lesson-plan/dissecting-owl-pellets). The book *Owl Moon,* by J. Yolen (1987), can be paired with the owl pellet exercise. It captures the magic of a woodland adventure by taking the reader on a special journey with a girl and her father as they trudge through the snow on a very cold winter night to see the Great Horned Owl and listen to its call.

Diet helps to explain a lot about the physical structure of animals. Some animals have limbs for movement, while others have wings. Some animals have fur, scales, or feathers for protection and insulation. Some animals have strong jaws and large, sharp teeth, while others do not even have teeth at all.

In some animals, their structure gives them an advantage over their competitors for food. Some animals, like leopards, are lean and muscular and can run fast. They also are smart and can climb trees from which to pounce on their prey. Sharks, one of the oldest organisms in the oceans, have an enduring success story and have left a rich fossil record. Structurally, they have skeletons of cartilage, not bone; they have gill slits and pectoral fins; and they are built for speed because of their torpedo-shaped bodies. They are eating machines, consuming on average over 11 tons of food a year, consisting of sea lions, seals, small-toothed whales, sea turtles, and fish. They have a well-developed sense of smell. And they have several hundred teeth, which are replaced if lost or broken. Over its lifetime, a shark will go through 30,000–50,000 teeth (Nguyen, np). Other great hunters are alligators (with U-shaped snouts) and crocodiles (with V-shaped snouts). Their teeth also are replaced when lost or broken. These amazing animals are built to be successful in their ecosystems, and they illustrate the many variations and adaptations that exist in the animal kingdom.

Today for humans, food is readily available in stores, with fewer families living on farms and producing their own food for survival. Most people get their food from supermarkets or from fast-food establishments, and students often do not have a clear picture of where this food comes from—milk from cows, eggs from chickens, bread from grain, etc. *How Did That Get in My Lunchbox? The Story of Food* (2011) by C. Butterworth explores where food comes from and provides an engaging look at the steps involved in the preparation of common foods such as bread for sandwiches, vegetables, fruit, etc. This book is a gateway to many science topics, such as following food to market, diet and the human digestive system, etc. In addition, there are health tips, which can lead to lessons that examine the "nutrition facts" on food labels. This information will introduce students to a host of new terms—vitamins, calories, fat content, sodium, protein, portion size, and ingredients.

Adaptations. These are coping mechanisms that help plants and animals survive and thrive. They include special behaviors and physiologies to deal with harsh conditions such as extreme heat and cold, lack of oxygen at high altitudes, and scarcity of water and space. Cacti have modified leaves called spines, and roots that spread out close to the surface (some prickly pear roots spread 10 to 15 ft away). This is to maximize access to scarce rains that often come hard and fast during specific seasons of the year. *Cactus Hotel* and *Desert Animal Adaptations* are books that get the conversation going about plant and animal adaptations. Stick insects "disappear" in the rain forest because they use camouflage, and some butterflies have wings that look like leaves. These adaptations increase the organisms' chances for survival. For more about the rain forest, Gibbon's *Nature's Green Umbrella* is a good place to begin.

Consider how frogs catch their prey. What adaptations do they have? As amphibians, they can hunt on land and in water. Their tongues are designed like a party blower that quickly rolls in and out. In addition, their tongues have a sticky substance on the tip that prevents the prey from flying off before the frog has had a chance to retract its tongue and enjoy its meal. This exercise is a fun way to get students' attention about specialized structures in plants and animals. The materials for each pair of students include a party blower, a Velcro dot, a piece of string about a meter long, and a small piece of felt (2 cm × 2 cm). The students construct a frog's tongue that will catch a fly with the materials provided. If some students have difficulty with the task, the directions are simple: Stick the Velcro dot to the end of the party blower and tape the piece of felt to the end of the string. As one partner blows, the other partner holds the string with the felt on it. In their science notebooks, they draw the model of a "frog's tongue," make predictions, and then record how many "flies" they actually catch. The goal is to see how many "flies" can be caught.

After all pairs have built and tested their tongue models, the students come together and discuss why some were successful in capturing their food while others were not. How are human tongues different from those of frogs? What adaptations do frogs have that make their tongues ideal food-catching devices? And if frogs did not have the ability to coil and recoil their tongues, what would happen to them?

Space and Home Range. These are needed for organisms to move around, obtain food, have access to water, and avoid predators. They also need a place to rest and raise their young. Bears, for example, need a place to *hibernate* in the winter for as long as 100 days without drinking, eating, urinating, defecating, or moving. In the summer in preparation for hibernation, they gorge on carbohydrate-rich berries and other foods to put on weight, gaining up to 30 pounds a week. In the fall, bears respond to their nesting instinct and begin to gather leaves, twigs, and other plant materials to make nests in dens (burrows, caves, hollowed-out trees) that they have selected. The space is small, but that is the way they like it. They curl up into a ball, head pressed into their chest, and their back to the elements. If the bear has cubs, the den becomes the family's home for the next several months. *Time to Sleep* (2001) by D. Fleming is an inviting, colorful book that might be a good ending to a lesson on hibernation. With the approaching winter, the bear says, "I smell winter in the air. . . . It is time to crawl into my cave and sleep. . . ."

So what does it take to make a home for animals? For bears it is a den, for chipmunks and ground squirrels it is a burrow, and for birds it is a nest. To make a den their home, bears use a variety of materials to make it as soft and comfortable as possible. Birds, depending on their sizes, build nests of similar materials to the bears and also use anything else that is available, such as bits of string, cloth, or paper.

What does it take to make a nest big and strong enough to hold adult birds, their eggs, and then their young? Students can test their ideas by making a "nest" to see how many marbles it will hold. They work in groups to build a nest using 15 strips of paper (all the same size: 2.5 cm wide and 16 cm long), an empty 1-pound plastic container from the deli department of a grocery store (in which to build the nest), and a number of marbles of the same size. The group members develop a model of their nest first in their science notebooks before actually constructing it so they can keep track of their ideas before testing them. After they decide on a design (how they are going to arrange the paper strips over the opening of the container), they build the nest. They then place the marbles gently in the nest, one at a time. When the nest collapses, they redesign it and start over. In this modeling exercise, students try to meet the challenge of what it takes to build a nest that will hold a specific number of marbles.

It is important to note that K–5 students study specific examples of animals. Throughout the early elementary grades the emphasis has been on physical characteristics as a way to group animals. In the upper grades, the concept of diversity is further developed when vertebrate and invertebrate organisms are introduced. It is at this time that the groundwork for classifying animals is laid. The resulting taxonomies include insects, reptiles, amphibians, birds, fish, and mammals.

Designing an animal is an exercise that will encourage students to think about the diversity of life, animal adaptations, and their physical characteristics. This exercise asks students to design an animal that is suited to a specific biome. First, students select the biome and the general location where their animal will live; they then decide what their animal will look like, taking into consideration the conditions mentioned in Figure 7.3. Also, they consider what the physical features will be, including body covering, feet, teeth, coloring, legs, and general body shape. Students then can construct a diorama of that biome and place their animals in it (http://www.wikihow.com/Make-a-Diorama).

Conclusion

Introducing students to the big picture of the biosphere and its different biomes provides them with insights into where they live. Additionally, they begin to recognize the interdependence that exists on Earth as they learn more about the relationships that plants and animals share, their needs, and the climatic conditions that contribute to their survival and how they continue to adapt and change.

The core ideas in the life sciences afford many clues and strategies for studying plants and animals in their natural settings. The concepts of living and nonliving initiate the life science study. The crosscutting concepts of patterns, scale, systems, cycles, etc., become evident as students investigate the dynamic nature of the various ecosystems and the diversity of life forms. The nature walk—described in great detail, involving active learning strategies—can open students' eyes to how the web of life around them functions and can give them a snapshot of the life science core ideas.

Your Turn

1. Find your grade level in Figure 6.1, Overview of Crosscutting Concepts, Topics, Disciplinary Core Ideas, and Student Performance Expectations for Grades K–5, for the life sciences.
    - Select a life science (LS) topic and take note of the student expectations for that topic.
    - How would you go about teaching this topic to your students?
    - Use the 5E science lesson-planning template (Figure 3.3) as a guide. Individually, or with colleagues, fill in the information

based on the topic that has been selected, keeping in mind the form of inquiry that you would like to promote while focusing on this life science topic.

2. A description of a science loop was presented in Chapter 3. The *I have* and *who has* statements may or may not be appropriate for your students, so develop a science loop of your own focusing on a life science topic. The template for a loop can be found on the website in Word format so that it can be modified.
   - Model how the loop is played so the students know what they are expected to do. The goal is to get students engaged by listening to what is being read; then they have to decide if they have the information requested.
   - At first, the going will be slow. But once the students catch on, they help one another, and the more they participate, the faster the loop will be completed. Students within the same grade levels can compete with one another, and the times can be posted on their classroom door.

3. In the classroom, have students look through recent copies of newspapers and magazines to find stories that focus on the life sciences (e.g., environmental issues). Have them report on what they have found, and ask them to write a related follow-up article for the local newspaper. Or have them role-play a reporter covering the story for the local TV or radio station.

4. Review the book's website for different types of resources (lessons, games, songs, books, writing ideas, etc.) that target various grade levels, from how plants grow to animal movements and their tracks. Check out these and others such as Antarctic birds, PowerPoints addressing animal coverings, and the cycle of life on the food chain.

5. As a home science activity, ask students and parents to do the following when they go to the supermarket in order to look for ways that packaging of products adds to the amount of waste we generate. They should locate three items that are particularly wasteful and three that are not—with little or no packaging, or packaging made from recycled materials. In addition, ask them to read the food labels on their favorite cereal or snack and compare that information to the labels on dried fruit or granola bars.

8

Games

A Context for Meaningful Science Learning and Communicative Language Usage

© FlairImages/Thinkstock Photos

As we play, we learn. And as we grow, our play gets more complicated. We add rules and goals. The result is something we call games.

—Will Wright

Introduction

In recent years, the United States has witnessed a growing student engagement crisis in our schools. One way to motivate learners for the 21st century is to turn to the new literacy of the digital world coming from popular culture. As part of this world, many students today readily play video games that involve problem solving, and that focus on an array of topics (Gee & Levine, 2009).

The latest buzzwords pervading educational blogs are *game-based learning* and *gamification*. Brain research has supported the claim that using games is one of the best ways to activate learning (Tate, 2008). While playing games, students interact using their communication skills and their senses that stimulate the brain to retain information.

Students in today's classrooms are tech-savvy and adept at using technology in productive ways. Electronic games have long been popular with students—the competitiveness, the flashing lights, and all the bells and whistles are appealing qualities. For many who support the use of games, playing them is not their only educational value; how they cut across home, community, and school settings, and connect to books, music, movies, and the real world are also important factors.

It is clear from surveying teachers that many of them have decided to take advantage of gaming in their classrooms. Whether the games employ technology or rely on more traditional formats such as boards and pieces, or are those that involve matching terms with definitions, they seem to be equally applicable. The reasons why teachers are embracing games are many, but the most important ones are getting the students' attention, engaging them in learning content and skills, and providing contexts for communicative language production. Sykes (2013) notes that using games for language learning highlights the "critical nature of learner-driven experiences that are authenticated through play and participation" (p. 32). When teachers use meaningful games—video or traditional—their roles change to those of mentors and guides, which are more in line with inquiry learning.

The New Literacy: Digital Video Games

For many, playing video games has developed into a new "literacy" because of its interactive quality of connecting students to virtual worlds. With the increasing interest in digital literacy, the use of video games in the classroom is on the increase. Commercial games build in an entertainment value that students find extremely attractive. There are games, however, that may not address directly the specific science and language objectives that teachers may want to target. A brief description of gamification along with simulations and digital games follows.

Gamification

Many businesses such as fast-food restaurants and supermarkets employ gamification in the form of promotions—for example, collecting *Monopoly* puzzle pieces for prizes. Why do businesses utilize these games? What makes them so popular with the public? The goal of gamification is to motivate customers to buy at their establishments by offering fantastic rewards. Similarly, Catalano (2012) notes that educational games are increasingly being used in classrooms across the United States to reach students. He continues that gamification, simulations, and games can be viewed as "a continuum, or a Venn diagram . . . [of] overlapping circles—but they are notably different" (np).

Gamification is a new term that simply means adding game elements to something that already exists. To "gamify" something in education is to apply gaming principles to motivate and inspire student learning (Catalano, 2012). Teachers already engage in gamifying when they have students earn stickers, chits, and/or points after they have completed their work, followed directions, shown respect for others, etc. Students respond positively when learning is structured like a game because they understand that the outcome matters. It should be noted that some view gamification in education as bribes and devoid of intrinsic value, leading at best to short-term learning (Catalano, 2012).

Simulations. These have been around for a long time. *SimCity* (1989) is one example that has been used in schools extensively. In this simulation, students build and sustain cities. Students are placed in situations from which they have to disentangle themselves. By using different thinking skills and implementing them through the characters they play, they make their way out of these circumstances. These experiences can be extremely engaging, and they get students to recognize the importance of putting their thinking skills to work.

Digital Games. In education, digital games go back to 1985, when *Where in the World Is Carmen Sandiego?* came on the market. Like simulations, digital games are rule-bound, but even more so. Students intrinsically want to beat the other players and "win." Most games have the potential to teach, and students playing games have the potential to learn. Games immerse students into new roles and worlds that help them understand concepts in a different way, but Cowan (2010) and many others think that this is especially true of electronic games.

A more recent example is *Quest Atlantis* (http://crlt.indiana.edu/projects/completed-projects/transactive-art). In the fourth-grade unit, students are in a virtual world in which they use scientific information and tools to solve problems in an aquatic park that has serious ecological problems. In assuming roles of the virtual characters, students develop ideas about how to address the pollution in the fish habitats and propose informed solutions. Student engagement increases when they participate in games like *Quest Atlantis*. Students learn the language of science as they evaluate the information provided and make decisions regarding solutions. According to the research conducted by Barab, Zuiker, Warren, Hickey, Ingram-Goble, Kwon, and others (2007), students learn the science behind the game, and they transfer their learning to achievement on standardized tests.

A survey involving K–8 teachers (majority K–5) was conducted to determine the degree to which digital games reached underserved students in their classrooms (Joan Ganz Cooney Center, 2012). In the survey, over half of the teachers reported that they used digital games at least 2 or more days a week. Nearly 70% said that lower-performing students connected better with content in the curriculum using digital games. Teachers also noted that digital games on computers and iPads made it easier to teach students from diverse populations and to assess their knowledge. And they reported that many of these games were aligned with the Common Core. The survey respondents, however, did list several shortcomings that included cost, lack of access to technology, and the emphasis placed on them to prepare their students for standardized tests (http://www.joanganzcooneycenter.org/wpcontent/uploads/2013/10/jgcc_teacher_survey_analysis_final.pdf).

To get teachers familiar with digital language, Gee and Levine (2009) recommend that they consult several websites. The first, http://wiki.classroom20.com, offers free workshops and live conversations, and www.cast.org/teachingeverystudent/ideas/tes, from the Center for Applied Special Technologies, seeks to deliver a curriculum to meet every student's needs.

Additionally, teachers interested in using digital games in their classrooms should check the website http://www.games2teach.wordpress.com, which offers a game evaluation framework to select, review, and sample activities. Sykes and Reinhardt (2012) have developed a game journal activity that may prove helpful.

As shared by the surveyed teachers, commercial games can be expensive; money is needed to buy games and their associated hardware, as well as to maintain their upkeep. Even free science games online for primary grades at http://www.primarygames.com/science.php and http://www.sheppardsoftware.com/periodictable_0_click_all.html on elements and the periodic table still require equipment to access them during the school day.

The next section deals with games that have many advantages and are much cheaper. They do not incur costs for the games and do not require special equipment. Many of these games also encourage movement and get students to exercise as they participate rather than merely looking passively at expensive game consoles. Most important, these games are free and often result in many of the same educational outcomes and enjoyed in a relaxed atmosphere.

Games for the Science Classroom

Video games are not the only games for students to play. Whatever type of game that teachers implement in their classrooms, "their real value lies in leveraging play and exploration as a mode of learning" (Levassur, 2011, np). Games perform a variety of roles in promoting science and language learning, from warm-ups at the beginning of class to keeping students on task when class is formally over. However, their role should be considerably more substantial.

Games are used as a way to practice, review, and/or recycle previously taught science content and skills, and to contextualize language usage. With the shift in language learning from developing individual linguistic skills to developing communicative competence, game-based strategies in the science classroom fit the bill in getting students to produce meaningful communicative language (Chen, 2005). Games that involve students in communicative language focus on exchanges of information and ideas. In this context, students may discuss the differences between two rock samples—*Which one has cleavage, and which one does not?*—and offer their evidence for their respective claims.

In addition, games motivate students to learn science, sustain interest, and encourage the spontaneous use of language in a relaxed environment. Even when a game's focus is on spelling academic terms, students are more interested in learning how to play the game than in worrying about the terms (Wright, Betteridge, & Buckby, 2005). Students become emotionally invested in games, and their goal is to win or to help their group win. The games also build group spirit and activate spatial skills along with kinesthetic movements. Last, games can be played anywhere, in and out of classrooms; they can even be taken home and shared with parents and other family members.

Generally, students embrace games enthusiastically. Games are intriguing because of the challenges they present. Nonetheless, teachers should be cognizant of their level of difficulty in order to prevent discouraging students from participating. Students should understand the game rules and be familiar with the science and language skills needed to meet the challenges, thereby ensuring that they experience various degrees of success. To minimize these challenges, teachers should (1) model how the game is played; (2) highlight and explain the appropriate science vocabulary to avoid any misunderstandings; (3) give clear directions beforehand so that the game is not interrupted by student questions; (4) begin with games that students already know; (5) consider putting students in pairs initially to support one another; and (6) have resources such as word/phrase walls, anchor charts, nonfiction books, and textbooks available.

Let the Games Begin

Classifying educational games into categories can be problematic because the categories often overlap. For the purposes of this book, science educational games are those that provide a learning context for students to engage in, practice, and review science information. "Gamers play cooperatively. They play competitively. They share tips and tricks. They work together" (Flickinger, 2014). Rollins (2014) calls these opportunities "success starters." They are excellent ways to immerse students into new science topics and to ignite their curiosity. These success starters may involve reading books such as *Mom and Dad Are Palindromes: A Dilemma for Words . . . and Backwards* (Shulman, 2006), *What Is Science?* (Dotlich, 2006), *A Visitor for Bear* (Becker, 2008), and *Hatchet* (Paulson, 1987). Or teachers can use games to demonstrate how sometimes they are not fair. The topic of fairness is particularly important when students conduct comparative and experimental investigations.

Rollins (2014) also suggests that having students simply pull cards from a bag with terms or phrases on them—for example, on strip mining—and share their reasons why they support it or not, gets them thinking. Similarly, students can draw names of pretend animals and explain how they adapt to environments that have been struck by a catastrophic event such as a flood, earthquake, or tornado. They can use cartoon strips such as *Peanuts*, *Pickles*, or *Mutts* to explain orally or in writing what they think is the message being presented.

Six major categories of educational science games that require no equipment, hook students on science, and target different language skills are described below (Jacobs, nd). When reviewing each category, teachers should consider (1) where the game will take place (inside the classroom or outside on school grounds, in a park, at home, etc.); (2) the appropriateness of the game for the students who will participate; (3) how long the game will last (10 minutes, a class period, or more); and (4) the level of participation required. This last point, Sousa and Tomlinson (2011) note, is critical because of the potential for negative reactions from peers. Students may hesitate to participate fully for fear of being made fun of. Conversely, positive feedback from teachers and peers gets students involved; there is nothing like success to get students enthused about learning science.

1. In *games calling for sorting, ordering, or classifying*, students are given a collection of materials such as rocks, buttons, leaves, or balls. Generally, students have many experiences putting objects into different groups or piles. In science, teachers might find exercises that focus on dichotomously grouping objects a pleasant alternative. It is a two-by-two classifying system. In this book, it was introduced in Chapter 7, when students examined different types of seeds and did a seed sort (see Figure 7.6).

It may be helpful to use and model for the students sentence frames such as *I divided this pile of objects using the property of size—tall and short.* In the next round of the game, use *I divide each pile* into two more groups, and the game continues until each object is in its own group. This way students can recite the properties of each group of objects, such as *I have a ____ that is big, dark, and rough.* Any objects or materials can be used, but healthy treats (e.g., slices of apples and pears, or orange sections) that have different properties can be placed in plastic bags and sorted; they can then be eaten after the game is over. Teachers can add more rules to the game to make it more competitive and challenging.

2. *Seeking information games,* also called "guessing games," usually include one student who has science information and a partner who has to guess what it is by asking "yes" and "no" questions. The *Backs Have It* game operates off this basic principle. The guesser faces away from a partner who has a laminated card on a string hanging from his or her back, and the guesser has to determine what the information or picture is by asking "yes" or "no" questions. The game is over when the correct information or pictured object or organism is identified. Refer to Figure 8.1 for more details about how the game is played.

Figure 8.1 The Backs Have It Game

I. Objectives:

Science Objective: The students will pose yes/no questions using science terms to identify the object or organism in the picture on the card.

Language Objective: The students will ask and respond orally to yes/no questions based on what is pictured on the card.

II. Materials:

A set of pictures of animals, plants, scenes of different habitats, different seasons, etc., from old calendars, magazines, state park or wildlife agencies, and *National Geographic.*

© GlobalP/Thinkstock Photos

Have the pictures laminated. Punch holes in the upper-right and left corners and tie a string through each hole, leaving enough length for students to place the picture over their heads to rest on their backs.

III. Directions:

Part A

1. Students work with a partner.
2. One member of the pair places the laminated card on the back of his or her partner. Do *not* let the partner see what is on the card.
3. The student with the card on his or her back will try to discover what is on the card. This student asks yes/no questions such as:
   - *Is it an animal? Is it a plant?*
   - *Does it eat plants?*
   - *Does it live on land? Does it live in a marine ecosystem?*
   - *Does this organism live in a freshwater ecosystem?*
   - *Is this organism terrestrial?*
   - *Is this organism a producer? Is this organism a consumer? Is it a predator? Or prey?*
   - *Does this organism get its food during the day? At night?*
   - *Is it winter? Spring? Summer? Fall?*
   - *Is the picture of a specific biome?*
4. The winners will be the pair that discovers what is on the partner's back first.

Part B

When the student identifies what is on the card correctly, the student answering the yes/no questions reads any additional information that may be on the card. For example:

- The habitat of the organism
- Where it lives and what it eats
- The types of adaptations it has, if any, to survive
- Animal and plant facts

3. *Looking for information games* are yet another type in which the students seek information, give information, and/or listen for information. A variant of this game is a scavenger hunt. This type of game or scavenger hunt can easily be used at the beginning of the school year to get students acquainted with their school campus. For example, the Can You Find These Things in Your School? game can be used to find the library and librarian, the nurse, the main office and the principal, science lab, cafeteria, etc.

The game involves students circulating around the classroom or building, asking and answering questions, and collaborating with classmates to fill in all the cells on the scavenger hunt sheet. Students are given a sheet requesting specific information that they are to find. To verify that they found the information in each cell on the sheet, signatures are generally required. The goal is to have fun while finding the information in all the cells, and the first student or group that has the grid filled in is declared the winner.

The Science Textbook Scavenger Hunt game is presented in Figure 8.2. Using a search-and-find game strategy, students are asked to locate different features in their science textbook to familiarize them with, for example, the table of contents, glossary, appendix, and style used to emphasize important science information, along with main and subheadings. Such a game can be used with other science books (e.g., *Oceans* by S. Simon [2006]) and science stories (e.g., *The Boy Who Made Dragonfly* by T. Hillerman [1993]).

Another game—Science Laboratory Equipment Scavenger Hunt, designed for familiarizing students with science equipment and safety—is presented in Figure 8.3. Teachers can include those items that are appropriate for their students. The *I am . . .* format offers a different twist to this game. The template for this game and the scavenger hunt for science textbook game can be found on the companion website, http://resources.corwin.com/ReinhartzGrowingLanguage, in Word format.

Last, Figure 8.4 is a guide for planning a nature scavenger hunt game and offers many ideas including what to observe, collect, do, photograph, and display during this experience.

4. *Matching information games,* as the name implies, can involve students in matching words to pictures, or words to definitions. After a lesson on cloud formations, for example, one version is to give students an envelope with cards that have cloud names, and other cards that have pictures of these clouds. They place the cards face down randomly and then turn them over to match the cloud name with its picture. These cards can be color-coded by using different color,

Figure 8.2 Science Textbook Scavenger Hunt Game

Name: ______________________________

Date: ______________________________

Class: ______________________________

Title of Textbook: ______________________________

Directions: Using your science textbook, respond to the following questions by filling in the information requested on this sheet.

On what page does the table of contents begin? What is the title and number of the section that sounds most interesting to you? Why? Tell a classmate or adult in the room. Name that person here.	Why are some of the terms in bold print? Explain the reason(s) why to a classmate, using an example from the textbook.	What is the title of Chapter _____? What are three subheadings? List them here.	Is there an appendix? If so, on what page does it start?
How many chapters are in the textbook?	What is the title of the textbook?	What is the last "S" entry in the index?	How is the textbook organized?
What is the definition of _____?	What is the color of the major headings of each part, and what color is used for subheadings?	In the review section at the end of Chapter _____, what is the first question? Write it here.	Where in the textbook are the resources listed to obtain more information? What resources do they include? Write one example here.
Review the textbook. What catches your attention and why? List them here.	Find a picture in Chapter _____. What does the caption under the picture say? Read the caption to another person in the room and share why you think captions are important under pictures or diagrams. Name that person here.	What are two special features of the textbook? List these features here.	How many pages are in the textbook? Write that number here.

Source: Adapted and modified from ShellysScienceSpot.com.

Figure 8.3 Science Laboratory Equipment Scavenger Hunt Game

Name: ______________________ Date: ______________________

Directions: Next to the correct clue, draw a picture or write in the space the names of the science equipment. How many can you figure out before the time is up?

1. I am used to measure mass.	
2. I am used when a student's clothes catch fire.	
3. I make things bigger so they can be seen more clearly.	
4. I am used to protect clothes in the science lab.	
5. I am used to measure the temperature of a substance or object.	
6. I am used to measure liquids (volume).	
7. I can be a real grind.	
8. I am used if something in the laboratory is on fire.	
9. I am used to make things hot.	
10. I am worn to protect the eyes.	
11. I am used to measure.	
12. I am glassware that has a narrow top and a wider bottom.	
13. I am glassware that is open at one end and closed at the other and holds small amounts of liquid.	
14. I am made of glass, and specimens are mounted on me in a liquid.	
15. I am a narrow container that is used to measure the volume of a liquid.	

Source: Modified from *Engage the Brain Games, Grades 6–8 Science*, by M. L. Tate, 2008. Thousand Oaks, CA: Corwin.

same-size index cards for students to match names with pictures. Another version is to provide students with a set of cards with science vocabulary on one half of them and definitions on the other half. The students shuffle them and then arrange them randomly, face down, on a flat surface.

In both examples, students work in pairs or small groups and alternate turning over two cards at a time during each round to determine

Figure 8.4 Designing a Nature Scavenger Hunt

I. Planning a Scavenger Hunt: Things to Consider

1. **Location:** Where will the students carry out the hunt? Discuss the rules of the scavenger hunt game (for example, look and leave live things alone and feathers where you found them).
2. **Students:** The scavenger hunt list should be age-appropriate. Generally, young students may become frustrated when they cannot find the items easily; older students often enjoy the challenge. Decide whether the hunt will include competition and science prizes for the winner(s) who check off all the items on the list.
3. **Duration:** How long will the scavenger hunt last? This impacts the number of items on the list to find.

II. Scavenger Hunt Ideas

The possibilities for a science scavenger hunt are endless! The following are some ideas for designing a nature scavenger hunt.

1. Things to See/Observe

- Insects, including butterflies, dragonflies, grasshoppers, birds, and ants
- Spider webs
- Leaves from specific trees—an oak or maple, for example
- Frogs, toads, and lizards
- Flowers—wildflowers or annuals plants
- Mushrooms
- Feathers or abandoned birds' nests—students just observe them and do not touch or remove them
- Something *camouflaged*, such as a walking stick insect or a moth that blends in with the surroundings
- At the ocean, seashells and seaweed and possibly jellyfish and horseshoe crabs (just observe them)

2. Things to Collect[1]

- Butterflies, ladybugs, dragonflies, or other insects (once you have observed them up close, release them)
- Fossils, colored rocks, quartz, and/or flat river rocks
- At the coast, seashells and small pieces of driftwood

3. Things to Do

- Draw a flower and make a dandelion chain.
- Make a leaf or tree bark rubbing.
- Get up early to watch the sun rise; write a description of a sunset.
- Use a compass to find a specific location (orienteering).
- Look at pond water under a microscope.
- Stargaze with binoculars or a telescope.
- Record a birdsong or other animal sound (also the rustling of leaves).

(Continued)

Figure 8.4 (Continued)

- Find a chrysalis and watch a butterfly emerge from it.
- Go to the zoo and find a fact about a favorite animal and write it in your science notebook along with a brief "story," "song," or "poem."
- Respond to questions, record descriptions, and draw pictures in the nature section of the science notebook.

4. Things to Photograph

- Birds at a birdbath, birdfeeder, or birdhouse
- Squirrels or other small animals scurrying around
- Animal tracks
- Sunset or sunrise
- Waterfalls, mountains, boulders, lakes, beaches, wetlands, and swamps (with someone in the picture!)
- Water and wind erosion

5. Make a Display

- Display student science nature notebooks as well as pressed leaves, tree bark and leaf rubbings, pictures taken, written descriptions, etc.
    - Let them display their collection of objects in a *display case or diorama* that they create. Items that can be used might include seashells, rocks, or other materials collected, along with pictures taken. See http://www.knowitall.org/naturalstate/html/Dioramas/Dior-2-1-a.cfm for ideas.

6. Tools and Materials to Take on the Scavenger Hunt

- Plastic bags for collecting specimens
- Camera, if possible, to take pictures of what cannot be collected
- Science notebook with a nature section and pens/colored pencils—make notes and sketches to remember what was observed
- A snack because scavenger hunting is hard work, so a snack is a welcome treat in the field!
- Sunscreen and insect repellent
- Baby wipes or hand sanitizer
- Net to catch flying insects
- Binoculars to observe birds and other animals
- Magnifying glass to see details of leaves, flowers, etc.
- Field guides to identify trees, flowers, rocks, birds, etc.
- Backpack to carry materials, leaving the hands free

[1]Promote observation skills by identifying different types of trees, leaves, and/or flowers. (Look for regional field guides in your school library or on enature.com.)

Source: Adapted and modified from Nature Scavenger Hunt, http://www.hometrainingtools.com/a/nature-scavenger-hunt. Used with permission.

if there is a match. After a few rounds, students begin to remember where particular words and pictures or definitions are on the table, and subsequently make matches.

Figure 8.5 presents an example of an earth science matching game. It lists seven earth science terms and their respective definitions. These terms and their definitions are written or typed on cards, and sets are copied for students to play the game with a partner or group members. Concentration games operate similarly. The main idea is to make a match.

The template for matching games is also online in Word format.

Figure 8.5 Matching Earth Science Terms With Their Definitions

Terms	Definitions
Core	The central part of the Earth below the mantle
Crust	The outermost layer of the Earth
Deposition	The process in which wind, water, and gravity move sediment to new places
Igneous rock	A type of rock that forms from melted rocks that cool and harden
Mantle	The thick, rocky part of the Earth that makes up 70% of the planet
Metamorphic rock	A type of rock that forms because of changes caused by heat, pressure, or chemicals
Sedimentary rock	A type of rock that forms when sediments harden

Available for download from **http://resources.corwin.com/ReinhartzGrowingLanguage**

Yet another form of a matching game involves students exchanging cards or objects to complete sets that they are building. On the Quizlet website, there is a whole host of flashcards on a variety of science topics—adaptation, food chain, stimulus and response, animal coverings, energy, and many other topics—that are ready to be printed, cut out, and used with students.

5. *Completing puzzles, word searches, and more traditional games* (e.g., *Monopoly*) involve students in responding to questions. If they answer them successfully, they move forward, unless on the path there is a message to move back a specific number of steps, similar to *Clue* or *Sorry*. Scrabble is another one of the most popular games that focuses on spelling. Students can spell out recently acquired science terms. Whatever game format that is in use, there must be rules to follow so students are clear about what they are expected to do.

There are board game templates in the shape of bones, flowers, and hearts at the following sites: http://www.mes-english.com/games/files/bones.pdf; www.mes-english.com/games/files/flowers.pdf; and http://www.mes-english.com/games/files/hearts.pdf. Many more are offered by Game Boards for Homemade Educational Games at http://donnayoung.org/homeschooling/games/game-boards.htm. Teachers can write on different segments of the templates, starting with directions, picking up a card that tells students what to do, etc. The science questions can be written on blank index cards. Within a short amount of time, science games are created.

Students can be game makers as well as players. Ideas for making science games are endless. According to Allen (2008), when students create games and play them, they double their time with the science content. *Bingo* is one example. Teachers provide students with bingo cards containing nine blank spaces, and the students draw or write science information randomly in the spaces. Students also draw or write the same information on blank index cards that are then placed in a bag. As a class review, students are given the filled-in bingo cards and take turns randomly picking the index cards from the bag. One student pulls out a card and shows the picture or reads the information to the others; those who have the match on their cards cover the spaces with a bean. When they cover three spaces in a row—horizontally, vertically, or diagonally—they shout out "bingo!" To win, the student reads the information in the covered spaces on his or her card. If the winner has difficulty reading, he or she can ask for a "lifeline" for assistance. In this review, students are dealing with science information several times, and in several different ways.

Playing the game *Can You Top This?*, students working in groups individually are given a stack of caps from Snapple 16-oz glass bottles. Students read the information in the caps and decide which is the most outrageous, interesting, amazing, or awesome piece of science information. After each student decides on the cap to "top this," he or she reads it to the members of the group. Examples are, "Tigers have striped skin, not just striped fur," and "*Ferret* comes from the Latin word for little thief." The group votes on which piece of information or fact meets the criteria of "topping this," and its reader wins that round. All the caps, except the winning one, are then pushed to the center of the table, face down. Each student then takes five caps, and the game continues as previously described. In this game, students are reading, speaking, making decisions, and learning something they did not know before.

6. In *role-playing,* students take on roles that encourage them to think and use their imaginations. It also is a way for students to develop and practice language and social skills (eye contact, listening, taking turns, etc.) in a nonthreatening environment. This is particularly appropriate for quieter students, who now get a chance to express themselves.

For all students, dressing up, using props, and rearranging the furniture to play a specific character in a specific situation can be not only fun but educational as well. When role-playing, students are representing and experiencing the character and communicate more fluently and confidently. Role-playing games offer unique combinations that integrate experiential learning with content learning, which generates interest and understanding (Jarvis, Odell, & Troiano, 2002).

To get the game started, teachers determine the settings and the group of characters that students play. Students assume the personalities of the characters they select, and through them actively engage in sharing science information that provides a degree of authenticity to the role-playing scenario.

Students use their background knowledge to play a role, but they may need to do some additional research to play it better (e.g., going to the school or community library, searching online, etc.). A role-playing game, for example, might focus on a scientist (e.g., Louis Pasteur, Marie Curie, Charles R. Drew, etc.) and his or her contributions. In this scenario, students may need to research the scientist's life and times and his or her contributions or awards. So they are learning twice: once when they do the research and then when they role-play the scientist.

Because role-playing involves speaking from a character's point of view—whether it is a real or imaginary person, or an animal—and uses a variety of visual, spatial, linguistic, and bodily modalities, students comprehend at deeper levels as they get into their characters (Gregory & Parry, 2006). Additionally, they use talents that may not have been tapped as they express themselves during rehearsals or formally in front of audiences. In doing so, students are experiencing the "real-world" side of science by dealing with often complex issues. In particular, role-playing goes beyond textbook science because students express their feelings, offer different perspectives, and develop a sense of presence when they perform in front of others (Role Play, http://serc.carleton.edu/introgeo/roleplaying/reasons.html).

Even when students confront emotionally charged issues such as pipelines to transport oil and gas, fracking, or global warming by playing a Sierra Club member, CEO from the oil and gas industry, parent, or general citizen, they are expected to be objective and not interject their opinions. To prepare students for their roles, developing a scaffold and modeling a character will prove helpful. Role-playing should help students to better understand these issues.

Charades, discussed in Chapter 2, are a form of role-playing. The teacher divides the class into two groups randomly, not by gender or level, that play against each other. Before role-playing begins, it is helpful to review what gestures and nonverbal communication "look like." In the lists below, the left column has the words to be acted out, and the right has the corresponding gestures.

Word or Phrase	Gestures
Hello	wave
Goodbye	wave
it is cold	put your arms around your shoulders
it is hot	fan yourself with your hand
No	shake your head from left to right
Friction	rub your hands together
Rotate	turn around in place
Bird	flap your arms
electric circuit	hold hands with several students to make circle

In this exercise, a student from each group pulls a card with a picture or a science word on it, and acts it out. The students have to use nonverbal communication and gestures to get their group members to identify the picture or word. The group that correctly first acts out the picture or the term wins a point for that round. The group with the most points at the end wins the game (Tate & Phillips, 2011).

Games of any type do not teach themselves. As Barab, Gresalfi, and Arici (2009) contend, their real value is realized when teachers join in with students in motivating them with appropriate feedback and highlighting key concepts. These authors continue that for games to be beneficial they require students to engage in transformational play that sparks interest and leads to deeper engagement with the science content. Educational games produce unexpected science and language-learning outcomes when students undergo transformational play (Barab, Gresalfi, & Ingram-Goble, 2010).

Stealth learning, coined by Laura Sharp (2012), is a clever way to use nontraditional approaches such as games to get students to think they are merely playing when they really are learning. Embedded in gaming strategies are opportunities for students to make choices, take risks, and learn by doing, while at the same time meeting local, state, and national educational standards. A gaming environment offers a variety of learning contexts in which students explore, investigate, and build science knowledge, and often results in increased achievement (Sharp, 2012).

Whatever the type of game that is planned and implemented in science, they all have a purpose, are relevant, get students "doing," and stimulate interest that students find satisfying. Students become emotionally invested when they play games because they often feel in control by having choices about how to work their way out of situations and solve problems, as well as researching the background information on a character. The bottom line for planning, creating, and employing games is to have students learn in ways that make them feel comfortable and come away empowered with a better understanding of science.

Conclusion

Content does matter, and games can support teaching it. Science content will be meaningful to students if it is contextualized, so they can recognize how it relates to their lives. In doing so, it gives students opportunities to transfer skills learned in game-based situations to using them in real life. Games provide a bridge to students' questions such as *What does learning about ____ have to do with me?*

Using electronic games or traditional games is not an either/or situation; it is a matter of using both. If teachers do not have the equipment, then the educational games presented in this chapter provide alternative ideas for integrating game-based learning into their science classrooms. Even if teachers have the technology, traditional games as well as electronic ones can still be integrated into their 5E lessons. There is nothing like a challenging game to motivate students to learn science. Some games require students to find the missing science information and demonstrate social skills, while others create opportunities for them to solve problems. At the same time, the games also help students grow their language as they develop their cognitive skills. Games immerse students into the content with greater engagement.

Throwing bean bags as part of a game or playing charades, for example, gets students to think and act quickly. Additionally, game narratives and characters during role-playing are especially powerful in developing language literacies and can serve as catalysts for discussing science concepts (Sykes, 2013). Game-based learning should be a fundamental component of the planning process that serves the strategic purpose of adding value to students' learning experiences.

Your Turn

1. What role do games play in your science classroom? What types of games do you use? Electronic? Traditional? Both? None?
   a. Develop a survey with a few questions to ask your students. The survey can be done orally, or students can respond in writing. Some ideas for questions might be, "Why do you like playing video and board games? What motivates you to keep playing them?"
   b. Analyze their oral or written responses and consider them as you plan future science lessons using game-based learning strategies.
2. Review the tips on designing a nature scavenger hunt and plan one for your students and their parents. See Figure 8.4 for suggestions. Jot down ideas for addressing the following:
   a. Getting parents involved in the planning phase, and then getting them to participate in the outdoor event.
   b. Writing a letter to parents informing them of the purpose, and how they can get their children ready for the outing.
   c. Determining the materials needed and where to house them (e.g., scavenger hunt backpacks).
   d. Identifying ways to determine if the hunt was an educational success for all students. Develop a survey for students and parents to complete.
3. With a group of colleagues, go to the website http://atlantis remixed.org/ to become familiar with the *Atlantis Remixed* (ARX) learning and teaching project. It uses 3D multi-user environments to engage students, ages 9–16, in educational tasks. The ARX project, sponsored by the Gates Foundation, combines strategies used in commercial games with lessons from educational research on learning and motivation, and is compatible with the Common Core and learning standards.
   a. On the homepage find and read:
      - About ARX
      - Explore the game
      - Learning can be fun
      - FAQ contact
   b. Find the *Quest Atlantis* manual.
   c. Find the directions for "How to Download *Quest Atlantis*" (2012).
   d. What do you think? Can you use any of these resources? If so, how? Brainstorm ways that would be beneficial to your students.
4. Return to Figure 6.1, Overview of Crosscutting Concepts, Topics, Disciplinary Core Ideas, and Student Performance Expectations for

Grades K–5 (page 130). Find a science topic that you can teach that you have not used in previous "turns." Develop a traditional game, and find an electronic one.

a. To get students engaged in a science topic, select one of the games presented in the chapter that you have not used before.

b. For the electronic game consider checking the following websites: Kids.gov games on animals, the Earth, energy, and space; PBS science games at http://www.pbs.org/parents/education/science/games/preschooler-kindergarten/; and/or the Smithsonian for the habitat game at http://www.ssec.si.edu/games/habitats, which requires technology that asks the students to drag and drop animals into the best habitat. Check the website for more links.

c. Once you pick a game from each,
   - In what 5E phase will these games be used?
   - In what ways will you determine that students have a better understanding of the science information after playing the games?

5. In this book, find the following:
   a. Where do you find explanations of inquiry science teaching? List the chapters and page numbers.
   b. Where do you find the explanation for the science and engineering practices (D1) crosscutting concepts (D2), and disciplinary core ideas (D3)?
   c. Find Figure 1.6, the Language and Science Framework. Review the list of "student behaviors" and label the ones that relate best to D1, D2, or D3.
   d. Find at least six examples that demonstrate that language and science form a synergy that enhances student learning in both.

6. You may want to go online and read about EdSurge at https://www.edsurge.com/guide/gaming. It offers *The Ultimate Guide to Games in School*. This site also includes resources to assist educators to incorporate gaming into their science instruction.

PART III

Enhancing the School–Home Connection

9

School–Home Science Connection

© Ablestock.com/Thinkstock Photos

[N]o school can work well for children if parents and teachers do not act in partnership on behalf of the children's best interests.

—Dorothy H. Cohen

Introduction

The school-to-home connection is extremely important. Research says that families with children who do well in school have routines at home, participate in family discussions, have parents involved in the school's instructional program, monitor out-of-school activities, and show they value education by communicating it and creating a place where their children can do their schoolwork (Lawrence Hall of Science, Parent Portal). Research also says that the most successful schools are those that provide several ways for parents to get involved in the instructional program, "greatly improving the quality of schools in both low- and high-resource communities" (Parent Portal).

Successfully engaging parents in their children's education yields exponential educational benefits for them. Children's success in school is a shared responsibility of both the school and the family. The process begins with the vision of having parents as partners in their children's learning, and then establishing ways for that partnership to be activated, nurtured, and to thrive (Center for Comprehensive School Reform and Improvement, 2014). The science classroom is an ideal place for this partnership to begin.

Science teaching and learning is a family affair that builds on students' cultural and linguistic experiences. To support these experiences, teachers should ask themselves three questions: (1) *How can I engage students in culturally relevant science lessons?* (2) *How can I relate science topics to the students' home and community experiences?* (3) *How can I affirm the backgrounds of my students and their parents using the funds of knowledge in the science classroom?* (González, Moll, & Amanti, 2004; Pang, Lafferty, Pang, Griswold, & Oser, 2014).

The answers to these questions can help to galvanize the school–home partnership. This partnership will provide a context for developing a strategic, culturally sensitive science curriculum that speaks to household social and economic activities locally. These activities describe students' daily home life, and they represent important resources for teachers to consider.

Partnering With Parents

The goal of collaborating with parents and other family members is a basic tenet of the *Framework* (2012), which states:

> Teachers pursuing a culturally responsive approach to instruction will need to understand the sense-making practices of

particular communities, the science-related values that reside in them, and the historical relationship that exists between the community and local institutions of education. (p. 284)

The end result of implementing such an approach validates students' lives, providing a valuable resource for teachers to use in science instruction.

Finding answers to these questions and making science learning more meaningful begins with identifying the sociocultural assets that students bring to the science classroom, including their cultural experiences, beliefs, artifacts, arts and crafts, vocabulary, history of storytelling, and role models. Linking students' funds of knowledge to science content contextualizes what they are learning by using examples from their lives. Thus, unfamiliar science concepts become more relevant to students as they manipulate everyday materials such as cooking utensils, different fabrics, and foods they eat. In the beginning of a lesson on magnets, for example, students can test household items such as refrigerator magnets, forks, plates, chopsticks, hammers, and/or tortilla presses for magnetic properties. The goal is to get students to see that science is all around them, including in their homes, yards, and neighborhoods. There are many resources for parents on the Lawrence Hall of Science website, including readings on active learning and science education, ideas for building a strong math and science foundation at home, and ways to support their children and their school (http://www.lawrencehallofscience.org/parents/foundation.html).

Doing Science Is a Family Affair

Building on student assets requires the involvement of parents in the teaching–learning science paradigm. McGough (2013) offers an example of how she involved parents in her science classroom. She shares a journal entry from one of her first graders, Riley. He wrote in his "family science journal" about an experiment that he did at home using Pop Rocks and different kinds of soda. In addition, Riley wrote questions and asked different people in his family to help him respond to them. McGough goes on to describe how a student–teacher–parent relationship got started by using family science journals. The journals became vehicles for generating conversations, raising new questions, and recording information discussed at school to home and home to school.

A family science journal (or, in my words, notebook) could include information about animals, specifically how animals adapt to their environment. For example, in science class students learn about animals that live in cold regions of the world and have blubber to keep them warm. Students can write in their family journals or notebooks how important blubber is to insulating animals from the cold in areas such as the Arctic and Antarctic. Begin the brainstorming session with the students by asking them how people protect themselves in cold weather, and record their ideas (gloves, coats, socks, long underwear, etc.) on an anchor chart. Next, ask how animals protect themselves from the cold (fur, thick layers of fat/blubber, etc.). Ask the students to model the protection of blubber with household items. List their ideas (e.g., solid fat or lard wrapped in a towel around their arm) on an anchor chart. Zero in on the solid fat or lard idea so they can investigate it at home. Pose the question, *How can we test how blubber protects animals?*

Use another anchor chart to stimulate students' ideas about the role of blubber that they will be exploring at home. To help ensure that this home science investigation is a success, prepare and send home the handout on the next page.

Family science journals or notebooks integrate different disciplines and provide opportunities for students to (1) implement the crosscutting concepts of cause and effect, (2) write informative and explanatory texts, and (3) respond to questions that come up during investigations.

Another idea of doing science at home starts with sending home a "science bag" with inexpensive materials for activities. These bags should be sturdy enough to be reused, and should be returned by students on specific due dates or when an activity is completed at home. Ashbrook (2012) refers to these take-home bags as "send-home science." Depending on the science topic being studied in school, teachers can write out simple instructions for what to do—if needed, have it available in the home language as well—and include materials such as the following:

- An onion, a lemon, a cinnamon stick and ground cinnamon, and three or four coffee beans to examine. The student surveys family members and neighbors about their favorite smells and their reactions to the different scents.
- Two or three green beans or a zucchini squash to be cut up with the aid of a family member to look at the seeds. The students can draw what they see and answer the question, "Where do

Exploring How Blubber Works in Animals

I. Directions:

A. Materials:

© Purestock/Thinkstock Photos

- A large bowl of ice water on a table covered with newspaper
- A 1-lb can of solid shortening or lard
- A large spoon
- A clock or watch with a second hand
- Plastic gloves or bags

B. Have a family member do the following:

1. Place the glove or bag on the child's hand, making sure it is snug around the wrist.
2. Dip his or her hand in the ice water. Do not go too deep. How does the hand feel?
3. Use a clock to see how long the child can keep his or her hand in the ice water. Record the amount of time in the table below.
4. Using the spoon, take one third of the shortening or lard and spread it over the child's hand with the glove or bag on it. Repeat this step two more times (see table below).

Amount of shortening or lard used	Time the hand was kept in ice water
Without any shortening/lard	
1/3 of the shortening/lard added to hand	
2/3 of the shortening/lard added to hand	
3/3 or all of the shortening/lard added to hand	

5. Write a story about what the child did and learned about how shortening/lard (blubber) protected his or her hand, and how blubber protects animals in cold climates. As the child writes his or her story, the following questions should be used as a guide:
   - How long was the hand *without* the shortening/lard kept in the ice water? How did it feel?
   - How did the hand feel with the first amount of shortening/lard (1/3) spread on it? How did it feel each time when more shortening was added?
   - In what way did the shortening/lard act like fat or blubber?
   - What are some of the animals that have blubber for protection to insulate them? Write down three examples, and where they live.

seeds come from?" Send home a copy of the book *How Did That Get in My Lunchbox?* by C. Butterworth (2011) with one or two students each week until all of them have had a chance to enjoy it with the whole family. Check out the companion website, http://resources.corwin.com/ReinhartzGrowingLanguage, for more information on how to use this book. And you can get additional resources and related activities for doing science at home at http://www.rif.org/documents/us/How-Did-That-Get-in-My-Lunchbox.pdf.

- A small toy car to be run on different surfaces, such as the kitchen floor, carpet, or outside on the sidewalk, dirt, or grass. As they test the car on these different surfaces, they answer the questions, "Where did the car move the longest distance?" "Shortest?" "Why?"

A second-grade teacher, Liliana Aguas, provided several ways to involve parents. These opportunities included hosting *cafecitos* (coffee times), publishing parties to showcase her students' writing, and gaming sessions in which her students taught their parents how to play different types of games. For her, parental engagement is essential to "validate the cultural capital and wealth of knowledge that ELL parents possess" (p. 2).

There are many other activities that students can do at home, listed in Figure 9.1, from blowing bubbles to sailing soap ships in an aluminum pan. Parents, teacher education students, and/or retired educators can be recruited to refresh these bags and put the supplies needed for the next science experience(s).

These activities involve inexpensive materials that are readily available. There also are other ideas and topics included on the companion website, http://resources.corwin.com/ReinhartzGrowingLanguage, that teachers might find helpful.

Whether it be a family science night outside to view the sky, in the school moving through science centers, reinventing the . . . bridge, and/or doing labs with Dad, they all take family involvement to a new level and bring the school and community closer together (Havers & Delmotte (2012); Ogens & Padilla (2012); Owens & Sullivan, 2012). Often, the local community college, university, and/or astronomy clubs sponsor events such as viewing the night sky—they supply the speakers, and all teachers have to do is to line up the parents and the students. These events are one way to reinforce the school–home connection. Thomas and White (2012) write in their article "Aligning the STARS: A Partnership Brings a Community Together for a Night of Astronomy" about how to get this type of event off the ground.

Figure 9.1 Doing Science at Home

The science activities are organized from the easiest to the most difficult. In each entry, there are a few science facts and explanations. The goal is to pair these with topics being studied in class, giving parents and other family members opportunities to explore, question, and spend time together. Getting the family and their child(ren) to see science in simple things such as toys, books, and objects around the house while having fun is most important.

I. Getting the Big Picture

Looking at objects closely is an important part of science, and a magnifying glass lets us see things we do not even know are there. It also helps us see how objects are similar or different from one another.

What you'll need:

A magnifying glass
Your science notebook

What to do:

A. Use your magnifying glass to see: pieces of paper, soil from the yard, a few leaves, and dead butterflies, beetles, etc. Check to see what's in the soil. How many different objects can you find in the soil? Under the leaves? What do you see on the front and backsides of the leaves? Draw the patterns of the leaves and butterfly wings.

B. Draw pictures, or describe what you see, in your science notebook.

II. It Is About Force, Straw, and a Potato

What you'll need:

1 raw potato
1 or more *paper* straws
Your science notebook

Question to guide the investigation: Can a paper straw go through a raw potato? Here's an easy way to learn about inertia and momentum.

What to do:

A. Put the potato on the table or counter and have a family member hold it firmly with one hand, making sure the palm of the hand is not underneath the potato. (If the potato has wrinkles and/or deep crevices, soak it in water for about half an hour before beginning this investigation.)

B. With a fast, strong push, stab the potato with the straw.

What happens? Did the straw bend? The straw should go into the potato. If it did not, try again with another straw—maybe a little faster or harder this time.

C. *Science focus*: An object remains at rest (the potato) or keeps moving (the straw) unless it is acted upon by some external or outside force.

III. Soap Power

Have you ever tried using soap to power a boat?

What you'll need:

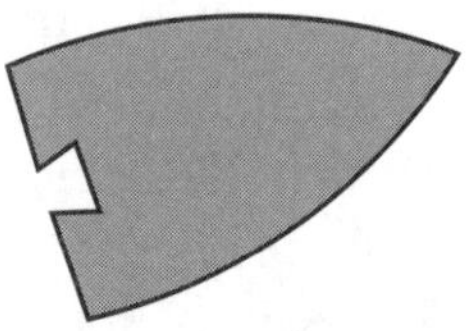

1 index card
Scissors
A baking dish (or sink) half full of water
Liquid dish detergent
Your science notebook

What to do:

A. Cut out a boat like this (see picture above) from the index card. Make it about 6 cm long and 4 cm wide.
B. Place the boat gently on the water in the dish or sink.
C. Pour a little detergent into the notch at the end of the boat. Observe what happens. What did you see?
D. If you want to repeat the investigation, wash out the baking dish (and sink) carefully, or guess what? Your boat will not go.

Science focus:

A. The boat should zip across the water. Water molecules are strongly attracted to one another and stick close together, especially on the surface.
B. This creates a strong but flexible "skin" on the water's surface that is called *surface tension*. Adding soap disrupts the arrangement of the water molecules and breaks this skin, making the boat go forward.

IV. Blowing Bubbles

Blowing bubbles is fun. Who doesn't enjoy it? You can make bubbles at home that have beautiful shapes and colors!

What you'll need:

8 tablespoons of dishwashing liquid (Dawn works best)
1 quart water
1 drinking straw (or a plastic wand that comes with the bubble mixtures, or make a loop out of pipe cleaners in different shapes)
1 shallow tray
1 tin can, open at both ends (be sure there are no sharp edges)
Your science notebook
Newspaper for under the tray to absorb any water that spills over

What to do:

A. Mix the dishwashing liquid with the water in the shallow tray.
B. Move your straw or wand slowly across the surface of the solution. Now blow.
C. Once you make a bubble, touch it gently with a wet finger. What happens?
D. Make another big bubble. Touch this one with a dry finger. What happens?
E. Try making bubbles with a pipe cleaner, shaping it into a circle, square, triangle, etc. Be sure to have a handle on it. Dip the shape into the soapy solution so that you get a soap "window" across it, and blow gently into it to form a bubble.
F. Look closely at the bubbles that are made. What colors do you see? Do the colors change? If yes, why do you think so? If no, why?
G. If the wand you use has a square shape, what shape will the bubble be after you blow?

Science focus:

A. Bubbles are bits of air or gas trapped inside a liquid ball.
B. The surface of a bubble is very thin. Bubbles are particularly fragile when a dry object touches them. That's because the soap film tends to stick to the object, which puts a strain on the bubble.
C. So if you want your bubbles to last longer, keep everything wet—even the sides of the straw.

(Continued)

Figure 9.1 (Continued)

V. Insect and Spider Alert!

Some insects help us, some annoy us, and some are dangerous. But insects tell us a lot, and so do spiders.

What you'll need:

An insect guide and a spider guide from the library—preferably ones with pictures

A magnifying glass

Your science notebook

What to do:

A. With a family member, search your home and neighborhood for insects and spiders. Look around your front door, in cracks in the sidewalk, on lamps, on lights hanging from the center of the room, on plants inside the house and outside, in crevices in drawers, and in corners of rooms. *Just look*—do not touch them.

B. With the assistance of a family member, try to identify the types of insects and spiders you have spotted using the guides. Are they ants? Mosquitos? Silverfish? Flies? Ladybugs?

1. Ants tell us how they work together as a community. What do you observe/see? Watch ants scurry in and out of their anthills or find some spilled food on the sidewalk. What do you think? Do they eat their food on the spot, or do they carry it back to their anthill? When an ant finds food, it runs back to the hill to "tell" the others. As it runs, it leaves a trail that other ants in the hill can smell. The ants find the food by smelling their way along the trail.

2. What is the difference between an insect and a spider? Why do you think spiders spin webs? What are webs made of?

C. Draw a picture of what the web looks like in your notebook and formulate questions with the assistance of a parent or other family member to learn more about spiders.

Science focus:

A. Insects do what they do to survive. They are constantly looking for food. Some insects are both good and bad. Termites, for example, destroy houses by eating the wood. But they also break down old trees, keeping the forest floor from becoming too cluttered with dead trees.

B. Spiders and insects are not from the same class. Spiders are in the arachnida class, and insects are in the insecta class.

C. Spiders have eight legs, and insects have six legs. Generally, insects have wings to move (there are exceptions; for instance, ants). Insects have three body parts (head, thorax, abdomen) and spiders have two (cephalothorox, abdomen). And spiders do not have antennae, whereas most insects do.

D. To demonstrate these differences, create a model of an insect and one of a spider using play dough and pipe cleaners.

Once the models are built, talk about the body parts for insects (head, thorax, abdomen) and form three balls, one for each part; generally they are different sizes.

Now make six legs out of the pipe cleaners.

Last, make a set (two) of antennae for smelling and feeling.

Make a model of a spider: Spiders have 2 body parts and 8 legs and for the 8 eyes, poke holes in the play dough.

E. Make a Venn diagram comparing and contrasting insects and spiders—looking at the models for clues and finding out what they have in common.

VI. It Floats!

Why does a big cruise ship and a feather float?

What you'll need:

1 solid wooden building block
1 plastic cap from a bottle
2 pieces of aluminum foil (heavy duty, if you have it)
1 chunk of clay
1 pair of pliers
1 bathtub (or sink) filled with water
Your science notebook

What to do:

A. Working with a family member, hold the wooden block in one hand and the plastic cap in the other. How do they feel?

B. Do you think the wooden block will float, or will it sink? Will the plastic cap float, or will it sink? Make your predictions after discussing with your parent. Write your predictions in your notebook. Draw what you think will happen.

C. Put both of them in the water to test your *predictions*. What happened? Put both of them under the water. What happened?

D. Take a piece of aluminum foil and squeeze it into a solid ball as tightly as you can— using pliers, if possible. Drop it in the water. Did it float or sink?

E. Get another piece of foil about the same size and shape it into a little boat. Place it on top of the water. Did it float? Did it sink?

F. Now use clay. Make a ball. What do you think/predict will happen when you drop it in the water? Draw/write your predictions in your notebook. Now try it. What happened?

G. Shape the clay ball into a boat. What do you think will happen? Will it float? Will it sink? Draw/write your prediction in your notebook. Now put it in the water. Did it float? Sink?

Science focus:

A. The clay and foil balls sink because they are squeezed into small shapes, and only a small amount of water is trying to hold up these objects.

B. When you spread out the clay or foil, it floats because the mass is supported by a lot more water.

Source: Adapted and modified from Activities at Home. Retrieved from http://www2.ed.gov/pubs/parents/Science/Home.html. Used with permission.

Engaging parents and family members of older students can be a tricky process. Fearing embarrassment, often students do not want their parents at school. Patricia Littlejohn (2012) in a recent article talks about involving parents of older students and how she successfully organized family science nights for 10 years. Once you get the word out through the students and public media, teachers are more likely to get parents involved. By engaging parents early in the school year, they are more willing to talk to teachers about issues of concern. A by-product of Littlejohn's science nights is to have students recognize and appreciate their parents' skills and experiences such as organizing, designing, and taking on science night challenges. Another result she noticed was that students took more interest in class because of their successes outside the classroom.

Being creative also can mean exploring the outdoors on Saturday trips to local science museums, with parents in some cases providing transportation and serving as guides and chaperones. Such experiences become ready-made science classrooms all year round as students make observations and comparisons when turning over rocks they see along a trail, or watching local animals at play (see Figure 8.4 for additional ideas). In addition to their natural encounters, children and parents can test their design skills by making kites and paper airplanes in order to understand the basic principles of flight. There can be competitions involving which planes fly the greatest distances and explaining why, or which kite did not get off the ground, and why.

Involving Parents in School Science Activities

Involving parents in their children's science learning takes many forms, from serving as assistants on science walks around the school or neighborhood to working one on one with students, monitoring a science station, and/or listening to students read. As noted in Chapter 1, students are always eager to share their ideas, whether they relate to science stories they have written or responses to questions they recorded in their science notebooks. Such experiences not only benefit the children, but their parents as well. Parents become partners as they work with their children to solve science problems; make observations during investigations; record data; tell stories of how common ailments were addressed when they were young children; and share typical foods they ate, how they were prepared, and where they were grown.

How do you get parents involved? Teachers do not have to do it alone. Sharing your ideas with campus colleagues and administrators makes connecting with parents a family affair at the building level. Next is to check with your school's parent–teacher association (PTA or PTO). Its members often can provide organizational, financial, and people-power support. If they are not up and running, teachers can work with interested parents in sponsoring science events.

But with or without these resources, it is essential to initiate communication with your students' parents. One way is to prepare and send home a monthly or bimonthly newsletter in both English and the home language, highlighting upcoming events and tips for parents while including invitations to participate in classroom and school activities. Newsletters from Resources for Educators are a good place to start. The *Home & School CONNECTION* is a reproducible newsletter packed with ideas for any family to use to promote their children's reading, writing, and language skills (http://www.rfeonline.com/content.cfm?dept=11). For example, in a 2011 issue there are tips for developing thinking games under the Parent to Parent section for "parents on the go." Or in another newsletter—*Reading Connection,* from Resources for Educators—parents are encouraged to involve their children in family conversations and to narrate everyday activities. These newsletters can be used schoolwide so principals can help to support teachers' efforts to engage parents at their campuses.

You can also host regular open-house meetings for parents (with or without light refreshments) to discuss ways to support their children at home doing science activities. Figure 9.2 offers tips that teachers can share about ways parents can support their children at home. It is in Word format on the website so teachers can tailor the list to meet their needs.

The examples in Figure 9.2 of questions to ask, ideas about getting students to make predictions, and collecting pictures from old magazines, etc., are all ways to involve students in identifying patterns through observations, cause-and-effect situations, and analyzing and interpreting data.

Figure 9.3 lists home science activities that parents can do with their children, including taking a field trip and making beautiful music.

In addition, develop and maintain a web page with science home activities, upcoming dates relevant to science such as Earth Day, science fairs, and places where parents can meet and get ready for their roles within the school. Parents can support teachers in many ways, such as cutting out pictures of animals, plants, mountains, or streams

Figure 9.2 Tips for Parents to Support Their Children at Home

I. Ask questions:

A. Why do birds make nests?

B. What materials do birds use to make their nests?

C. How does electricity help us?

© cowboy5437/Thinkstock Photos

II. Have children make predictions:

A. Looking in the newspaper, online, and/or on mobile phones, predict the weather for the next 2 days.

B. Ask children to predict how tall the plant will grow by the end of the week.

C. Go out and fly a kite with your child. While flying the kite, ask how high the kite would fly.

III. Start collecting actual materials and objects to use and to identify patterns, colors, textures, similarities, and differences:

A. These collections can include seeds, leaves on the ground, Snapple caps, Kid Scoop pages, short articles from the science section of the newspaper, etc.

B. They can also be pictures, graphs, and diagrams from magazines and newspapers (*USA Today* includes many graphs).

C. They can record sounds. Use a mobile phone or recorder to capture environmental sounds such as dogs barking, birds chirping, cats meowing, wind blowing, and rain falling. Parents can ask the following questions to develop their children's listening skills as they walk to school or wait for the school bus:

What do you hear?

- Any animal sounds?
- People talking?
- Plants moving?

Can you make the sounds that you heard?

Can you invent a family secret sound, like a series of taps or whistles?

Check out www.calmsound.com for other sounds in nature.

With family members, play the game *Can You Name That Sound?*

IV. Promote observation skills:

A. Look for differences in shapes, patterns, colors, animals, plants, etc., around the house, neighborhood, and parks.

B. Search for insects in sidewalk cracks, in the soil, on lights, and on plants (ants, spiders, flies, and ladybugs).

1. Make puppets of these animals out of socks, string, pipe cleaners, and construction paper for body parts using glue and a needle and thread (under your supervision)
2. Create your own animals (see Chapter 7).

C. Check out the ants as they move to and from their anthill. What do you see happening? What senses do they use? (Sense of smell; they find their way back to the anthill by smelling the food along the trail.)

V. Focus on changes that take place in nature.

For example:

A. When plants are in sunlight and are watered, what happens inside them? What is the process called that uses chlorophyll, sunlight, carbon dioxide, and water?

B. When fall comes, leaves turn yellow and then brown and drop to the ground. What causes the leaves to change color? What is the science behind this change?

C. When it rains, water runs down hills into the street. What happens to the soil it runs over? Where does it go?

© Jose Luis Pelaez Inc/Thinkstock Photos

from magazines and newspapers; putting science games together; organizing science supplies for specific lessons and materials donated to the "science shower"; and stuffing "send-home science backpacks." Figure 9.4, also on the website in Word format, features several materials that can be included in students' science backpacks. It is essential to have enough backpacks with different materials and supplies to carry out specific science exercises. This way students have opportunities to take them home and experience several of them throughout the school year. Also, students can assist in refurbishing the backpacks when they return them to the classroom by using a checklist to replace the materials they have used.

Some of these materials can be obtained from sports organizations that have used balls or other equipment that they may be willing to donate.

Freudenberg (2012) in her article calls them "science sacks" for second graders. She provides a comprehensive graphic that includes the science theme and communication tasks including describing,

Figure 9.3 Checklist of Things to Do

Ideas for Home Science Activities	Place Check Mark When Completed (✓)
I. Take a "field trip" around your residence. List at least three items in each room and identify a science connection. A. What science is in the bedroom? For example, the wooden end table is made from a natural resource that comes from trees. Light bulbs (depending on the type) are made of metal, glass, and tungsten. (The handout "Make a Light Bulb," at http://www.mineralseducationcoalition.org/pdfs/dig/lightbulb.pdf, includes some very interesting information.) Bed coverings may be made of cotton, which comes from cotton plants. B. What science is in the kitchen? For example, food in the refrigerator comes from different animals and plants—milk and cheese come from cows, eggs come from chickens, corn tortillas come from corn plants, and flour tortillas come from wheat plants. C. What science is in the bathroom? For example, soap used to wash your hands, water for a bath or shower, and paper cups come from natural resources that are so important to humans.	
II. Make beautiful music. A. Can you play an instrument? B. What materials in the house can create sounds? (Bells, rattles, wooden spoons, paper clips, aluminum pie pans, etc.) C. How can we use these materials to make an instrument? (Materials: cardboard rolls, dried peas/beans, pebbles, sticks, string, tape, etc.) D. Can you make a loud, soft, dull, or light sound with your instrument? Show and explain what is done to make a specific sound. E. Can you create a song/rap with your instrument? Write the words in your home science notebook and share it with members of the family.	

Figure 9.4 Send-Home Science Backpack Supply List

A magnet	Tuning forks
Children's gently used paperback science book	Mirrors made with Mylar
String, yarn	Thermometers (F° and C°)
Box of Total cereal	Rain gauges
Plastic bowls from frozen dinners	Prisms
Hand lens	Potting soil
Toy cars, trucks	Small plastic containers for planting seeds
Flashlights	Seeds of different types—flowers, bean, corn
Aluminum foil	Index cards
Unopened tomato soup cans	Pencils, pens, crayons
Rubber balls of different sizes	Rulers
Pipe cleaners of different colors	Plastic wrap
Cellophane tape	Handheld microscopes
Beans of different sizes and shapes (corn, bean—dried soup bean mixes)	Plastic container of bubble solution
Balloons of different shapes (mostly round ones)	Insect magnifying cases
Rice	Safety goggles
Measuring cups	Glue
Straws	Assorted paper
Hula hoops	Notepads for parents to provide feedback
	Brief information sheet about what is to be done with materials included in the backpack

comparing, measuring, charting, and predicting. Teachers may need to call upon parents or bilingual colleagues at school and in the central office for assistance in preparing bilingual posters, signs, and PowerPoint presentations.

Communication is another important dimension of fostering a trusting school–home connection. What better way to generate communication with parents and their children than by doing science at home, and to bring the results back to the classroom? These experiences provide a context for family members to talk to one another as they work together. Communication is generated when students, for example, take a magnet home to check which objects are attracted to the magnet. They can keep track by completing the following two-column sheet.

Directions: Write the name of the object or draw a picture of it in column 1. Place a check (√) in the "Attracted" column if the object moves toward the magnet. Place a check (√) in the "Not Attracted" column if the object does not react to the magnet.

Objects Tested	Attracted	Not Attracted

During this exercise, family members discuss what takes place when the magnet touches an object, and in doing so they may use terms from academic science such as *magnets, north and south poles, attract/attraction, repel/repulsion,* and *magnetic force/field.* They also apply inquiry skills of observing, comparing, and experimenting.

Steps for Fostering and Sustaining a School-to-Home Connection

A first step is to establish a language-rich, hands-on science classroom where students find learning exciting, enjoyable, relevant, and risk and anxiety free. Once students are hooked on science, they will be more than eager to participate in classroom activities and more willing to take science home and share it with their parents and other family members. Other steps include the following:

1. Create a nonthreatening learning environment that encourages students to get involved in science experiences and to use the skills of listening, speaking, reading, and writing. They make predictions, discuss them, write about them in their science notebooks, and read what they have written to their teachers, peers, and family members. Being involved in such learning environments demonstrates that students are valued, bring important assets to the science classroom, and are afforded a context to be academically successful.
2. From the beginning of the school year, be in contact with parents on an ongoing basis, using telephone calls and/or home visits if appropriate, as well as written and online communication.
3. Decide with students what they will share with their families from that day's lesson. Using an anchor chart will focus the

students' attention on the topic and what they will be doing at home. Family members also will receive an invitation to participate and an introduction to the science topics. The following is a sample of a letter to be sent home to parents:

> Dear Members of My Family,
>
> I want to invite you to work with me on a science project at home. In my science class this week, we have talked about how animals adapt to their environment, and my teacher read the story *Animal Adaptations for Survival* by Elizabeth Rose. At home, I am to identify animals that live in our neighborhood. I am to
>
> - Write in my notebook or say the names of the animals that live in our neighborhood.
> - Describe in writing in my notebook or just talk about how they have adapted to their environments.
> - Write or orally answer the following questions: *What covers their bodies? Where do they live? What color are they? What do they eat?*
>
> My project is due on ____________________.
>
> My teacher asks that you sign below to show you have worked with me on this project.
>
> Signature: ________________________________

When the assignment is due, ask the students to read from their notebooks (depending on their reading level), or have them tell what they did at home to complete this exercise. Listening to what they read or say will provide insights about family members' involvement in the science assignment.

Using this approach, family members do not only get involved in science learning of their relative; more important, the children have a reason to talk with them and share their ideas. Building a strong school–home connection becomes a communication tool that is critical to students' academic success. If families are reluctant to participate, for whatever reason, arrange for "surrogate family members" such as upper-grade students in the school, parent volunteers, and/or teacher education candidates from a local college. Surrogate family members serve a valuable function when they (1) read students' notebook entries, (2) listen to their oral descriptions and explanations, and (3) respond and provide feedback (McGough, 2013). Establishing this feedback loop between students and adults demonstrates that students have ideas valued by people who will listen to what they have to say, which builds self-esteem and in turn confidence to communicate. All those involved will learn new things about themselves and their world.

Conclusion

Parents make a difference, and they are extremely important to their children's learning! And the school–home partnership is a two-way street that sometimes requires teachers and school administrators to go the extra mile to involve parents. The place to start is in the science classroom.

Family science investigations conducted outside the formal science classroom become a foundation for students to learn science, and to get them to integrate language into their learning. The opportunities to connect with parents and family members are endless. Exploring the night and day skies, enjoying the outdoors, building something (models), and growing something provide contexts for asking who, what, where, when, how, and why questions. While students explore materials and get new ideas, they and their parents come to better appreciate learning science and their roles in it.

González and his colleagues (2004) express the importance of having a trusting relationship with parents. They sum it up best when they say that such a relationship can become the catalyst for exchanging "knowledge about family and school matters, reducing the insularity of classrooms, and contributing to the academic content and lessons" (p. 85).

In addition to the resources cited in the February 2012 issue of *Science and Children*—"Doing Science at Home," "Tips for Parents," "Checklist of Things to Do," and "Send-Home Backpack Supply List"—there are a myriad of others that may prove helpful to parents and teachers. The sky is the limit for finding ways to get parents connected to the school and the science classroom—and, most important, to their children. But it takes a willingness to find the time to implement the ideas shared in the chapter and not get discouraged if at first parents do not respond. Be persistent: Many parents will eventually realize that the opportunities, whatever they are, are too good to pass up.

Making parents your partners takes good communication and interpersonal skills, openness, and understanding (Froschauer, 2012). When communication between the school and home is in sync, teachers gain a better understanding of their students' abilities and talents.

Your Turn

1. How can the following ideas be successfully implemented with parents and family members at your school? How can teachers build alliances and make a positive connection with them?

   a. Review the science exercises and 5E lessons in the previous chapters and identify a few that are a part of your students' science instructional program. Determine how you would partner with parents to help their children learn more about these topics.

   b. Check the Lawrence Hall of Science's website for ideas to strengthen the school–home connection, specifically the information that is part of the Parent Portal 20 Ways to Support Your Child and Her School. Pick three that can be implemented.

2. What is your vision of an effective and productive school–home partnership? Brainstorm answers to this very important question and use a graphic organizer to map your ideas.

   a. What does your vision look like? How would you explain it to parents at the beginning of your school's open house, or in a letter?

   b. Repeat this process with colleagues and administrators to learn their vision for growing an effective parent–educator relationship. Conduct this process with parents to determine what their vision and expectations are about building and sustaining a positive home–school connection. Implementing the results from these sessions may contribute to a win-win situation for all involved.

3. You unknowingly heard the following conversation between two teachers as they were leaving your superintendent's presentation about the district's new initiative to get parents more involved in their children's education:

   "As a teacher, I believe there should be a continuous line of communication with parents, but I can't do all the work to make it happen."

   "I know parents want to get involved but often don't have the time, and many of the teachers at my school then become apathetic—thinking if the parents don't care about their own children, well why . . . ?"

   "So how do we achieve what I think we both want—a collaborative partnership between parents and teachers that leads to academic success for their children?"

"Perhaps begin with getting input from the students; see what they say about how to keep the lines of communication open and making their parents partners in their education. Let's ask students a few questions in our classes and see what they say. I think once we review their responses, we can prioritize them and determine next steps."

a. Now it is your turn to keep the conversation going between these two teachers. What do you think can be done to make their school initiative work? Role-play your ideas with a colleague.

   You may want to implement some of these strategies for enhancing the school–home connection, or you may have other innovative ideas that could require extra funding. Explore the website http://www.edutopia.org/grants-and-resources#graph1 for grants to finance these projects and additional teachers' resources. Pick two grants that support your goals, complete the applications, and submit them and then identify two resources to explore further.

   A. Educational grants:

      Classroom grants from the Association of American Educators—grants are available up to $500.

      Classroom newspaper subscription grants from *USA Today*—classroom subscriptions to the e-edition of *USA Today.*

      Compete for a Green Thumb challenge grant—several $500 grants are available to benefit the country's most inspiring K–12 gardens.

      Field trip grants from Target—up to $700 for out-of-school field trips.

      Grants to increase access to healthy foods from the No Kid Hungry Foundation—grants range from $5,000 to $10,000.

      Grants for STEM programs from American Honda Foundation—grants range from $20,000 to $75,000.

      Math and science grants from Toshiba America Foundation—grants are $5,000 or less.

      Thank a Million Teachers: school Supplies and PD grants—grants are available up to $2,500.

      Good luck!

B. Resources:

Science News for Students—https://student.societyforscience.org/sciencenews-students

SciStarter—to contribute to science

STEM-Works—offers links to virtual field trips, interactive lesson plans, and fun activities for all grade levels.

PART IV

Assessing Learning

10

How Do We Know That Students Know?

© monkeybusinessimages/Thinkstock Photos

To know something is not just to have received information but to have interpreted it and related it to other knowledge one already has.

—Richard J. Stiggins

Introduction

Historically, assessment has played a major role in detecting and highlighting differences in student learning. The implementation of these types of assessment experiences produced winners and losers. In such an assessment climate, some students build a winning record while others experience a losing one, which often continues to follow them throughout their school years. The focus on assessment should not be on sorting students; rather, it should be on supporting them in meeting the science expectations required in the standards. Teachers should view assessment through a different lens—from one that verifies learning to one that supports learning (Stiggins, 2007). Seeing assessment in this way requires a shift in thinking. This shift from judging to focusing on making changes takes place during the planning rather than at the implementing stage.

Maximizing student science learning outcomes begins when lesson objectives are written giving insight into the formative and summative assessment strategies that will be implemented. Assessment, according to Gottlieb (2006), is a process of planning for learning, gathering, and analyzing "information from multiple sources over time so that the results are meaningful to teaching and learning" (p. 1). When assessment is fair and valid, it becomes the conduit to educational success for all students. In classrooms with a heterogeneous mix of students, teachers are faced with different backgrounds, learning preferences, and language and cognitive levels. This student mix affects how they learn and how they measure their learning. The litmus test for effective assessment for learning is one that informs students about their progress (Stiggins & Chappuis, 2008).

Assessment Drives Science Teaching and Learning

Do the following student questions sound familiar? *You want us to do what? Why do we have to do this? Where do we begin?* If yes, there may be a mismatch between what and how science is taught, and how students perceive it. Using a variety of assessment strategies brings teaching and learning closer together. The student questions cited above may be red flags that something is not working, and that students are not getting it. Assessment is the third leg of the teaching and learning stool. Teachers can use information generated from assessments to guide them in finding out about what students know, are learning, and need to learn.

There is no one assessment strategy for all students and all learning situations. Assessments are used to make instructional decisions when planning—deciding what strategies to implement and selecting resources to use. After teaching a science lesson(s), assessment information lets teachers know if things are working or if adjustments need to be made. The closer the match is between instruction and assessment, the closer teachers and students are to understanding what they know. To assist teachers in navigating the assessment process, there are many strategies to inform their instructional practices.

Summative and Formative Assessments

In 1967, Scriven coined the terms *summative* and *formative assessments* and described them. And a year later, Bloom used formative assessment in his book *Learning for Mastery* as a tool to improve the teaching–learning process. From the works of Scriven and Bloom, these terms continue to permeate the literature on assessment. Along with diagnostic assessments, they constitute the three major types of assessment that have been used in schools. The differences between formative, summative, and diagnostic assessments include the objectives for collecting data and how and when they are collected.

Summative Assessments

For Dunn and Mulvenon (2009), summative assessments collect information about students' "academic progress at the end of a specified time period (i.e., a unit of material or an entire school year) and for the purposes of establishing . . . [students'] academic standing relative to . . . established criterion" (p. 3). Typically, summative assessments include traditional pencil-and-paper unit or end-of-year tests and/or long-term projects. Effective as summative assessments are, they have their limitations. They tend to uncover learning issues long after teaching a specific topic. Using a unit summative assessment to turn learning around can be problematic. Time is lost waiting until the end of a unit to find out what students are having difficulty with or did not learn, and often jeopardizes the students' chances to improve their academic performance.

Summative assessments have many names, from high-stakes mandated tests to final end-of-course exams, which are designed by states, school districts, and/or individual schools and teachers. These measures are tied to content standards that students are expected to meet. For comparative purposes, scores on mandated tests are compiled according to teachers, grade levels, schools, and/or school systems. Summative assessments are valuable tools, but they need to be supported with formative measures. Formative assessments get teachers beyond scores on tests to more meaningful data to approach and measure student learning. They provide some degree of assurance that continuous learning and relearning and teaching and reteaching are taking place throughout the school year.

At the classroom level, summative assessments determine student cumulative learning over time. These cumulative measures prove helpful, especially when a series of benchmarks are built in to guide teachers and students toward the summative goals. The question is not whether to use summative assessments or not, but to use both summative and formative strategies. Periodic formative checks along with meaningful feedback to students—for example, having them submit updates on their science projects before the due date—will prove helpful to students to keep them on track in meeting the academic expectations.

Formative Assessments

Formative assessment is aligned according to Greenstein (2010) with three principles: It is student focused, instructionally informative, and outcomes based. The first principle of formative assessment focuses on how students receive information. Formative assessment helps teachers to identify students' learning styles and preferences, track achievement, and select instructional activities that offer students many ways to excel.

The second principle is that formative assessment guides instructional decision making. It informs teachers about their effectiveness in designing lessons and the degree to which their teaching is aligned with planned science and language objectives, science content, and strategies selected and implemented. Last, formative assessment closes the gap between what the students know and the desired instructional outcomes. Questions that teachers ask to keep formative assessment transparent include: *What does the curriculum standard "look like" in the science classroom? What criteria will be used to measure if the students have met the standards? What type of feedback is there, and how often is it given to students? What action will teachers take to move students closer to meeting the established standards?*

"Formative assessment is . . . used by teachers . . . to adjust ongoing teaching and learning to improve students' achievement of intended instructional outcomes" (McManus, 2008, p. 3). Filsecker and Kerres (2012) go one step further in describing the role of formative assessment as a process of informing action by incorporating feedback loops to support learning complex topics. To some degree, formative assessments function very much like a tutorial system or scaffold to support learning.

Formative assessments are integral to instruction. A seminal study conducted nearly 2 decades ago reported that the use of formative assessments leads to significant learning gains for all students, but especially low-performing ones (Black & Wiliam, 1998a; 1998b). Using evidence from formative assessments gives teachers valuable information about student progress in "real time." They do not have to wait days or even weeks before ascertaining what students know, where the gaps in their learning are, and/or what still needs to be acquired before moving on. In addition, students understand what they are to do on a daily basis, know the criteria for meeting expectations, and have many opportunities to make changes. More recently, school districts have implemented web-based formative assessment tools to inform parents and their children about their progress.

Formative assessments should go beyond providing evidence of recollection and focus on higher-order cognitive tasks that encourage students to express their ideas and comprehension through oral and written communication. Throughout the formative assessment process, teachers should select challenging science investigations, exercises, and/or assignments, and provide students with constructive and quality feedback as they coach them in ways to improve.

There are many examples of formative assessment, including observations, questioning, discussions, science notebooks, daily quizzes, visual representations (graphic organizers), and peer and self-assessments using rubrics. The evidence from these instructional activities forms the individual "puzzle pieces" for teachers and students to use to assess their learning.

Formative Assessment Strategies: Before, During, and After Instruction

Establishing incremental requirements and giving students timely and meaningful feedback make assessments more effective to gauge student progress. Research studies have provided evidence that formative assessments make a difference in learning outcomes for all grade levels (Greenstein, 2010). In addition, formative assessments are highly correlated with teachers adjusting their teaching to accommodate students.

Formative assessments come in many different forms, depending on their purposes. They should be integral parts of the planning process. Learning about students and who they are often goes beyond what is written down in their school records. Teachers who use formative strategies become better acquainted with their students, leading to the establishment of a baseline for best instructional practices.

Accessing and Assessing Prior Knowledge Before Instruction

Accessing and assessing prior knowledge is critical to ascertaining what students already know and are able to do. Gathering such data leads to the creation of instructional exercises that play off students' strengths and address their weaknesses. Teachers who learn that their students lack the prerequisite skills, possess misconceptions, and/or have a weak understanding of a science topic are in a better position to direct their energy and resources toward implementing strategies that differentiate and scaffold instruction.

K-W-L. There are many ways to assess student prior knowledge before embarking on a science topic. One simple strategy is using a K-W-L (or K-L-E-W) chart (refer to Chapter 3). It can be implemented on a chalkboard, flip chart, overhead projector, PowerPoint slide, and/or handout. Asking students what they "**k**now" about a science topic—for example, matter—during a class discussion can reveal aspects of their past experiences that may include family, culture—art, music, language, and literature—and what is important to them. Recalling what they know activates background knowledge, and teachers can take this opportunity to have students make predictions about what they think they will be learning about the science topic. Also, making predictions leads to understanding "**w**hat" they want to learn about the topic. And after instruction, students orally or in writing tell what they have "learned." This serves as a springboard to the next learning steps. Teachers assess whether students got it or not and can then address any misconceptions that were shared (Instructional Strategies Online, 2004–2009).

Whether on the original K-W-L chart or a variation such as K-L-E-W, teachers record what their students say in each column. If students are proficient writers, they then can write their answers in reply to questions on sticky notes and place them on a class chart, in their science notebooks, or write on individual handouts. Students' oral and/or written responses provide more information about what they are thinking and how they organize their ideas. This information reveals the cognitive levels and language functions that are critical for planning upcoming science lessons.

Culturally Responsive Formative Assessment (CRFA). The CRFA assessment builds on students' past experiences, which can be beneficial to teachers (Keeley, 2014). The goal of a culturally responsive formative assessment is not only to uncover what students already know, but to find out what science ideas they bring to the classroom. In addition, such a strategy before formal science instruction reveals students' reading and comprehension skills, along with their learning preferences and styles. Once these preferences are known they can be used to support students as they acquire new information, organize their thinking, and communicate their understanding. Teachers can make use of these learning preferences—writing, singing, drawing, speaking, etc.—to find out their favorite ways to learn science. When students are comfortable expressing their ideas, they are more likely to be at ease when building models, telling stories, talking, and/or using technology.

Figure 10.1 presents an example of CRFA in which students are presented with a set of pictures and asked to respond to what they see. The goal of this exercise is to find out the students' initial ideas as they relate to the pictures of animals and plants. The pictures selected offer insights into what the students know about them and engage them in discussing them in the context of their home and cultural environments. The exercise gets the students talking, which sparks new ideas. This, in turn, keeps the cycle of thinking and talking going.

More important, after uncovering students' ideas before formal teaching begins, appropriate scaffolds can be assembled. This strategy offers a variety of formative assessments with the aim of having all students share their ideas, through which a window into their thinking is opened.

Formative Assessments During Instruction

Formative assessment focuses on the collection of "streaming" data about how students are doing. It fills in the blanks, letting teachers know where students need support before teaching the lesson.

Observing Students. This is an important part of assessment in science. Reviewing plans students developed to solve problems and build models; listening to students talk about strategizing how to win the game; and seeing if they are following the safety protocols are some

Figure 10.1 Example of Formative Assessment Probe

What are you thinking of when you look at these pictures?

@ HitToon/Thinkstock Photos

@ Yuriy Tsirkunov/Thinkstock Photos

@ jehsomwang/Thinkstock Photos

@ HitToon/Thinkstock Photos

@ Sana-design/Thinkstock Photos

@ zacky24/Thinkstock Photos

@ Happy_Inside/Thinkstock Photos

Available for download from **http://resources.corwin.com/ReinhartzGrowingLanguage**

of the ways to observe students. Evidence gathered during observations should influence instructional decisions about how science topics are taught.

What does it take to be a good observer? What do you look for? To be active observers, teachers need to survey their classrooms, watch their students, and make informal notes that will drive future planning and instruction. At first, they look for students who seem confused, not engaged, and/or off task. Next, they observe specific groups of students. And finally, they focus on individuals. Teachers will find it helpful to list student names on a sheet of paper, leaving a space after each to record what has been observed in note form.

Another helpful technique is to have a "teacher observation science notebook" in which information from observations is logged. Pages of the notebook should have two columns. The left column is reserved for the notes on what has been observed. The right column is for jotting down ideas about ways to address individual and/or group learning issues. Reflecting on why students are off task, not following directions, or consistently not completing class and/or homework assignments is a form of brainstorming that gives rise to ideas for remediating these issues. These considerations guide future instruction that involves either the whole class or individual students.

Becoming a "good" observer means recognizing what has been overlooked by more traditional assessments such as pencil-and-paper assignments, tests, and/or formal one-on-one encounters. The information gleaned from classroom observations affords ways to move students along in the learning process.

Figure 10.2 includes six columns. The first lists student behaviors, followed by two columns to indicate if these behaviors are present or not, a reflection column to record thoughts, a column for identifying language proficiency, and a final column for notes on ways to support students. Chapters 1 and 3 include several descriptors of what students should be doing in science classrooms. It would be helpful for teachers to review these behaviors to enhance their observation skills.

Think-Pair-Share (T-P-S). T-P-S is an effective formative strategy. It calls upon students to consider science issues and/or to respond to provocative questions and then discuss them with their partners. It also encourages students to think about a science question and formulate ideas that will lead to refining and deepening their understanding of it. After they have time to think, they share and discuss their ideas with their partners. Read- or write-pair-share functions similarly, but instead of just *thinking* about specific science issues or responding to questions, students *read* or *write* about these issues or questions and share this information. Teachers model how to get information from science books such as *Three Kinds of Water* by K. Scraper (2006), and share it.

Figure 10.2 Sample Science Classroom Observation Instrument

Student Behaviors	Observed Yes, Present	Did Not Observe No, Not Present	Reflections Ideas for Ways to Support Students to Improve	Level of Language Proficiency (B, BI, I, A, AH)	Next Instructional Steps
What are the students doing? A. Actively participating in planning and carrying out science investigations. B. Being on task and focused on assignment or exercise. C. Collaboratively working with others. D. Respectfully listening to classmates. E. Observing, measuring, collecting, and recording data in science notebooks. F. Using different tools/equipment, materials, and science skills. G. Following safety protocols. H. Playing group roles and responsibilities (PI, MM, MD, RR). I. Communicating orally and in writing. J. Using a variety of methods to record information—drawings, notes, graphs, and charts.					

How does T-P-S work? Teachers present students with a science issue or question, preferably higher order, and give them time to think about it. Teachers set time limits for each of the three phases of T-P-S. Also, teachers should consider using hand signals (closed fist to stop talking, crossed fingers to get with partners, and open palm to share) to move through each phase. Switching partners several times throughout the school year is beneficial for all students.

It becomes a formative assessment strategy when teachers walk around the room and listen during think-pair-share exercises and determine the extent to which the students are enhancing their listening, speaking, turn-taking, respecting others' points of view, asking clarifying questions, and rephrasing statements skills. Monitoring students' discourse—for example, about environmental issues—is the first step in gathering science and language information. The next step is to have the pairs share with the entire class what they learned—for example, about animals and plants that are endangered. Another way to extend T-P-S is to trade partners and have them share their ideas again, thereby building on their original statements. Last, a science notebook element can be added to the T-P-S exercise. By reviewing what students have written and/or drawn in their notebooks, teachers gain a deeper understanding of how students are processing ideas and integrating them into their existing schema (e.g., how they organize and categorize their thoughts and recognize relationships).

Think-pair-share gives students time to mentally "mull over" new ideas and "rehearse" what they are going to say to their partners and the whole class. Like wait time, T-P-S gives students a chance to think, which in turn increases the quality of their responses. In addition, teachers have opportunities to assess how students organize, make sense of, and synthesize ideas before, during, and after instruction.

Science Notebooks. These can be used to formatively assess student learning. They "give teachers access into students' thinking—what they do and don't understand, what misconceptions they have, and the organizational skills they are using" (Gilbert & Kotelman, 2005, p. 29).

Often, the more traditional forms of assessment are not designed to determine the types of conceptual understandings that are called for in NGSS. As students write and/or draw in their notebooks during and after conducting an investigation, they develop a deeper understanding of crosscutting science concepts and processes through active construction of knowledge. Science notebooks are integral to instruction and serve as direct measures of student understanding, based on what has been taught. Yet the literature suggests that teachers do not perceive them as formative assessments to improve teaching and learning because of the limited guidance they received in using them.

Many educational sources refer to science notebooks as being interactive. Hence, the right side of the notebook is for information given in class (input; notes, lab sheets, handouts, directions, etc.) using the Cornell note-taking system, and the left side is the output (brainstorming, student questions, tables, graphs, etc.) to demonstrate students' levels of engagement and understanding. (For more information about interactive science notebooks, go to http://jyounghewes.tripod.com/science_notebooks.html.) Regardless of the format, science notebooks are rich formative assessment tools that include descriptive narratives about collaborative science investigations. These narratives include language, science information, and actual experiences being studied that provide evidence of academic growth in many areas of the school curriculum beyond science.

Chapter 2 emphasized that science notebooks are more than mere "trunks" to stuff with information. They are thinking tools for students—tools that guide instruction, enhance literacy skills, and support differentiated learning (Marcarelli, 2010). As they review specific sections of science notebooks, teachers look for evidence of overall quantity and quality of student-generated artifacts in them. These artifacts include responding to questions with writing and drawing what they observe, completing tables, plotting data on graphs, etc. These entries provide opportunities for the students to relive the science experiences by describing them. Once these entries are compiled, teachers need to model how to retrieve this information at a later time so that notebooks become an integral part of instruction (i.e., living documents), and not just extra work. And using scaffolds such as sentence prompts and frames (*The _______ and the _______ are the same because they both have _______. Or, They are different because the _______ has _______, but the _______ does not.*) and "think alouds" (when teachers respond to extend what students are saying by asking, for example, "What is another type of soil besides sand?"), structure notebook entries.

In Gabriela's science notebook, the 8-year-old student drew a picture of a deer. Under "physical characteristics," she wrote:

> "The ears are a triangle the tell as lpke rectangle. The horns are lpke. The color is brown purte the size is medium."

Under the "external characteristics," she wrote:

> "Deer have two eyes and two horns and 4 legs and one tale and one nose and one moude."

Gabriela described the deer using physical characteristics. She used phonetic spelling to portray the details of the deer she drew. And she followed many of the formal writing protocols, such as capital letters at the beginning of sentences, periods, and appropriate science vocabulary. Generally, grammar and spelling rules seemed to be of less concern to her, in order to allow her creative ideas to flow, and to help her feel comfortable sharing her ideas and drawings. From an analysis of Gabriela's notebook entries, it is evident that she has an understanding of the terms *physical, external,* and *characteristics.* Her teacher can feel reasonably confident that Gabriela has grasped the concept of physical characteristics of animals.

Another student—Ivan, an 11-year-old—constructed a model for light and shadow in his science notebook, as shown in Figure 10.3. Using a flashlight to represent the sun and plastic cubes to portray a building, he simulated a shadow, which he drew in his notebook. He then validated his model by going outside three different times during the school day to observe the shadows made by the real sun.

The two notebook entries provide examples of how teachers can access students' science knowledge and skills. Science notebooks are treasure troves of information from students like Gabriela and Ivan. To maximize the use of science notebooks by students and teachers, see Chapter 2, which offers additional tips on how to set them up and how to use them while teaching. Notebooks can be valuable tools to assess student thinking and how that translates into comprehending the science topic under study.

Figures 10.4 and 10.5 present rubrics for science for grades K–3 and 4–5, respectively. The first one uses faces on stars for the criteria or levels of proficiency that students complete. The second is more extensive and

Figure 10.3 Model of Light and Shadow

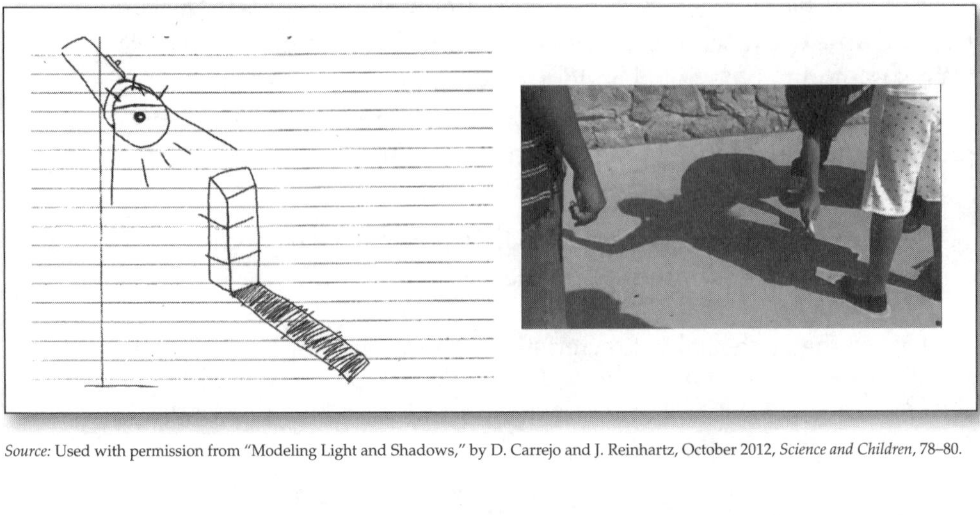

Source: Used with permission from "Modeling Light and Shadows," by D. Carrejo and J. Reinhartz, October 2012, *Science and Children,* 78–80.

Figure 10.4 Science Notebook Self-Assessment

I listen and follow directions.	 Every time I listen and follow directions.	 I usually have to be reminded.	 I sometimes have to be reminded.
I try my best in everything I do.	 I always try my best.	 I usually try my best.	 I sometimes try my best.
My science notebook is neat and organized.	 I always keep my notebook neat and organized.	 I usually keep my notebook neat and organized.	 I sometimes keep my notebook neat and organized.
My science notebook has drawings.	 I have all the drawings, and they are neatly colored and labeled.	 I have all the drawings, but some may not be neatly colored and some labels are missing.	 I do not have all the drawings; many labels and colors are missing.

Figure 10.5 Scoring Science Notebook Rubric for Intermediate Grades

Student Name: ______________________________ Date: ______________

Tasks	Level of Proficiency/Criteria			
	4—Well Done	**3—Good**	**2—Satisfactory**	**1—Not Satisfactory**
Overall Quality and Appearance	Work is of the highest quality.	Work is consistently good.	Work is occasionally untidy.	Work is often untidy, incomplete, or off target.
Table of Contents including titles and page numbers	Is careful to record all required activities into the table of contents.	Is careful most of the time in recording required activities into the table of contents.	Is careless and needs to do a better job in recording the required activities into the table of contents.	Is extremely careless in recording required activities, with many entries omitted in the table of contents.
Science Content demonstrates understanding through written science entries	Demonstrates an understanding of all science content and used most of the science vocabulary.	Demonstrates some understanding of the science content and used some of the vocabulary correctly.	Demonstrates very little understanding of science content and used a limited number of the science vocabulary.	Demonstrates a limited understanding of science content and used only a very few of the science vocabulary correctly.
Drawings/Sketches	Required drawings are generally large, accurately labeled, and have relevant detail.	Required drawings include a few incorrect labels, are not always carefully drawn, and/or have little detail.	Required drawings are too small, not labeled, and/or are very untidy with limited detail included.	Required drawings are consistently missing, and when included are too small, not labeled, and/or are very untidy.
Readiness to use science notebook	Science notebook is ready every time it is required.	Science notebook is sometimes ready to use when required.	Science notebook is often not ready to use when required.	Science notebook is not ready when required.
Attitude about using the science notebook	Always is positive about using the science notebook.	Often is positive about using the science notebook.	Usually positive about using the science notebook	Often is negative about using the science notebook.
Notebook Tasks	Consistently stays focused on the task. Is self-directed.	Mostly focused on the task and what needs to be done.	Often is focused on the task that needs to be done.	Rarely is focused on the task and lets others do the work.

Source: Adapted and modified from Science Notebooks in K12 Classrooms.

Available for download from **http://resources.corwin.com/ReinhartzGrowingLanguage**

goes deeper into what is expected, along with criteria for scoring science notebook entries—penmanship, written entries, and drawings.

Three Quick Questions. Britton (2011) shares her formative assessment strategy that she uses to determine the degree to which students learned the science information presented. Three questions based on previous lessons are written on the board before students enter the science classroom. Students are given index cards, and they write the questions and the answers to these questions on them. The teacher collects the cards, "grades" the answers as correct or incorrect, and returns them to the students. The scores are recorded, but not calculated into their final term grades. As a class, students review the questions and write the correct answers on their cards. The students keep the cards, which serve as study aids for quizzes, science notebook entries, and/or games. Teachers analyze the answers from the three-question assessment and can determine what science content should be presented next, and how.

After grading these cards, teachers know who needs extra help, and if the majority of them missed a question; then the concept is revisited and may be retaught. The information gained from these cards as a formative assessment is invaluable and "requires only a small amount of time; even in a class of 30 students, the three questions can quickly be assessed and marked" (Britton, 2011, p. 17).

Building Models and Telling Their Stories. When given the task of building a model, students are presented opportunities to show their ideas in a three-dimensional form. "Models are bridges that connect concrete learning by using physical objects to correspond to abstract ideas" (Carrejo & Reinhartz, 2014a, p. 11). They also provide a means for students to make transitions from concrete to abstract by constructing relationships that form the basis for using graphs, tables, and formulas (Carrejo & Reinhartz, 2014a).

As students test their ideas, their models change. Assessing conceptual change in students' thinking as they build and revise their models can be achieved by having them tell their "stories" (Carrejo & Reinhartz, 2012; 2014a). Over time, these stories provide insight into the students' line of thinking and offer opportunities to measure conceptual understanding—as their models change, so do their stories.

Alternative Formative Assessments

These are chances for students to demonstrate their science knowledge that lead to possible products such as writing song lyrics, poems, and/or science stories; creating travel brochures, concept maps, and/or web pages; making collages, mobiles, and PowerPoints; and designing models, posters, and flowcharts. Creating products allows students to apply their science knowledge, but also to present it in new ways, giving teachers another set of learning tasks to formatively assess.

Student Discourse. Schleigh (2014) assessed student discourse using individual thought sheets designed "to involve students in a silent argument about ideas," which she says is an important strategy for language learners (p. 47). The NGSS emphasis is on engaging students in scientific arguments to develop conceptual understanding, acquire scientific behaviors, and exhibit science and engineering practices. The goal of having students take part in pre- and postwriting exercises focusing on scientific arguments is to have them think about an idea and develop claims based on evidence they have collected during an investigation they designed. Here, discourse also acts as the catalyst for conducting investigations, evaluating the findings, or coming up with ideas or claims based on evidence; and if there is no evidence to back up the claims, the process starts over.

The Science Loop. As discussed in previous chapters, the science loop is yet another way to assess student understanding of terms and definitions. It involves reading out loud and listening to the information printed on cards, and as students participate, teachers can assess their level of engagement, attitude, and language fluency. As active loop participants, students put their science and language knowledge and skills to work. As students respond, teachers listen to them read the information on their cards, and in doing so gain an awareness of their levels of language and science functioning.

Teacher Feedback: The What and the How

When teacher feedback is mentioned, several ideas come to mind. Most people think of it only as explaining the reasons behind a certain grade, motivating students to learn, and/or offering students ways to improve. It tends to be all of these, but not all feedback is created equal. There are different ways to deliver feedback to students—orally and/or in writing, with general, specific, formal, and informal comments. Who is to receive the feedback, and for what reason, determines the form that the feedback takes.

Adjectives often used to describe feedback include *effective, quality, constructive, targeted,* and *formal/informal.* "Effective, constructive, or quality" feedback should lead to students taking on more of the responsibility for their learning and identifying ways to improve it (Assessment Toolkit Resources). It should be timely and based on criteria that explicitly describe the desired outcomes. It should also include abundant examples to illustrate key behaviors or skills, leave time for questions, be sensitive to the student body and other nonverbal language (e.g., gestures), model identified steps on how to address areas of concern, and brainstorm with students about how to build on their accomplishments to progress.

When feedback is mentioned in this chapter, it is in the context of giving impetus to adapting and adjusting instructional strategies to accommodate student needs and to communicate to students ways to increase their learning. Checking spelling, marking responses as correct or incorrect, and giving praise do not alone constitute meaningful feedback to students and may have little impact on their performance. It takes a combination of feedback strategies to influence student learning positively.

For example, in the formative assessment strategy of asking three questions, students' responses are scored, but not formally as grades. Rather, they get feedback via their index cards individually and as a class; students are provided explanations so they can see where they were on target and where they made mistakes. By retaining these cards for study purposes, this exercise becomes a learning experience and not just one to get the correct answer.

Feedback is a powerful motivator. But as Hattie and Timperley (2007) note, it is the type of feedback along with the way it is given that makes it differentially effective. Feedback takes planning and should be consistent. In addition, it should be nonjudgmental, supportive, and specific to unpack the notion of excellence for students. Thus, over time students assume more and more responsibility for their own learning, which is one of the important goals of education.

Using and Constructing Rubrics

Rubrics list knowledge, behaviors, and skills that students need to demonstrate, as well as criteria for determining the level of achievement. They ratchet up the assessment process by offering levels of mastery. And they certainly go beyond checking off behaviors and completed tasks. Rubrics go hand in hand with science and language lesson objectives. Since objectives identify student behaviors and specify what the students will be doing, the constructing of rubrics begins with objectives.

The more specific the objectives are in targeting what students will be doing and how they will be doing it, the better the rubric will be. Good objectives for a unit on sound might read that the students will make a musical instrument using at least three different materials with three different pitches. They also will explain in writing or orally why the sound levels differ. These objectives are loaded with assessment information. First, the students have to make something; next, it has to yield sounds at three different pitches; and finally, the students have to put into their own words the science behind the achievement of the different pitches, and share their explanations with partners and possibly the whole class. A rubric with several entries can be constructed based on these lesson objectives to access what students have learned about sound.

In constructing a rubric for these objectives, learning tasks are listed in the left column of a table and may include the following:

a. The student builds an instrument using at least three different materials—aluminum pie pans, dried beans, string, wire, paper towel holders, dowel sticks, wooden spoons, etc.
b. The student makes sure his or her instrument has at least three different pitches.
c. The student organizes his or her thoughts.
d. The student communicates orally to a partner and/or the class the science ideas behind why the instrument has three different pitches.

Across the top of each column the criteria or levels of proficiency are described: Well Done (A), Good (B), Satisfactory (C), and Not Satisfactory (D–F). It is this combination of the identification of learning tasks and expected student behaviors that provides an assessment grid for teachers.

Using rubrics can be extremely helpful in identifying the knowledge, skills, and behaviors that students are expected to learn and master, along with the criteria/standards that show the degree of the students' accomplishments.

Figure 10.6 presents a rubric that teachers can use for observing students in science. The criteria for assessing these behaviors are also included: 1 = to a very limited degree, 2 = to some degree, 3 = to an adequate degree, and 4 = to a great degree.

The Exemplars K–12 website (http://www.exemplars.com/resources/rubrics/student-rubrics) offers three science rubrics for students to complete. The first two self-assessments, Seed (2012) and I Get It (2009), are fun and inviting for younger students, and the third, What I Need to Do (2009), is designed for older students.

Figure 10.6 Rubric of Student Behaviors in the Science Classroom

Student "doing" science. To what degree is the student . . .	1	2	3	4
Actively involved in singing songs and repeating rhymes?				
An active listener and demonstrates by using a pointer to pick out pictures that match science vocabulary words?				
Responding to yes/no questions using nonverbal communication skills?				
Using the skills of observing, exploring, and predicting when given materials/objects?				
Using models to explain science events?				
Using visuals to describe and/or explain what he or she is thinking?				
Activating prior knowledge when using different visuals, real objects, and print materials?				
Responding using single words or simple phrases to describe and explain models?				
Learning vocabulary by using an interactive word/phrase wall, drawing pictures, and participating in anchor chart development?				
Working cooperatively in teams/groups to accomplish a task?				
Demonstrating cooperation by working with other students, listening to one another (showing respect), and making group decisions?				

1 = to a very limited degree 2 = to some degree 3 = to an adequate degree 4 = to a great degree

Conclusion

Assessment drives teaching and subsequent student learning. Assessment for learning impacts what and how teachers teach and students learn, and assessment is the reciprocal of effective teaching and vice versa. The synergism that teaching and assessment share provides valuable information about what is to be learned and if the teaching of it was successful.

Assessing students can be very challenging for teachers because it requires making instructional decisions before and after the teaching act. The assessment process is made easier and less stressful when teachers write and follow science and language lesson objectives. By planning ahead of instruction, teaching and assessment become reciprocal processes. When teachers employ instructional strategies that promote student learning and collect information to determine if the instruction was appropriate, then much of the guesswork related to assessment is eliminated.

Assessment strategies can lead to tweaking future objectives based on ongoing teaching and learning with the goal of improving student achievement. Teachers should welcome assessment strategies because they serve as a road map for how to move forward instructionally. *Before instruction,* formative assessment offers insights into students' learning preferences, how they organize information, and how they communicate their understanding. When they are used *during instruction,* assessment strategies provide teachers with an understanding of their students' levels of science learning and communication skills. And *after instruction,* teachers get a picture of what adjustments in instruction they may need to make before moving on to enhance student success.

Your Turn

1. Do you consistently observe your students as they are working with partners or in groups? If so, do you have a way to organize observations? If not, try using Figure 10.2.
   a. Plan to observe your class and prepare an observation guide like the one in the figure, or if possible develop an observation notebook as described in the chapter.
   b. Once you have observed students for at least 30 minutes, analyze the data and summarize what you found.
   c. Were you at all surprised?
   d. Highlight the items that you would like to address; then, next to them, brainstorm ways to do so.

e. Consider including an agenda item for the next grade level or team meeting to generate additional ideas.

f. You may want to try using Figure 10.6 to get you to think about to what degree students are engaging in the tasks listed.

2. You have been asked to be a panel member at an upcoming professional meeting to discuss student assessment. As you think about this topic and what you will say, it might be helpful to consider the following questions:

   a. *What are my ideas about assessment—what does assessment mean to me?*

   b. *Do I think I "assess for learning"? What does this mean to me?*

   c. *Do I agree with Stiggins when he suggests that the assessment climate in our schools needs to move away from sorting students (winners and losers) to supporting them? Yes or no? Why?*

   d. *Do I also think he is referring to a shift away from focusing on students to focusing on teachers and how they plan and deliver instruction?*

   e. *As a panel member, I am told I will have 5 minutes to summarize my main points. What will they be?*

3. Analyze a science lesson or series of lessons (unit) you have planned and taught. Make a "t" table with the left column labeled "What have I learned from this lesson(s)?" and the right column, "How can I apply what I have learned?" Use the following questions to stimulate your thinking:

   a. *Would I change anything? If yes, what would it be: content, the way it was presented (instructional strategy), and/or materials used?*

   b. *How would I align the science content in this lesson(s) with lower and/or upper grades? How would I go about opening up dialogue with colleagues to discuss the science curriculum at my school so assessment for learning becomes the goal?*

   c. *What objectives provided the most success for all my students?*

   d. *Were there areas of overlap? What are ways to extend the science topic without using the same investigations, questions, and exercises across the grade levels?*

4. In Ruth's science class, students are learning about birds, and she describes the process: "As I begin to think about what the students need to learn and do, I refer to the content and language objectives and identify what will be assessed." Ruth is thinking about formative and summative assessments and begins to consider the exercises needed to implement them. Below are exercises that Ruth's students will be doing:

   a. From the list below, create a rubric using a four-point scale to assess student learning:

      - Read a book and identify five things you learned about birds.

- Draw at least three different kinds of birds, with different beaks and feet.
- Write down the most likely place each bird would live.
- Select three habitat cards from a deck and three bird cards from another deck, both of which you have created or acquired. Place each bird in a specific habitat and explain why.

b. Construct a rubric.

Tasks Grading Scale/Criteria				

c. What, if anything, do you notice is missing from Ruth's planning? What will help her to better assess what her students have learned about birds from these exercises?

Epilogue

The Mind is not a vessel to be filled, but a fire to be kindled.

—Plutarch

This quote is at the heart of my book. Science can be a spark for engaging students because it has a built-in set of motivators. *Growing Language Through Science, K–5: Strategies That Work* is founded upon the notion of meaningful and relevant "doing" that motivates students to investigate things that they truly want to because they see the virtues in doing them (Azzam, 2014). Students who enjoy what they do will freely let their teachers and classmates know what they are doing, and why. When approaching science teaching from this perspective, using language skills becomes a natural pairing with science learning.

Having teachers appreciate the purpose and need for planning gives rise to answering students' oft-asked question, "What's the point to learning this?" Planning meaningful science lessons—with attention to language—that engage students offers them an invitation to learn.

Just as anchor charts are developed collaboratively with students, so it is with motivation. As Wormeli (2014) suggests, motivation is something that teachers create *with* students, not something they do *to* them. Having students focus on goals they had a hand in choosing takes engagement, motivation, and learning to a whole new level (Serravallo, 2014). Getting students' attention using motivational strategies prepares them for growing language through science, because motivation does matter!

Today's science classrooms should focus less on sorting students and more on supporting them. By using science as a catalyst for language usage, all students have a better chance of not falling behind and succumbing to a losing streak that makes them stop trying. Teachers should embrace a new vision of success for their students that taps into their learning potential.

This book is filled with strategies that have a track record of success with elementary school students. These strategies have worked to motivate students to use their language as they immerse themselves in science exercises and investigations. More resources and ideas can be found on the companion website, http://resources.corwin.com/ReinhartzGrowingLanguage.

As teachers continue to adjust their plans and search for better ways to reach their students, we are reminded of John Cotton Dana's plea that they "never stop learning." In language-rich science classrooms, the lifelong learning journeys for students and teachers are just beginning.

References

Achieve, Inc. Washington, DC. Retrieved from http://www.achieve.org

Activities at home. Retrieved from http://www2.ed.gov/pubs/parents/Science/Home.html

Aguas, L. (2013). Hands-on science lessons in the elementary classroom. *Education Update*. Association of Supervision and Curriculum Development (ASCD). *55*(4), 6–7.

Aguas, L. (2013). In the classroom with Liliana X. Aguas: Promote parent engagement. *Education Update, 55*(6), 2–3.

Alborough, J. (2002). *Duck in the truck*. New York: HarperCollins.

Allen, R. (2008). *Green light classrooms: Teaching techniques that accelerate learning*. Victoria, Australia: Hawker Brownlow.

American Association for the Advancement of Science (AAAS). Science for all Americans: Education for a changing future. Retrieved from http://www.project2061.org/publications/sfaa

Anchor charts rubrics. http://www.cornerstoneliteracy.org/newletter-archive/anchor-charts and http://grrec-k-3literacy.wikispaces.com/file/view/Anchor+Chart+Participants+Handout.pdf

Anderson, L. W., & Krathwohl, D. R. (Eds.) (2001). *A taxonomy for learning, teaching, and assessing: A revision of Bloom's taxonomy of educational objectives.* New York: Longman.

Annenberg Learner. *Learning science through inquiry: Frequently asked questions.* Retrieved from http://www.learner.org/workshops/inquiry/resources/faq.html

Ansberry, K., & Morgan, E. (nd). *Picture-perfect science: Favorite children's picture books for teaching science in grades K–6*. Retrieved from http://commoncore.dadeschools.net/docs/science/Elementary%20Science/PPSFavoriteBooksK-6.pdf

Arizona Finalized English Language Proficiency (ELP) Standards. (2013). Retrieved from http://www.azed.gov/english-language-learners/elps

Ash, D., & Kluger-Bell, B. (2000). Identifying inquiry in the K–5 classroom. *Foundations: A monograph for professionals in science, mathematics, and technology education* (Chap, 10, Vol. 2). Arlington, VA: National Science Foundation, Division of Elementary, Secondary, and Informal Education.

Ashbrook, P. (2012). Send-home science. *Science and Children, 49*(6), 26–27.

Assessment Toolkit Resources. Giving assessment feedback. Retrieved from http://www.itl.usyd.edu.au/assessmentresources/pdf/Link8.pdf

Aston, D. (2014). *A seed is sleepy*. San Francisco, CA: Chronicle Books.

Azzam, A. M. (2014). Motivation to learn: A conversation with Daniel Pink. *Educational Leadership*. *72*(1), 12–17.

Badders, B. (2013). New standards create professional opportunities. *NSTA Reports*, *25*(7), 20.

Banchi, H., & Bell, R. (2008). The many levels of inquiry. *Science and Children, 46*(2), 26–29.

Barab, S. A., Gresalfi, M., & Arici, A. (2009). Why educators should care about games. *Educational Leadership*, *67*(1), 76–80. Alexandra, VA: ASCD.

Barab, S. A., Gresalfi, M., & Ingram-Goble, A. (2010). Transformational play: Using games to position person, content, and context. *Educational Research*, *39*(7), 525–536.

Barab, S. A., Zuiker, S., Warren, S., Hickey, D., Ingram-Goble, A., Kwon, E.-J., Kouper, I., & Herring, S. C. (2007). Situationally embodied curriculum: Relating formalisms to contexts. *Science Education, 91*(5), 750–782.

Baxter, J., Ruzicka, A., & Blackwell, S. (2012). Inquiry takes time. *Science and Children, 50*(1), 42–47.

Becker, B. (2008). *A visitor for bear*. MacDonald, K., illustrator. Sommerville, MA: Candlewick Press.

Bencze, J. L. (2010). Promoting student-led science and technology projects in elementary teacher education: Entry into core pedagogical practices through technological design. *International Journal of Technology and Design Education*, *20*, 43–62.

Bentley, M., Ebert, C., & Ebert, E. S. II. (2000). The natural investigation: A constructivist approach to teaching elementary and middle school science. Stamford, CT: Wadsworth Thompson.

Benoit, P. (2011). *Temperate forests*. New York: Scholastic.

Benson, B. (1997). Scaffolding (coming to terms). *English Journal, 86*(7), 126–127.

"Best practices" of science teaching. Retrieved from http://www.phy.ilstu.edu/pte/311content/effective/best_practice.html

Biomes of the world. Enchantedlearning.com. Retrieved from http://www.enchantedlearning.com/biomes

Black, P., & Wiliam, D. (1998a). Assessment and classroom learning. *Assessment in Education*, *5*(1), 7–74.

Black, P., & Wiliam, D. (1998b). Inside the black box: Raising standards through classroom assessment. *Phi Delta Kappan*, *80*(2): 139–148.

Bloom, B. S. (1968). *Learning for mastery*. Los Angeles: University of California Press.

Bloom, B. S., Engelhart, M. D., Furst, E. J., & Krathwohl, D. R. (Eds.) (1956). *Taxonomy of educational objectives. The classification of educational goals, Handbook I: Cognitive domain*. New York: D. McKay.

Bloom's taxonomy "revised" key words, model questions, and instructional strategies. (2006). Retrieved from http://www.colorado.edu/sei/documents/Blooms_Taxonomy-verbs.pdf

Bradley, K. B. (2003). *Energy makes things happen*. New York: HarperCollins.

Britton, T. (2011). Using formative and alternative assessments to support instruction and measure student learning. *Science Scope, 34*(5), 6–21.
Brophy, J., & Good, T. (1986). Teacher-effects results. In M. C. Wittrock (Ed.). *Handbook of research on teaching* (3rd ed.). New York: Macmillan.
Brown, M. W. (1999). *The important book.* New York: HarperCollins.
Butterworth, C. (2011). *How did that get in my lunchbox? The story of food.* Somerville, MA: Candlewick Press.
Bybee, R. E. (1997). *Achieving scientific literacy.* Portsmouth, NH: Heinemann.
California State Board of Education: Content Standards. (2012). Retrieved from http://www.cde.ca.gov/be/st/ss/index.asp
Calmsound. Retrieved from http://www.calmsound.com/#!country-garden/cjzy
Cardak, O., Dikmenli, M., & Saritas, O. (2008). Effect of 5E instructional model in student success in primary school 6th year circulatory system topic. *Asia-Pacific Forum on Science Learning and Teaching. 9*(2), 1–12.
Carlsen, W. S. (2007). Language and science learning. In S. K. Abell & N. G. Lederman (Eds.), *Handbook of research on science education*, 57–74. Mahwah, NJ: Lawrence Erlbaum.
Carmi, R., & Stamper, J. B. (2002). *Amazing magnetism* (Magic School Bus Chapter Book No. 12*).* New York: Scholastic Paperbacks.
Carrejo, D., Cortez, T., & Reinhartz, J. (2010). Exploring principal leadership roles within a community of practice to promote science performance of English language learners. *Academic Leadership Live: The Online Journal, 8*(4).
Carrejo, D., & Reinhartz, J. (2012). Modeling light and shadows. *Science and Children, 50*(2), 78–80.
Carrejo, D. J., & Reinhartz, J. (2014a). Facilitating conceptual change through modeling in the middle school science classroom. *Middle School Journal, 46*(2), 10–17.
Carrejo, D. J., & Reinhartz, J. (2014b). Teachers fostering the co-development of science literacy and language literacy with English language learners. *Teacher Development, 18*(3), 334–348.
Carson, R. (1965). *The sense of wonder.* New York: HarperCollins.
Catalano, F. (2012, August 21). What's the difference between games and gamification? [Web log comment]. Retrieved from http://blogs.kqed.org/mindshift/author/frankcatalano/
Center for Comprehensive School Reform and Improvement. Getting parents involved in schools. (2014). Retrieved from http://www.education.com/print/Ref_Getting_Parents
Chen, I-Jung. (2005). Using games to promote communicative skills in language learning. [Electronic version]. *The Internet TESL Journal, XI*(2). Retrieved from http://iteslj.org/Techniques/Chen-Games.html
Cherry, L. (2000). *The great kapok tree.* New York: Houghton Mifflin Harcourt.
Chin, C., & Chia, L.-G. (2004). Problem-based learning: Using students' questions to drive knowledge construction. *Science Education, 88*(5), 707–727.
Climate Kids, NASA's Eyes on the Earth. Retrieved from http://climatekids.nasa.gov/
Colburn, A. (2004). Inquiring scientists want to know. *Educational Leadership, 62*(1), 63–67.

Commission on Excellence in Education. (1983). *A nation at risk: The imperative for educational reform.* Washington, DC: U.S. Department of Education.

Common Core Standards. (2012). Washington, DC: National Governors Association Center for Best Practices, Council of Chief State School Officers (CCSSO). Retrieved from http://www.corestandards.org/the-standards

Common Core Standards: Overview—Depth of Knowledge. Retrieved from http://www.stancoe.org/SCOE/iss/common_core/overview/overview_depth_of_knowledge/dok_bloom.pdf

Concept to Classroom. (2004). Inquiry-based learning. Retrieved from http://www.thirteen.org/edonline/concept2class/inquiry

Cooper, J. (1992). *Magnets (science secrets).* Vero Beach, FL: Rourke Publishing.

Cowan, D. (2010). Gates foundation funds handheld games promoting middle school literacy. Retrieved from http://gamasutra.com/view/news/27588/

Designing a nature scavenger hunt. Retrieved from http://www.hometrainingtools.com/a/nature-scavenger-hunt

Cronin, D. (2003). *The diary of a worm.* New York: HarperCollins.

Damjanovich, M. L. (2011). *Let's use force.* Retrieved from http://www.uen.org/Lessonplan/preview.cgi?LPid=28150

Darling-Hammond, L., Austin, K., Orcutt, S., & Martin, D. (2003). Learning from others: Learning in a social context. Retrieved from http://www.learner.org/courses/learningclassroom/support_pages/index.html

Denton ISD. (2011). Comparative investigations, McNair Elementary School, Denton, TX. Retrieved from http://www.dentonisd.org/Page/21169

Dewey, J. (1938). *Experience and education.* New York: Collier Books.

DeWitt, L. (1993). *What will the weather be?* New York: HarperCollins.

Doing Science. The process of inquiry, teacher's guide to information about the process of scientific inquiry (page 3 of 3). Retrieved from https://www.criticalthinking.org/pages/critical-thinking-development-a-stage-theory/483

Dotlich, R. L. (2006). *What is science?* New York: Henry Holt and Company.

Drapeau, P. (2014). *Sparking student creativity: Practical ways to promote innovative thinking and problem solving.* Alexandra, VA: Association of Supervision and Curriculum Development (ASCD).

Duckworth, E. (1987). "The having of wonderful ideas," and other essays on teaching and learning. New York: Teachers College Press.

Dunn, K. E., & Mulvenon, S. W. (2009). A critical review of research on formative assessment: Limited scientific evidence of the impact of formative assessment in education. *Research & Evaluation, 14*(7), 1–11.

Dyasi, H. (nd). What children gain by learning through inquiry. Retrieved from http://www.nsf.gov/pubs/2000/nsf99148/ch_2.htm

Ehlert, L. (1992). *Planting a rainbow.* New York: Houghton Mifflin Harcourt Books for Young Readers.

Elder, L., & Paul, R. (2010). *Critical thinking development: A stage theory,* with implications for instruction. Retrieved from http://science.education.nih.gov/supplements/nih6/inquiry/guide/lesson2.htm

Enature. Retrieved from http://www.enature.com/home

Endres, H. J. (2004). *Push and pull.* Minneapolis, MN: Capstone Press.

Enfield, M., & Mathew, E. (2012). Storybook science. *Science and Children. 50*(2), 46–49.

Exemplars K–12. Retrieved from http://www.exemplars.com/resources/rubrics/student-rubrics

Fabulous fourth grade. Retrieved from http://fabulous-fourth.blogspot.com/p/anchor-charts.html

Filsecker, M., & Kerres, M. (2012). Repositioning formative assessment from an educational assessment perspective: A response to Dunn & Mulvenon (2009). *Practice Assessment, Research & Evaluation, 17*(16). Retrieved from http://pareonline.net/pdf/v17n16.pdf

Fleming, D. (2001). *Time to sleep*. New York: Square Fish.

Flickinger, B. (2014, May 16). Social and emotional benefits of video games: Metacognition and relationships. Retrieved from http://blogs.kqed.org/mindshift/2014/05/social-and-emotional-benefits-of-video-games-metacognition-and-relationships/

Forehand, M. (2005). *Bloom's taxonomy:* Original and revised. In M. Orey (Ed.), Emerging perspectives on learning, thinking, and technology. Retrieved from http://epltt.coe.uga.edu/index.php?title=Bloom%27s_Taxonomy

Fowler, A. (1995). *What magnets can do*. New York: Children's Press.

Fowler, A. (1997). *Arctic tundra: Land with no trees*. New York: Children's Press.

Freudenberg, K. (2012). Science sacks: A parent initiative brings learning home with ease. *Science and Children*. *49*(6), 37–41.

Froschauer, L. (2012). Don't forget families. *Science and Children*, *49*(6), 6.

Game board templates. Retrieved from http://donnayoung.org/homeschooling/games/game-boards.htm

Game evaluation. Retrieved from www.games2teach.wordpress.com

Gee, J. P., & Levine, M. H. (2009). Welcome to virtual worlds. *Educational Leadership*, 66(6), 48–52.

Genesee, F., Lindholm-Leary, K., Saunders, W. M., & Christian, D. (2006). *Educating English language learners: A synthesis of research evidence*. New York: Cambridge University Press.

Gibbons, G. (1997). *Nature's green umbrella*. New York: HarperCollins.

Gilbert, J., & Kotelman, M. (2005). Five good reasons to use science notebooks. *Science and Children, 42*(3), 26–29.

Goldberg, C. (2008). Teaching English language learners: What the research does—and does not say. *American Educator*, *2*(2), 8–23.

González, N., Moll, L. C., & Amanti, C. (2004). *Funds of knowledge for teaching: Using a qualitative approach to connect homes and classrooms*. Mahwah, NJ: Lawrence Erlbaum Associates.

Gottlieb, M. (2006). *Assessing English language learners: Bridges from language proficiency to academic achievement*. Thousand Oaks, CA: Corwin.

Gottlieb, M., & Ernst-Slavit, G. (2013). *Academic language in diverse classrooms: Mathematics, grades K–2*. Thousand Oaks, CA: Corwin.

Gottlieb, M., & Ernst-Slavit, G. (2014). *Academic language in diverse classrooms: Promoting content and language learning: English language arts, grades K–2*. Thousand Oaks, CA: Corwin.

Graphic organizers and concept maps. Retrieved from http://www.temple.edu/studentaffairs/disability/faculty-resources.html

Greenstein, L. (2010). *What teachers really need to know about formative assessment*. Alexandra, VA: ASCD.

Gregory, G. H., & Parry, T. (2006). *Designing brain-compatible learning* (3rd ed.). Thousand Oaks, CA: Corwin.

Guiberson, B. Z. (1993). *Cactus hotel*. New York: Square Fish.

Guided Language Acquisition Design (GLAD). (2014). Training session: Color coding, observation sheets, and ABC science books. Santa Fe, NM.

Hattie, J., & Timperley, H. (2007). The power of feedback. *Review of Educational Research, 77*(1), 81–112.

Hauser, J. F. (1998). *Science play*. Charlotte, VT: Williamson Publishing Company.

Havers, B., & Delmotte, K. (2012). Lab with dad: A simple idea encourages family involvement. *Science and Children, 49*(6), 62–64.

Hechinger Report. (2011). Retrieved from http://hechingerreport.org/what-makes-a-good-science-teacher/

Hershberger, K., Zembal-Saul, C., & Starr, M. L. (2006). Evidence helps the KWL get a KLEW. *Science and Children, 41*(1), 42–44.

Hess, K. (2006). Applying Webb's depth-of-knowledge (DOK) levels in science. Retrieved from www.nciea.org

Hillerman, T. (1993). *The boy who made dragonfly*. Albuquerque: University of New Mexico Press.

Himmel, J. (2012). Language objectives: The key to effective content area instruction for English learners. Retrieved from www.colorincolorado.org/article/49646

Hislop, T., & Green, H. (2003). *Flicking with force*. Utah Education Network. Retrieved from http://www.uen.org/Lessonplan/preview.cgi?LPid=3195

Home & School CONNECTION. Retrieved from http://www.rfeonline.com/content.cfm?dept=11

Hutchins, R. (1953). *The conflict in education in a democratic society*. New York: Harper.

Instructional Strategies Online. (2004–2009). Retrieved from http://olc.spsd.sk.ca/De/PD/instr/strats/think/

Interactive notebooks. Retrieved from http://jyounghewes.tripod.com/science_notebooks.html

It is alive. Retrieved from http://crisscrossapplesauce.typepad.com/files/is-it-living-recording-sheet.pdf

Jacobs, G. M. (nd). Games for language teaching. Retrieved from www.georgejacobs.net

Jarvis, L., Odell, K., & Troiano, M. (2002, April). *Role-playing as a teaching strategy*. Retrieved from http://imet.csus.edu/imet3/odell/portfolio/grartifacts/Lit%20review.pdf

Joan Ganz Cooney Center. (2012). The teacher attitudes about digital games in the classroom. Conducted by the Games and Learning Publishing Council. Retrieved from http://blogs.kqed.org/mindshift/2012/05/new-survey-half-of-teachers-use-digital-games-in-class/

Johanson, P. (2004). *The forested taiga: A web of life*. Berkeley Heights, NJ: Enslow Elementary.

Justice, L. M. (2004). Creating language-rich preschool classroom environments. *Council for Exceptional Children, 37*, 28–34.

Just Science Now. What is inquiry? Retrieved from http://www.justsciencenow.com/index.htm

Keeley, P. (2014). Formative assessment: Assessment for all. *Science and Children, 51*(5), 32–35.

Kelly, G. (2007). Discourse in science classrooms. In S. K. Abell & N. G. Lederman (Eds.), *Handbook of research on science education*, 443–469. Mahwah, NJ: Lawrence Erlbaum.

Kisa, M. T., Stein, M. K., & Schunn, C. (2013). A framework for analyzing cognitive demand and content–practices integration: Task analysis guide in science. Submitted to *Journal of Research in Science Teaching*, October 28.

Krashen, S. D., & Terrell, T. D. (1983). *The natural approach: Language acquisition in the classroom*. New York: Pergamon.

Krasnic, T. (2012). *Mind mapping for kids: How elementary school students can use mind maps to improve reading comprehension and critical thinking*. Concise Books Publishing.

Lawrence Hall of Science. Parent Portal. Retrieved from http://www.lawrencehallofscience.org/search/node/parents

Lee, O., Quinn, H., and Valdés, G. (2013). Science and language for English language learners in relation to next generation science standards and with implications for common core state standards for English language arts and mathematics. *Educational Researcher*, *XX*(X), 1–11.

Levassur, A. (2011, October 27). Is gaming the new essential literacy? [Web log comment]. Retrieved from http://blogs.kqed.org/mindshift/2011/10/can-playing-games-teach-literacy/

Littlejohn, P. (2012). Never too cool for science: Involving parents of older children in the science classroom. *Science and Children*, *49*(4), 50–53.

Living and nonliving things—lesson for kids. Retrieved from https://www.youtube.com/watch?v=cPiNTkCmmv0

Llewellyn, C. (2004). *And everyone shouted "pull!": A first look at forces and motion*. Mankato, MN: Picture Window Books.

Macaulay, K., & Kalman, B. (2006). *A desert habitat*. New York: Crabtree Publishing Company.

Make a light bulb. Retrieved from http://www.mineralseducationcoalition.org/pdfs/dig/lightbulb.pdf

Making a diorama. Retrieved from http://knowitall.org/naturalstate/html/Dioramas/Dior-2-1-a.cfm

Manna, R. *Dissecting owl pellets*. Retrieved from http://www.scholastic.com/teachers/lesson-plan/dissecting-owl-pellets

Marcarelli, K. (2010). *Teaching science with interactive notebooks*. Thousand Oaks, CA: Corwin.

Marzano, R. J., Warrick, P., & Simms, J. A. (2014). *A handbook for high-reliability schools*. Bloomington, IN: Solution Tree.

Mason, A. (2005). *Move it!* Tonawanda, NY: Kids Can Press Ltd.

McComas, W. F., & Abraham, L. Asking more effective questions. Retrieved from http://cet.usc.edu/resources/teaching_learning/docs/Asking_Better_Questions.pdf

McGough, J. (2013). Journaling: A bridge between school and home. *Science and Children*, *50*(8), 62–67.

McHenry, N., & Borger, L. (2013). Effective use of inquiry in the elementary science classroom—implications for teacher directed professional development. *Electric Journal of Science Education*, *17*(1). Retrieved from http://www.ejse.southwestern.edu/article/view/10874

McKissack, F., & McKissack, L. (2009). *Counting in the taiga*. Berkeley Heights, NJ: Enslow Elementary.

McManus, S. (2008). (Ed.) *Attributes of effective formative assessment.* Washington, DC: Council of Chief State School Officers. Retrieved from http://www.ncpublicschools.org/docs/accountability/educators/fastattributes04081.pdf

McTighe, J., & Wiggins, G. (2013). *Essential questions: Opening the doors to student understanding.* Alexandra, VA: Association of Supervision and Curriculum Development (ASCD).

Mercuri, S., & Rodríguez, L. D. (2014). Developing academic language through ecosystems. In M. Gottlieb & G. Ernst-Slavit (Eds.). *Academic language in diverse classrooms: English language arts, grades K–2.* Thousand Oaks, CA: Corwin.

Minerals Education Coalition. (2014). Retrieved from http://www.mineralseducationcoalition.org

Mohr, K. A. J., & Mohr, E. S. (2007). Extending English language learners' classroom interactions using the response protocol. *The Reading Teacher, 60*(5), 440–450.

Mr. R's science poems and songs. Retrieved from http://sciencepoems.net/index.html#physics

Murphy, J. (2011). *Desert animal adaptations.* Minneapolis, MN: Capstone Press.

Music and rhyme station. Retrieved from http://www.preschoolexpress.com/music-station08/cloud-songs-rhymes-mar08.shtml

National Center for Education Statistics. (2014). English language learners. Retrieved from http://nces.ed.gov/programs/coe/indicator_cgf.asp

National Research Council (NRC). (2011). *A framework for K–12 science education: Practices, crosscutting concepts, and core ideas.* Washington, DC: National Academies Press.

National Research Council (NRC). (2012). *A framework for K–12 science education: Practices, crosscutting concepts, and core ideas.* Washington, DC: National Academies Press.

National Research Council (NRC). (2013). *A framework for K–12 science education: Practices, crosscutting concepts, and core ideas.* Washington, DC: National Academies Press.

National Science Teachers Association (NSTA). Retrieved from http://www.nsta.org/safety/.

Nature scavenger hunt. Retrieved from http://hometrainingtools.com/a/nature-scavenger-hunt

Nelson, R. (2004). *Push and pull.* Minneapolis, MN: Lerner Publishing Group.

Next Generation Science Standards: For States, by States (NGSS). (2013). Washington, DC: National Academies Press. Retrieved from http://www.nextgenscience.org/next-generation-science-standards

Nguyen, J. *Sharks.* Retrieved from http://www.prezi.com/_qe_gdney5uo/sharks

Ogens, E. M., & Padilla, C. (2012). It's traditional! How one district evening evolved into years of family science at the school level. *Science and Children. 49*(6), 47–49.

Overbaugh, R., & Schultz, L. Retrieved from http://ww2.odu.edu/educ/roverbau/Bloom/blooms_taxonomy.htm

Owens, C., & Sullivan, E. A. (2012). Reinventing the . . . bridge: Modifying the family science night concept mimics the engineering design process and connects families to the science curriculum. *Science and Children. 49*(6), 58–61.

Pang, V. O., Lafferty, K. E., Pang, J. M., Griswold, J., & Oser, R. (2014). Culture matters in science education: A festival creates culturally relevant learning opportunities for students and parents. *Science and Children, 51*(5), 44–51.

Paulson, G. (1987). *Hatchet* (first in a series of five). New York: Bradbury Press.

Pearson, S. (1988). *My favorite time of year.* New York: HarperCollins.

Pop rocks experiment. Retrieved from www.stevespanglerscience.com/content/experiment/poprocks

Primary games. Retrieved from http://crlt.indiana.edu/projects/completed-projects/transactive-art/

Project share: Knowledge knows no boundaries. Retrieved from http://projectsharetexas.org/print/4413/all-content

Quest Atlantis. Retrieved from http://crlt.indiana.edu/projects/completed-projects/transactive-art/

Quinn, H., Lee, O., & Valdés, G. (2012). Language demands and opportunities in relation to next generation science standards for English language learners: What teachers need to know. Stanford, CA: Stanford University, Understanding Language Initiative at Stanford University (ell.stanford.edu).

Quizlet website. http://quizlet.com/; (http://quizlet.com/subject/stimulus-and-response/).

"Rainforest rap" (original). Retrieved from http://www.youtube.com/watch?v=m4bNrIIe0bk

Real trees 4 kids. Retrieved from http://www.realtrees4kids.org/teacher.htm

Resources for educators. Retrieved from www.rfeonline.com/content.cfm?dept=11

Revell, J., & Norman, S. Retrieved from http://www.php.com/quote/don13

Role play. Retrieved from http://serc.carleton.edu/introgeo/roleplaying/reasons.html

Rollins, S. P. (2014). *Learning in the fast lane: 8 ways to put all students on the road to academic success.* Alexandria, VA: ASCD.

Rose, E. (2004). *Animal adaptations for survival.* New York: Rosen Publishing Group, Incorporated.

Rosenshine, B. (2012). Principles of instruction: Research-based strategies that all teachers should know. *American Educator, 36*(1), 12–19, 39.

Rosenshine, B., & Furst, M. (1971). Research on teacher performance criteria. In B. O. Smith (Ed.). *Research in teaching education,* 27–72. Englewood Cliffs, NJ: Prentice Hall.

Rothstein, D., & Santana, L. (2011). Teaching students to ask their own questions. *Harvard Education Letter, 27*(5). Retrieved from http://hepg.org/hel/article/507#home

Rowe, M. B. (1986). Wait time: Slowing down may be a way of speeding up! *Journal of Teacher Education, 37*(1), 43–50.

Rutherford, J., & Ahlgren, A. (1989). *Science for All Americans.* Washington, DC: American Association for the Advancement of Science (AAAS).

Samway, K., & Taylor, D. (2008). *Teaching English language learners.* New York: Scholastic, Inc.

San Diego County Office of Education. Scaffolding matrix for English learners. Retrieved from http://kms.sdcoe.net/differ/147/version/default/part/AttachmentData/data/m3_scaffolding.pdf

Saville-Troike, M. (1988). Private speech: Evidence for second language learning strategies during the "silent" period. *Journal of Child Language, 15*, 567–590.

Sawyers, S. (2011). What makes a good science teacher? *Hechinger Report*. Retrieved from http://hechingerreport.org/what-makes-a-good-science-teacher

Schleigh, S. (2014). Assessments in the arguments. *Science and Children, 51*(8), 46–53.

Science notebook. Retrieved from http://jyounghewes.tripod.com/science_notebooks.html

Science notebooks in K12 classrooms. Retrieved from http://www.sciencenotebooks.org/classroomTools/assessment.php

Sciencesaurus: A student handbook. (2006). Boston: Great Source Education Group, Houghton Mifflin Company.

Scraper, K. (2006). *Three kinds of water*. Pelham, NY: Benchmark Education Company.

Scriven, M. (1967). The methodology of evaluation. In R. Tyler et al., (Ed.), *Perspectives of curriculum evaluation*. Chicago: Rand McNally. American Educational Research Association (monograph series on evaluation, No. 1, 39–83).

Seger, W. (2012). Anchor charts—five essential features. Retrieved from http://nancymcneal.blogspot.com/2012/08/anchor-charts-five-essential-features.html

Serravallo, J. (2014). Reading time with goals in mind. *Educational Leadership, 72*(1), 54–59.

Sharp, L. A. (2012). Stealth learning: Unexpected learning opportunities through games. *Journal of Instructional Research, 1*, 42–48.

Shelly's Science Spot. Retrieved from http://www.shellyssciencespot.com/Worksheets/FirstDays/TextbookScavengerHunt.pdf

Sheppard Software. Retrieved from http://www.sheppardsoftware.com/science.htm

Short, D., Himmel, J., Gutierrez, S., & Hudec, J. (2012). *Using the SIOP model: Professional development for sheltered instruction*. Washington, DC: Center for Applied Linguistics.

Shulman, M. (2006). *Mom and Dad are palindromes: A dilemma for words . . . and backwards*. McCauley, A., illustrator. San Francisco, CA: Chronicle Books.

Silverman, B. (2012). *Grasslands (habitat survival)*. Minneapolis, MN: Capstone Press.

SimCity. (1989). Retrieved from http://www.bestoldgames.net/eng/old-games/simcity.php

Simon, S. (2006). *Oceans*. New York: HarperCollins.

Simon, S. (2006). *Weather*. New York: HarperCollins.

Slade, S. (2010). *What if there were no lemmings?* Minneapolis, MN: Capstone Press.

Smith-Hagadone. P. (2013). Can we be garbage free? *Science and Children, 51*(4), 50–54.

Sources of insight. Retrieved from http://sourcesofinsight.com/avoid-the-intelligence-trap/
Sousa, D. A., & Tomlinson, C. A. (2011). *Differentiation and the brain: How neuroscience supports the learner-friendly classroom.* Bloomington, IN: Solution Tree Press.
Stiggins, R. J. (2002). Assessment crisis: The absence of assessment for learning. *Phi Delta Kappan, 83*(10), 758–765.
Stiggins, R. J. (2007). Enhancing student learning. Retrieved from http://www.districtadministration.com/article/enhancing-student-learning
Stiggins, R., & Chappuis, J. (2008). Enhancing student learning. Retrieved from http://www.districtadministration.com/article/enhancing-student-learning
Stille, D. R. (2000). *Grasslands.* Chicago, IL: Children's Press.
Sykes, J. M. (2013). Technology—just playing games? A look at the use of digital games for language learning. *The Language Educator, 8*(5), 32–35.
Sykes, J. M., & Reinhardt, J. (2012). *Language at play: Digital games in second and foreign language teaching and learning.* New York: Pearson.
Steve Spangler Science. Dancing raisins. Englewood, CO: Steve Spangler, Inc. Retrieved from http://www.stevespanglerscience.com/lab/experiments/dancing-raisins-the-bubble-lifter
Steve Spangler Science. (2000). Energy beads. Englewood, CO: Steve Spangler, Inc. Retrieved from http://www.stevespanglerscience.com/lab/experiments/uv-reactive-beads#sthash.VQw0OgB3.dpuf
Suzuki, D. (2011). *Natural curiosity: Building children's understanding of the world through environmental inquiry. A resource for teachers.* Oshawa, ON: Maracle Press Ltd.
Tabarrok, A. (2011). Teachers don't like creative students. Retrieved from http://marginalrevolution.com/marginalrevolution/2011/12/teachers-dont-like-creative-students.html
Tagliaferro, L. (2006). *Exploring the deciduous forest.* Minneapolis, MN: Capstone Press.
Tate, M. L. (2008). *Engage the brain games.* Thousand Oaks, CA: Corwin.
Tate, M. L., & Phillips, W. G. (2011). *Science worksheets don't grow dendrites: 20 instructional strategies that engage the brain.* Thousand Oaks, CA: Corwin.
Taylor, J., & Villanueva, M. G. (2014). The power of multimodal representations: Creating and using visual supports for students with high incidence disabilities. *Science and Children, 51*(5), 58–65.
Teachers of English to Speakers of Other Languages (TESOL). (2005). Pre-K–12 English language proficiency standards in the core content areas. Retrieved from http://www.tesol.org/advance-the-field/standards
Texas Education Agency (TEA). (2010). *Lab and field investigations.* Austin, TX: Texas Education Agency. Retrieved from http://www.tea.state.tx.us/WorkArea/DownloadAsset.aspx?id=2147486150
Texas English Language Proficiency Assessment System (TELPAS). (2011). Retrieved from http://ritter.tea.state.tx.us/rules/tac/chapter074/ch074a.html and TEKS, http://www.tea.state.tx.us/index2.aspx?id=6148
Thomas, J., & White, K. (2012). Aligning the STARS: A partnership brings a community together for a night of astronomy. *Science and Children. 49*(6), 42–46.

Tobin, K. (1987). The role of wait time in higher cognitive level learning. *Review of Educational Research, 57*(1), 69–95.

Toolbox for planning rigorous instruction. (2009). Section 5: Thinking Bloom, 16–17. Retrieved from https://tpri.wikispaces.com/Bloom's+Question+Stems+for+Instruction

Vygotsky, L. S. (1978). *Mind in society: The development of higher psychological processes*. Cambridge, MA: Harvard University Press.

Wadsworth, O. A. (1800s). *Over in the meadow.*

Walker, C. H. (1992). *Plants and seeds.* New York: The Wright Group/McGraw Hill.

Weakland, M. (2011). *Magnets push, magnets pull.* Minneapolis, MN: Capstone Press.

Webb, M. L. (2002). Implied cognitive demand and depth of knowledge. Unpublished paper. Retrieved from http://www.education.nh.gov/instruction/assessment/necap/admin/documents/tirc_math_dok07.pdf

Where in the World Is Carmen Sandiego? (1985). Retrieved from http://www.carmensandiego.com/hmh/site/carmen/

Willard, T., Pratt, H., & Workosky, C. (2012). Exploring the new standards: How to form a study group to examine the next generation science standards. *The Science Teacher, 79*(7), 33–37.

Williams, M. M. (2009). *Use anchor charts for English language learners.* Retrieved from https://suite.io/margaret-m-williams/1tjn2at

Willis, J. (2003). *Dr. Xargle's book of Earthlets*. Chicago, IL: Andersen Press.

Wilson, C. D., Taylor, J. A., Kowalski, S. M., & Carlson, J. (2009). The relative effects of inquiry-based and commonplace science teaching on students' knowledge, reasoning, and argumentation about sleep concepts: A randomized control trial. ERIC DOC.524749

Wisconsin English Language Proficiency Levels. (2008). Wisconsin Department of Public Instruction. Retrieved from ell.dpi.wi.gov/sites/default/files/imce/ell/pdf/elp-levels.pdf

World-Class Instructional Design and Assessment (WIDA). (2012). Madison, WI: Wisconsin Center for Educational Research, University of Wisconsin.

Wormeli, R. (2014). Motivating young adolescents. *Educational Leadership, 72*(1), 26–31.

Wright, A., Betteridge, D., & Buckby, M. (2005). *Games for language learning* (3rd ed.). New York: Cambridge University Press.

Wright, W. (2006). Will Wright explains how games are unleashing the human imagination. Wired.com. Retrieved from http://www.wired.com/wired/archive/14.04/wright.html

Yolen, J. (1987). *Owl moon*. New York: Philomel.

Index